CONTEMPORARY WALES

An annual review of economic and social research

Volume 5

Editors
Graham Day
Gareth Rees

Technical Editor
Martin Read

Published on behalf of the Board of Celtic Studies
of the University of Wales

Cardiff
University of Wales Press
1992

First published 1992

British Library Cataloguing in Publication Data

Contemporary Wales: an annual review of economic and social research.___5___
1. Social sciences___Research #5. Wales
___Social conditions

942.9′0858′072   HN 398.W2 6

ISBN 0-7083-1156-3

ISSN 0951-4937

Cover photograph by Howard Williamson
Cover design by Strata
Typeset by Megaron, Cardiff
Printed in Wales by Gwasg John Penry, Swansea

CONTENTS

CONTRIBUTORS

Rodney Bull, Centre for Social Work Studies, School of Social and Administrative Studies, University of Wales, Cardiff.

Graham Day, School of Sociology and Social Policy, University College of North Wales, Bangor.

Sarah Fielder, Social Research Unit, School of Social and Administrative Studies, University of Wales, Cardiff.

John Giggs, Department of Geography, University of Nottingham.

Dylan Griffiths, Department of Government, University of Essex.

Caroline Lloyd, Centre for Industrial Relations, University of Keele.

L. Mainwaring, Department of Economics, University College of Swansea.

Duncan Mitchell, School of European Studies, University of Wales, Cardiff.

Charles Pattie, Department of Geography, University of Nottingham.

Ceri J. Phillips, Policy Studies Unit, Gwent College of Higher Education.

Malcolm J. Prowle, KPMG Peat Marwick McLintock.

Gareth Rees, School of Social and Administrative Studies, University of Wales, Cardiff.

Teresa Rees, Social Research Unit, School of Social and Administrative Studies, University of Wales, Cardiff.

Ian Shaw, Centre for Social Work Studies, School of Social and Administrative Studies, University of Wales, Cardiff.

Dennis Thomas, Department of Economics and Agricultural Economics, University College of Wales, Aberystwyth.

Huw Thomas, School of Planning, Oxford Polytechnic.

Anna Walker, Department of Sociology, University of Glasgow.

V.J. Wass, Cardiff Business School, University of Wales, Cardiff.

Howard Williamson, Social Research Unit, School of Social and Administrative Studies, University of Wales, Cardiff.

CALL FOR PAPERS

The editors are always pleased to receive papers for consideration for publication in *Contemporary Wales*. Although it is intended to continue to focus each volume on a specific theme, no area of social and economic research on Wales will be excluded from consideration. Contributions should, however, be written in a style which makes them readily accessible to non-specialists, avoiding as far as possible highly technical material. Those who are planning to submit a paper are encouraged to discuss their proposal with one of the editors at an early stage.

On acceptance of an article by the Editors for publication in this journal, copyright in that article is assigned to the University of Wales.

ERRATUM

The paper 'The Social Construction of Nationalism: Racism and Conflict in Wales', which appeared in volume 4 of *Contemporary Wales* under the name of David Denney, was in fact jointly authored with John Borland and Ralph Fevre. At the time of writing, all three were at the University College of North Wales, Bangor. Ralph Fevre has subsequently moved to the University College of Swansea and David Denney to Roehampton Institute in London.

EDITORIAL

This issue of *Contemporary Wales,* the fifth, is marked by both consolidation and change. By the time it appears, we will know the result of a General Election in which three out of the four parties likely to gain representation in Wales are committed to some form of devolution of power from Westminster. The year 1992 also marks the beginning of the single European market, which will have further, as yet undetermined, consequences for the status of Wales within the United Kingdom. In this context, a number of contributions to this volume deal with matters touching upon the political and social identity of Wales.

The impact of growing European integration, at least at the economic level, figures prominently in this issue's economic survey by Dennis Thomas. Apart from commenting on preparations for the single market and their implications for training and competition, the author notes the involvement of French finance and construction companies in plans for a new Severn Bridge, the importance of European funding to new developments in rural Wales, and the efforts being made to draw lessons from the performance of successful European regions, like Baden-Württemberg. The other theme which runs through the review is, inevitably, the impact of the downturn in the economy on Welsh business and industry.

Duncan Mitchell's account of the expanding network of institutional links between Wales and Brussels further develops the mapping of the distinctively Welsh institutional complex which was begun by Barry Jones and Jonathan Murdoch in the second volume. There Jones (1988) argued that the growth of Welsh institutions was not enough to underwrite a genuine Welsh identity, but served instead to integrate Wales more fully into the framework of the British state. However, Mitchell shows how the momentum of development has now taken on an important European dimension, opening up the possibility of a convergence with federalist forces within Europe which are seeking to redistribute political control away from the national level. Both the British government and, to some degree, the Welsh Office find themselves caught between the claims of an emerging federal centre, and pressures for a more effective local or regional voice. With the shape of Welsh local government itself under review, and the European Community in the throes of adjusting to its assimilation of a number of areas which may have a greater claim on its resources than Wales, Mitchell poses the question of who can best speak for the interests of the Welsh. At this stage, he suggests, the answer is far from clear.

No matter how this is resolved, as John Giggs and Charles Pattie remind us in their discussion of Wales as a plural society, the people of Wales are unlikely to speak with a single voice. They point out that in terms of the proportion of its population born outside its borders, Wales is and has long been exceptionally cosmopolitan, and as a result differences of 'ethnic' composition play an important part in diversifying Welsh society. Using data from the 1981 census, they provide a careful examination of the way in which spatial, class and ethnic or language patterns intersect, and show how different parts of the country exhibit distinctive socio-economic profiles. Whereas the English-born have a propensity to dominate positions of prestige in the rural parts of 'inner Wales', in the more industrial areas of both the south and north-east, elite positions are most accessible to individuals drawn from a literate Welsh-speaking background. It is those who are less literate in their use of Welsh, and the non-Welsh-speaking Welsh, who are most heavily concentrated in the least prestigious positions, and who may even find their 'Welshness' being put into question by those above them in the class structure. This creates some understandable resentment among the majority Welsh population, and makes Welsh 'identity' a troublesome concept. Giggs and Pattie touch on a number of the cultural and political expressions of this complicated situation. They also note how the growth of Cardiff as a centre for governmental and service functions within Wales, and therefore as the focus of elite positions, has tended to drain the more Welsh-speaking areas of the presence of many of those who might have been expected to play a key role in sustaining the language and culture against forces tending to erode it.

The two contributions which follow focus on developments at the opposing poles of this relationship. In his discussion of political responses to the increasing numbers of non-Welsh-born people residing in rural Wales, Dylan Griffith picks up some of the issues raised previously in volume 3. With getting on for a third of the population of rural Wales now born outside Wales, there is a great danger that its particular political and cultural characteristics will be diluted. In view of this, there have been various attempts by different authorities and pressure groups to exert some control over the migration process, for instance by modifying the system of planning and development controls. Since from a British perspective they are seen as restricting individual freedom of movement, these have not gained the support of central government. Lack of effective action increases the political pressure from within Wales for legislation, and encourages some to adopt more extreme forms of 'direct action' against in-migrants or those (such as estate agents) who are thought to be sponsoring inward movement. As Griffiths notes, the level of politicization around cultural and language issues is further heightened by the appearance of counter-movements, such as those in Dyfed who oppose the extension of Welsh-medium education at primary level.

Huw Thomas provides an insight into the changing role of Cardiff. His case study of the development of the Atlantic Wharf site shows how the effort to maintain a significant industrial or manufacturing role for the city appears to have been abandoned, with the acceptance of a mixture of housing, office and leisure functions for the dock area. With the backing of the Welsh Office and the then Secretary of State for Wales, the change of direction was orchestrated by the County Council, with limited resistance by the City. An uncritical press coverage contributed to the marginalization of local opinion; both small business and the people of Butetown were sidelined by a well-organized coalition of public and private interests.

The next group of articles deal with aspects of women's role in the contemporary Welsh workforce, a theme addressed in earlier volumes by Winkler (1987) and Rees (1988). Teresa Rees and Sarah Fielder document the very limited extent to which women have succeeded in penetrating Wales's 'top jobs'. The record is even worse than that of England, and the difference cannot be explained simply in terms of a different industrial and occupational structure, since there are particularly poor figures in areas like health service management and secondary education. In both public and private sectors, Welsh employers have made less progress towards implementing equal opportunities policies than employers elsewhere in Britain. Rees and Fielder examine the reasons for these findings, and the extent to which work practices and career pathways are constructed so as to advantage men. Women in Wales are just beginning to create the networks and contacts which may help to counteract this bias, but with female participation rates still comparatively low, and so few 'top women', the distance yet to be travelled is huge.

Caroline Lloyd and Anna Walker provide accounts of two kinds of work which are very closely identified with female labour. In the clothing industry, discussed by Lloyd, a sector which at the time of her study was expanding in Wales, 86 per cent of employees are women. Predictably, they tend to be confined to the lower levels of the job hierarchy. Skilled tasks are associated with male employees, to such an extent that the feminization of a particular job, for example cutting, signifies its loss of skilled status. More advanced technology has enabled the employment of larger numbers of women, but wage levels are low and the industry is reluctant to train labour to a high standard. The picture of women's jobs as low-wage, low-skill is sadly familiar, although in this particular case we do not find the usual correlate of large numbers of part-time employees. This is because the nature of the labour process in the Welsh clothing firms is thought by employers to be incompatible with the uncertainty of part-time work. However, in practice employment patterns are quite varied.

In her case study of the hotel trade in a local labour market, Anna Walker does observe a great deal of part-time and casual working. This she explains in terms of the flexibility required to adjust to the irregular nature of demand for hotel services. It is mainly women who are employed to meet this need, and once again definitions of 'skilled' work, which are associated with clearly defined jobs, are constructed in such a way as to favour men. Female employees are usually expected to turn their hands to a variety of tasks. Although her findings show that there are clear gender differences, Walker argues that they are not adequately explained by prevailing models of 'dual' or 'segmented' labour market organization, and are better viewed as a continuum of positions.

Mainwaring and Vass return to the question of the economics of colliery closure discussed in volume 3, bringing up to date the story of British Coal's strategy for productivity through closure. In fact, they show that significant gains were made in the immediate aftermath of the 1984–5 strike, partly through closure of the least productive pits, but more through increased productivity in those that remained. They suggest that this result is compatible with a short-term policy of extracting a fast yield, capitalizing on the miners' defeat, prior to the abandonment of the South Wales coalfield, a section of the British industry that was not regarded as ripe for privatization.

The two remaining contributions are policy-oriented, reporting results from evaluation studies. In a wide-ranging review of developments in the field of special needs housing, Ian Shaw and his colleagues highlight the degree of turbulence in the policy environment, with health and social services and local government all undergoing major change associated with the introduction of new criteria for performance monitoring, quality assurance and strategic planning. The new Welsh agencies are seeking to make their mark in a volatile situation, where a broad consensus about the purpose of housing for categories in special need overlays considerable fragmentation and variation at the operational level. Day-to-day management of different kinds of special need necessitates a range of strategies for coping with limited resources. Resource constraints in relation to health provision set the context for Ceri Phillips and Malcolm Prowle's systematic appraisal of the costs and benefits of the anti-smoking component of the Heartbeat Wales campaign, designed to attack Wales's high levels of coronary heart disease. Employing the techniques of economic evaluation, the authors establish, within a wide band of assumptions, that the returns to this preventive measure were extremely positive.

With the appearance of this issue, Gareth Rees will be giving up his editorial role, to be replaced by Dennis Thomas. Gareth played a major part in arguing the case for a journal which would deal with social science contributions to understanding current economic and social issues in Wales, and we believe the development of *Contemporary Wales* has amply justified his confidence that there was both the audience and the level of activity among social scientists interested in Wales to support it. It is particularly gratifying to see topics which have been raised in past issues further developed in the pages which follow.

Graham Day
Gareth Rees

REFERENCES

Jones B. (1988) 'The Development of Welsh Territorial Institutions: Modernization Theory Revisited', *Contemporary Wales*, 2, pp. 47–61.

Rees T. (1988) 'Changing Patterns of Women's Work in Wales: Some Myths Explored', *Contemporary Wales*, 2, pp. 119–30.

Winckler V. (1987) 'Women and Work in Contemporary Wales', *Contemporary Wales*, 1, pp. 53–71.

1. WALES AND THE POLITICAL IMPACT OF '1992'

Duncan Mitchell

INTRODUCTION

Neville Chamberlain felt that Wales was not distinct enough an entity to warrant its own minister. Over the years the Principality has gradually asserted its identity, to the present point where some measure of devolution appears a real possibility. At another level, Europe has also struggled to find a sense of its own worth, and in recent years has also begun to lay claim to a degree of autonomy. This chapter seeks to establish what, if any, inter-relationship there may be between these trends. What does the mystic term '1992' mean in political terms? How does this relate to Wales? Is there evidence of change, and how may this influence the Welsh debate?

'1992' AND EUROPEAN INTEGRATION

The date of 31 December 1992 was laid down by the Single European Act (SEA) (Commission 1986), as the deadline for the completion of the Internal Market in the European Community (EC). The Act can be depicted as being primarily policy-driven, minimal institutional change included merely in order to facilitate legislation for the free movement of goods, services, persons and capital within the EC. Such an exclusively economic bias, however, provides at best a partial explanation of the SEA's motives and goals.

The Single Market programme was added into the deliberations of the Intergovernmental Conference (IGC), which drew up the SEA, by the Milan Summit of June 1985. Policy and institutional reform was by then already high on the EC's agenda. One of the primary influences in determining that agenda had been the European Parliament's (EP) Draft European Union Treaty of 1984, to which President François Mitterrand had lent his support. Essentially motivated by federalist goals, the Draft Treaty was too dramatic a step for member states to accept, but it was a vital background to the IGC's deliberations.

The IGC thus linked economic and political issues, and in the process dragged the UK unwillingly into the launch of a new phase in Euro-dynamism, partly through fear of losing the Single Market part of the package (which Mrs Thatcher viewed as a massive exercise in deregulation, *à la* Britain), and isolating itself into the bargain. Having opposed the convening of the IGC, but outvoted, the British government afterwards tried to dismiss the import of the political reforms. Yet the fusing of the Cockfield White Paper with institutional overhaul created a kind of symbiosis between economic and political processes which are more closely bound together today than ever. 'Whether the freeing of the internal market was being used as a stalking horse for political union, or whether it was seen as simply a pragmatic response to a pressing problem, it certainly had far-reaching implications' (George, 1991, p. 165).

The SEA itself was actually a great disappointment at the time to the EP and member states whose goal was European union. It seemed to many that an opportunity had been missed. The extension of majority voting in the Council of Ministers was restricted to those articles of the Treaty of Rome which were essential to the successful achievement of the Single Market. However, the SEA also broadened the EC's policy competences, bringing economic and monetary policies, social policy, policies for economic and social cohesion, research and technological development and environment policy into the treaties for the first time. The EP was given increased influence in the legislative process by means of the 'co-operation procedure',[1] and an element of co-decision with the Council via the 'assent procedure'. The Commission gained (strictly controlled) new powers to implement EC legislation. Community responsibilities were also widened to include the field of foreign policy and security cooperation.

The SEA and indeed '1992' must therefore be seen as symptoms, rather than causes or end-products. The Act may not have been a manifesto for political unification (despite the commitment to European Union in the preamble), but it can still be described as having 'clear maximalist/federalist implications' (Lodge, 1989, p. 36). The end of stagnation in the EC had released a mass of pent-up energy. Recent writings have reopened a debate about 'spillover', a concept central to the Neofunctionalist theory of European integration.[2] Neofunctionalism was developed in the 1950s and 1960s as a response to the establishment of European institutions. Leading proponents such as Haas and Lindberg advanced the thesis that 'integration within one sector will tend to beget its own impetus and spread to other sectors' (Tranholm-Mikkelsen, 1991, p. 4) with a cumulative effect resulting in increasingly supranational political and economic intercourse, and consequently supranational political institutions. Stagnation in the 1970s appeared to contradict this thesis, and Haas in particular virtually abandoned Neofunctionalism (Haas, 1976). However, spillover appears to be at work again in the aftermath of the SEA, as the steps taken to achieve the Single Market create pressures for action in other policy areas, such as regional and social policies. Functional integration in turn appears to be adding to pressures for greater institutional reform. One has only to look at the IGCs on economic and monetary, and political union, which resulted in the settlement at Maastricht in December 1991, to see theory in action. The depth of EC involvement in existing policy areas has also increased. Jacques Delors, the Commission President, told the EP in 1988 that within 10 years some 80 per cent of economic legislation would be enacted by the EC rather than by member states, and that social and fiscal matters might also be EC concerns. Helmut Kohl claimed that European Union was no longer a distant vision after the February 1988 Hanover summit. The EC integration process appears to have generated its own momentum, with a new focus of political authority appearing at the European level. This process is unlikely to be in a given direction or unbroken, as originally predicted by the Neofunctionalists, but may now be a little like riding a bicycle: if the rider stops he/she will fall off and therefore has no choice but to keep going forward (Emerson, 1989). Exclusion of the word 'federal' from the Maastricht agreement is therefore almost irrelevant.

The meaning of '1992' must be understood, not just as the Single Market programme, but as a wholly new phase in European integration, encompassing economic and monetary, and political union. It is in that context that this paper has been written. The significance of this new phase for national and subnational politics lies in the adjustments to established political patterns which need to be made if changes in the EC are to be addressed. Integration implies an element of centralization of political authority, even if that need not necessarily result in the creation of that Thatcherite bogey, the 'European superstate'. National executives have demonstrably lost individual control over the EC process where majority voting applies. EC intervention affects a large and growing number of policy sectors hitherto the preserve of national authorities. William Wallace describes the process of integration as leading to 'government as the sharing of powers between different institutions, groups and levels of loyalty and authority' (Wallace, 1990, p. 64). We may not be about to see the actual demise of the nation-state, but the EC is growing in relative importance. No one can afford to tip the rider off the bicycle, but there will be many grimaces as the wheels go over sensitive national sovereign feet.

ORGANIZATIONAL CHANGE IN WALES

The EC has long been important to Wales because of regional funding and policies connected with coal and steel, agriculture and fisheries, and transport (Jones, 1985). The EC was originally associated with fears of Welsh political and economic marginalization. In recent years, however, there appears to have been a qualitative change in Welsh 'Europeanization', and a new optimism that Wales can manage the benefits and disbenefits yielded by European integration.

The Welsh Office and its Agencies

The Welsh Office is responsible for the administration of a large number of policy fields in Wales, and therefore is at the centre of the Wales–EC relationship. The Agricultural Department (WOAD) administers the Common Agricultural Policy (CAP). A European Affairs Division (EAD) was created in 1973 for the administration of the European Regional Development Fund (ERDF). The EAD is nine years junior to the Welsh Office itself, but has progressively expanded in terms of size and role, and in its own sense of identity, especially in the last few years. Approximately 50 civil servants now work in the EAD, of whom 30 are involved with Community structural funds. The EAD's co-ordinating role within the Welsh Office is burgeoning as the scope of EC contacts with different departmental responsibilities expands (Jones and Keating 1991). Where the EC was once restricted to involvement in specific sectors, it is now affecting many more aspects of Welsh Office work, and in a far more visible manner. As a result, a determination to spread specialist knowledge of the EC across all departments has emerged, and this is clearly reflected by the Welsh Office's recruitment policy of attracting Welsh 'Europeans' via the HEOD(A) and European 'Fast Stream' intakes. The EC's present activity does not, therefore, give rise to public expressions of concern. Officials speak of the Welsh Office as having 'come of age', European developments being seen as an ongoing process which is unlikely to engender upheaval.

The Welsh Development Agency (WDA) was established in 1976 to deal with the economic regeneration of areas suffering from the decline of traditional industries. The Agency has exploited the latitude of its remit to develop a distinct role for itself, concentrating particularly on the EC. The

SEA marked a quantum leap forward for its work. Almost every aspect of WDA activity is now affected by EC programmes and legislation. In recent years a European division has been established in recognition of this 'explosion'. The WDA is also busy establishing links with organizations carrying out a similar or approximate role in other regions of the EC. Again, a purposeful optimism suffuses this work: reference is made to the extent of inward investment which the WDA has succeeded in attracting in recent years (*Western Mail*, 24 March 1990). Nowhere, however, is the changing strategy of the WDA clearer than in the 1991 decision to open an 'embassy' in Brussels (*Western Mail*, 17 October 1991). (Until 1991 the WDA had shared the costs of a Brussels-based consultancy with local authorities.) The need to expand its information-gathering and lobbying activities represented by the establishment of the Brussels office, which will begin work in January 1992, shows just how important activity at the EC level has become. The WDA is seeking collaboration from local authorities, who are also being asked to make a financial commitment (the office is to cost around £0.5m per annum), University Colleges and other organizations.

Local Government

Local government has been extensively affected by the evolution of the EC from the SEA onwards. The expansion of EC competences into areas affecting the work of local authorities (*Local Work*, March 1991) has led to a rash of European Liaison Officers being appointed by British local authorities, West Glamorgan being a recent example. The SEA also committed member states to an overhaul of the way in which the Community's structural funds were administered. One of the Commission's major aims is to develop a tripartite 'partnership' between itself, member governments and local or regional authorities (generally County Councils in the UK) in the drawing up of programmes for funding and the implementation of the funds allocated. This should in theory give local government a chair at the table and an opportunity to develop a much higher profile in relations with the EC: certainly, local authorities see things this way. The partnership concept also goes beyond regional funds to include much wider potential for local and regional authority involvement in a number of other EC policy areas. Welsh local government is having to revise its modes of operation accordingly, a difficult process which means a great deal of work for those involved and has added to pressures to re-evaluate existing Welsh Office and local government relations.

Contacts which Welsh local government has been building up over a number of years have also assumed a new substance. The Assembly of Welsh

Counties (AWC), which represents Welsh County Councils, is a member of a number of European organizations. Of these, the EC's Consultative Committee of Regional and Local Authorities (CCRLA), which was established by the Commission, and first met in 1988, is the only official body representing local and regional authorities directly to EC institutions. The AWC effectively nominates the one Welsh representative. The Commission has regularly consulted the CCRLA on matters of regional development and wanted to see its role institutionalized. The Commission tabled proposals to this end to the IGC on political union (Commission, 1991), and the Maastricht accord seems likely to incorporate the CCRLA formally in the treaty base of the EC as the 'Committee of the Regions'. There are to be 24 UK members of this body (out of a total of 189). How many of these will be Welsh representatives, and how they are to be appointed, are questions which will provoke fierce debate. The committee will have consultative status and will have to be asked for an opinion on legislative proposals relating to education, training and youth, economic and social cohesion, structural funds, transport infrastructure projects, public health and culture. The AWC's memberships of bodies such as the Atlantic Arc Commission, and the Conference of Peripheral Maritime Regions of the EC are additional means of expressing common interests and concerns, and reflect the growing need and desire of local government to deal beyond the national level. Certainly, if local government gains a voice at the European level via the Committee of the Regions, and allies in the Commission and EP, its visibility, authority and influence will be greatly enhanced.

Welsh Interests

The CBI's European interests are well established, the Single Market having been a long-standing theme in the business world. British business is also generally enthusiastic about Economic and Monetary Union (EMU). The CBI set up its own Brussels office at a very early stage and has played a major part in the European employers' federation, UNICE. 1992 has seen a redoubling of efforts to make Welsh business aware of the implications of the Single Market, but this is a quantitative rather than a qualitative change. The Wales Trades Union Congress (WTUC), on the other hand, has been dramatically influenced by the spur not only of the Single Market, but also by the Delors Commission's championship of the Social Charter. The WTUC is more than just a regional trade union organization: it lacks the full autonomy of the Scottish TUC, but is allowed to develop links independently with regional union organizations in other member states. Eight to nine years of assiduous cultivation have resulted in a broad network of Welsh contacts throughout the EC, as well as close co-operation with Welsh MEPs. 1992 has boosted these activities, but its effects also go much further. The Commission seeks to foster transnational and interregional projects, and encourages trade union involvement as part of its Social Charter/partnership ethos. This finds favour among British trade unions, which have been excluded from involvement in decision-making in the UK for over a decade. Three years ago the WTUC established a regional network with union organizations in Aarhus (Denmark) and Granada (Spain), with the aim of pooling information and expertise. Membership of this network has since mushroomed: regional organizations from most member states now have some representation at the annual meetings. The WTUC is gaining a voice in European affairs and sees the EC as an important forum for the advance of its interests. The work it undertakes with other regional organizations is not surprisingly described as 'vitally important' (WTUC, 1991, p. 10).

It would appear that revitalization of the Community has indeed 'spilled over' into a large measure of organizational change in Wales. European contacts can only multiply as the nation-state is increasingly by-passed. There also appears to be a developing belief that Wales will benefit from European contacts, but only if Welsh institutions can assert themselves, at the Welsh and UK levels as much as at the EC level. Whether this belief is based on more than optimism alone is not clear, but from the organizational viewpoint, integration is interpreted as much as a challenge and an opportunity as a threat. Growing EC influence is given: the real debate seems not to be over the positiveness of European integration as much as how best to manage this process.

THE REGIONS AND '1992'

Despite Welsh institutions' faith in their own capacities, Wales's status as a peripheral region is still an important factor. Cecchini's estimate of benefits accruing from the Single Market (Cecchini, 1988) has been strongly criticized for failing to deal with the fact that these gains will not be evenly distributed, and that some sectors and regions may well actually suffer (Cutler et al., 1989; Neuburger, 1989; Grahl and Teague, 1989). Regions with a concentration of declining industries or peripheral areas are certainly vulnerable. Unless action is taken to counter this problem, there is a danger that 1992 may increase Wales's economic marginalization. Member states are committed to doubling the EC's structural funds by 1992, but changing EC membership has meant that there are more relatively poorer regions, a situation exacerbated by

German unification. Questions have been raised as to whether the EC's funds can do more than simply prevent disparities from increasing overall (Marques-Mendes, 1990). What monies the EC does disburse to a region such as Wales may be psychologically important, but are small in absolute terms, and Wales faces growing competition for those funds. When EMU becomes a reality, as Maastricht makes inevitable, redistributive measures by national governments may be hampered by restrictions on the size of national budget deficits. As integration reduces national governments' ability to address the concern of regions, those regions will turn to the EC for an answer. If economic and political integration also accelerates the trend towards cultural homogeneity, regional disquiet will also be aroused. Regions will therefore need to strengthen their contacts with the new centres of authority, to gather information, lobby and extend networks of co-operation. Wales's ability to manage changes induced by events in Europe is thus equated with the ability to act independently in defence of its own interest at the European level.

The Commission is making efforts to minimize peripheralization: current efforts are most eloquently expressed in the concept of a 'Europe of the Regions'. Through 'partnership' the Commission aims to involve local and regional organizations in decisions affecting themselves wherever practicable. It was with this in mind that the CCRLA was created, and the establishment of the Committee of the Regions, with formal institutional status equal to that of the Economic and Social Committee will go some way to fulfilling this aim. The Committee's formal opinion, without receipt of which the Commission could not proceed, would acquire considerable weight. Ultimately there might even be an upper house in the EC, composed of regional representatives, with extensive legislative powers, although this lies in the distant future.

Subsidiarity is a principle which is likely to become one of the key items of 'Eurospeak' in the next few years. It is not a new word, deriving in part from the socio-philosophical language of the Roman Catholic Church (Wilke and Wallace, 1990). In the context of the EC the term has been in vague use for a number of years, but has become central to the debate since the SEA. The fears of the German *Länder* that growing EC authority might impinge on their own 'sovereignty' brought the issue to a head. The principle of subsidiarity allows no function to be allocated to a higher and larger level of authority if a smaller and lower level can perform that function adequately. Federalists have seized on subsidiarity as a means of allaying fears of centralization in a European Union. The British government interprets subsidiarity to mean that powers should remain with the member states unless a proven case for handing them over to the EC level exists. The federalist interpretation finds favour in many quarters. Chancellor Kohl has made this abundantly clear: 'Federalism and self-government at local level must have their place in a European Political Union. We are working towards a Europe characterized by diversity, in which traditional – particularly regional – identities have their place.'[3] Subsidiarity is therefore being used to argue for a democratic Community, based on decentralization of power from the national level, as well as accretion of power by the Community. At Maastricht the principle has found expression as 'decisions taken as closely as possible to the citizens'. A new Article 3b states that the EC shall act, rather than the member states, only if objectives can be better achieved 'by reason of the scale or effects of the proposed action' (Millar, 1991, p. 2).

The influence of the Commission should not be overestimated. Nor should one overestimate the power of German rhetoric. A Europe of the Regions, with functions distributed according to the principle of subsidiarity, is unlikely for the foreseeable future. There are pressures building in that direction, however. The rules of the game are changing, and it is no exaggeration to say that the SEA began a 'restructuring of the region–state relations' (Leonardi and Nanetti, 1990, p. 2). As Leonardi and Nanetti further comment: 'One cannot abolish all barriers to economic interaction among the Member States and at the same time maintain restrictions on subnational levels of government which prevent them from interacting across national boundaries' (ibid., p. 197). The weakening of the nation-state's stranglehold on channels of influence and communication between subnational and European levels may act *de facto* as a federalizing process. Pressures for a separate European identity for the regions, combined with a desire for flexibility and partnership on the part of the Commission constitute a pincer challenge to the national level of authority which could fundamentally affect national–regional relations.

WALES AS A REGION

The threat of peripheralization after 1992 requires Wales to organize its institutional order so that democracy and accountability are not impaired and so that the Welsh voice is heard. On whose terms will this be conducted?

Wales has certain structural disadvantages relative to, for example, the south-east of England. A concentration of declining industries, a large agricultural sector and a geographically peripheral position with poor transport infrastructure mean that Wales is not well placed to take advantage of the removal of barriers. Welsh interests have more in common with those of Scotland and the north-east of England. If Wales lacks the ability to be heard then all the Commission encouragement of the regions in the world will pass the Principality by. The priority for Welsh interests therefore has become the establishment of a clear and vocal Welsh identity at the EC level. The question is whether the present system is the best way to proceed. Who should speak for the Welsh?

Many comparisons are made between Wales's situation and that of the German regional states, the *Länder*. The Germans have an advantage in being familiar with the terms of the integration debate, being accustomed to the allocation of functions to different levels of government, and fully conversant with their own version of subsidiarity. The *Länder* have a considerable input into the German system through their own house in the Federal parliament, the Bundesrat. The regions have a direct say in federal politics and a measure of control over any EC legislation passing through the national level (Kellas, 1991), especially EC Treaty amendments. The *Länder* won additional rights *vis-à-vis* the EC as a result of the SEA (Paterson and Southern, 1991). There are also *Länder* offices in Brussels, well resourced and permanently staffed, which facilitate extensive lobbying and collaboration with each other and other EC regions in winning EC funds and, vitally, exerting considerable influence on the shape of future EC policies. The ability to act at the EC level is strengthened by their automatic representation on German delegations to the EC and their right to be present in the Council if *Land* interests are directly affected. *Länder* delegates sit on Commission consultative bodies and have a powerful presence in the CCRLA. Finally, the *Länder* have also been represented at the IGCs on EMU and political union. Not surprisingly the Germans are very keen on the idea of a Europe of the Regions, and will doubtless maximize the opportunity represented by the Committee of the Regions.

Wales's need to maximize its own influence has led to many envious comparisons between the status of Welsh and German regional representation. The accuracy of these comparisons may be debated, but not their political significance. True, Wales is indeed in a privileged position relative to English regions, none of which have their own representative in the Cabinet, or their own administration with separate powers. Wales also has more MPs at Westminster per head of population than England. The Secretary of State is able to push for Welsh interests at the top of the system, in Cabinet, and has privileged access to the EC via UK representatives in the Council and the UK permanent representation at the EC, UKREP. The Secretary of State also plays a figurehead role in attracting attention to the Principality. Agreements with Baden-Württemberg, and more recently with Catalonia[4] have been held up as examples of the gains from the EC which the present system brings.

It is questionable, however, whether the present system is the most democratic or efficient means of presenting the Welsh viewpoint in Europe. The Welsh Office has given Wales an identity of sorts but is itself a department of central government. At a time when the debate about democratic representation in the EC is raging, Wales is represented in the Council of Ministers via the British government. The Secretary of State, who is not directly accountable to Welsh voters in any case, is a 'junior partner' in this arrangement (Jones and Keating, 1991). EC institutions, particularly the Commission, are therefore hampered in trying to address Welsh interests directly, for fear of being seen as trying to undermine central government's authority. Welsh local authorities feel that 'partnership' gives them no more than a 'seat on wheels', to be pushed away from the table whenever their presence becomes undesirable. A Secretary of State can do no more than argue the Welsh case at the UK level; the view then put to the EC, by which the Secretary of State has to abide, is a collective UK view, which may subsume or even ignore Welsh needs. An illustration of this problem was the threat in late 1990 to South and parts of North Wales of losing Objective 2 (areas of industrial decline) eligibility for structural funds. The Secretary of State was urged by local authorities and MEPs to push the Welsh case but was constrained by pressure on the British government from other member states with poor regions, and also by the case for other British regions which were suffering more according to relative criteria. The present government has also been criticized by local authorities, MEPs and trade unions for frowning on Commission attempts to develop a dialogue with the Welsh CBI and WTUC, and on MEPs' attempts to develop a dialogue with the Welsh Office itself. Links with Baden-Württemberg have been dismissed, by such critics, possibly a little unfairly, as window-dressing.

Much is made by the AWC, despite central government opposition, of increasing co-operation between local government and the Commission, and as has been indicated, there are increasing links between Wales, other regions and the EC level, which by-pass the Welsh Office. Despite the Secretary of State's undoubted achievements, critics believe the status of the Welsh Office as a department of central government represents an obstacle to the efficient articulation of Welsh interests. Perhaps the most visible expression of this quarrel is over the issue of additionality. It is the aim of EC structural funds to act in addition to national measures, and not to be used merely as a subsidy for national expenditure. The UK does not account EC regional grants separately from total expenditure, making it almost impossible to see whether funds are reaching their prescribed destination. This in turn leads to the suspicion that EC aid is being diverted, at least in part, to subsidizing the Treasury.

The UK's response is that expenditure forecasts are drawn up anticipating an EC element, and that additionality is built in. Furthermore, 'top-slicing' in England and Wales keeps a certain proportion of EC funds for direct allocation to eligible areas. However, 'top-slicing' applies only to the ERDF, not the other structural funds, and in any case is still less than the total received from the EC.

The argument over additionality has recently concentrated on one particular Community programme, Rechar, drawn up in response to an initiative from UK coalfield communities, many of them Welsh, to promote redevelopment and retraining in areas affected by the run-down of coal mining. The UK is the largest single potential beneficiary of Rechar and has been offered £100m, of which approximately £18m could fall to Wales. However, the additionality controversy has led the British Regional Commissioner, Bruce Millan, to withhold Rechar funds from the UK. He has also blocked other regional aid to Wales until a settlement of the dispute is achieved. Millan has rejected British arguments and points out that such controversies happen only where the UK is involved. The Secretary of State is placed in an unenviable position, unable or unwilling to take a line contrary to that of the government. The campaign in Wales has consequently been left to local authorities, the WTUC and MEPs.

Battle lines are not entirely clearly drawn: there are Welsh Labour MPs who feel that the present system has its advantages. If Welsh interests are coterminous with those of the UK, then the status quo has a number of advantages in terms of representation in Cabinet and therefore all the weight of the UK in the EC. If however Wales as a region needs to put its own, different viewpoint to the EC (and this is increasingly the case), then the absence of a clearly separate Welsh identity may be a matter for concern. The Welsh Office's identification with central government may result in its also being by-passed, or at least challenged, creating a conflict at the Welsh level. The Secretary of State has reacted to calls for a Europe of the Regions and a clear Welsh voice with suggestions that Wales be represented on the Committee of the Regions by the Secretary of State and the head of the WDA. Would this reflect Welsh needs? However privileged Wales may be, relative to English regions, the present system, with its high degree of central control, arguably runs contrary to the debate about democratic accountability and subsidiarity which is taking place in other member states.

WELSH DEVOLUTION AND '1992'

Federalizing trends in the EC and the need to preserve democracy and accountability at all levels are closely linked to subnational units' concerns about economic and political peripheralization, and desires for greater representation at European level. We have seen how these concerns are particularly acute in the case of Wales, especially when one compares Wales with German Länder. There is already a pattern of contacts between various Welsh organizations, other regions and the EC, creating a kind of rivalry between these organizations and the Welsh Office. These tensions would be considerable were Wales 'just' a region. Yet Wales is more than this: it is a small, historic and cultural nation (Jones, 1985), which has aspirations to an independent political identity. It is in this context that the debate in Wales needs to be understood.

When the UK first joined the EC in 1973, devolution was a major political issue. However, in the first years of membership the EC was not seen as being linked to the devolution campaign, except in the negative sense that the EC might remove Wales one step further from the centres of decision-making. Integration-related concerns, Commission plans for partnership with sub-national levels of government, and a Europe of the Regions with special Welsh EC representation in a strengthened EC regional body, have more recently led to a new centre-left consensus in Wales, based on the positive realization that devolution and integration may actually be compatible.

The assault on the existing system comes from a number of directions. Wales is culturally distinct from England, not only because of its linguistic and nationalist elements but also because of the different ethos pertaining to employment and social issues which is reflected in Welsh electoral outcomes. Welsh economic concerns are also distinct from those of the English and particularly south-east England. The differences are reflected in the disparity between Welsh voting patterns and the overall UK result. Wales elects 38 MPs, yet at present less than a sixth of those MPs belong to the party in power at Westminster. The overwhelming dominance of the Labour Party in Welsh politics is also reflected in European elections, at which in 1989 Labour received 48.9 per cent of the vote in Wales against a Conservative vote of 23.4 per cent, and a Plaid Cymru vote of 12.9 per cent (Plaid Cymru's vote was concentrated in the north-west, where Dafydd Elis Thomas received a vote of 25.4 per cent (HTV Cymru Wales 1990)). At the local level Labour and Independents dominate District and County Councils, and hold all the seats on the AWC. (Labour has more than half of all the County, and nearly half of all District seats (*Municipal Journal*, 1991; *Western Mail*, 4 May 1991).) It could therefore be argued that Welsh interests are poorly represented at the British, and even less at the European level. The link between regionalism and European integration is thus reinforced. Britain's top-down, unitary system runs up against increasing European integration on the one hand, and increasingly related calls for decentralization on the other. The Welsh Office is caught in between. Margaret Thatcher's strident anti-Europeanism of the 1980s and the centralizing actions of her government acted as catalysts in tying Welsh and European issues together. John Major may be a more conciliatory figure, but the association is now established: Maastricht has done little to change impressions.

Many of the developments in Wales referred to earlier need to be understood in this light. Local authorities have found the 'partnership' system a frustrating experience, and although local authorities and the AWC speak of a reasonable working relationship with the Welsh Office, the constraints imposed on the Welsh Office by its relationship with central government have led many to conclude that accountability and efficiency would be better served by a separate Welsh voice. The AWC has thrown its weight behind the campaign for a Welsh Assembly and has built up its contacts via EC bodies such as the CCRLA, staking its claim as the forerunner of any elected Welsh regional body. The AWC views comparisons with the *Länder* as valid, and wants itself, rather than the Secretary of State, to be the Welsh voice in the Committee of the Regions not least because it sees itself as possessing democratic legitimacy which would place it on an equal footing with German representatives. The WTUC's links with regional counterparts form a whole network which the WTUC regards as far more wide-ranging and intensive than any of the Secretary of State's programmes. The EC offers Welsh trade unions a vision of influence denied them within the British system. The WTUC also supports the idea of a Welsh Assembly. Even the WDA's Brussels office, despite WDA denials, can be seen as an indication that a system forced to operate via UK channels, rather than direct Welsh representation, cannot adequately present the Welsh case.

Political parties are now also stressing the link between Europe and a Welsh identity. Plaid Cymru, originally opposed to EC membership, has radically revised its position over recent years, and is now campaigning vigorously on a platform of 'Wales in Europe'. Plaid has cultivated contacts within the European Free Alliance, which represents 18 parties from small nations and regions, and works with the Rainbow Group in the EP. Plaid wants Wales to be represented independently in a Senate of the Regions, which would form the upper house of a bicameral European Parliament, in the lower house of which Wales would have 15 MEPs. Wales would also gain the right to nominate one of the members of the Commission, and there would be an increased Welsh presence on the Economic and Social Committee (Plaid Cymru). Plaid has seen the opportunity in developing its credentials as a European regional party to shed its image of narrow linguistic and cultural nationalism. Whether Plaid will actually benefit electorally is open to question, given its wholehearted espousal of Europe at the 1989 European elections, in which it failed to win a single seat. However, the importance to Plaid's platform of the EC angle is clear.

The Unionist ethos in the Conservative Party makes it impossible for the Tories to subscribe to Welsh devolution, and attachment to concepts of sovereignty leads most Tories to a profound opposition to federalism in the EC. Nor is it in their interests to espouse devolution, given the 'English' nature of Welsh Conservative seats. The Conservatives are locked into a centralist logic which goes against the grain of present trends, but in any case '1992' will not produce a seismic shock for Welsh conservatism: it is not seen as being salient or decided enough an issue.

The Conservative case challenges a number of points in the devolutionist campaign. The EC is radically changing and developing, as is the world outside. Pursuing devolution and a more integrated Europe at such a time might run the risk of adding to bureaucracy and creating rigidities and conflict between the Welsh and UK levels, which could damage the Welsh interest far more than help it. If one accepts that this is the case, Wales would be much better off working within the UK framework for a pragmatic and evolutionary approach to the EC, which would continue to give Wales the influence at the EC level of the UK government.

The Labour Party has meanwhile used the discomfiture of Welsh Tories over devolution and Europe to its own advantage. Plaid Cymru campaigns, where successful, are most likely to benefit Labour in a non-radicalized political environment, where Labour is generally seen as the 'natural' party of government in Wales. However, Labour is, like the Conservative party, a national party, and is therefore even more vulnerable in some respects than the Conservatives to conflicts between its Welsh and English elements. Labour has its own rifts over Europe, and devolution would look much less attractive to a party which relies partly on Welsh over-representation for its strength in Parliament. European integration is therefore a double-edged sword for Labour in Wales, and were a future Labour administration to fail to satisfy Welsh demands, the devolution issue might once again become radicalized, to Plaid Cymru's advantage.

CONCLUSION

The convergence of devolution and European issues is very important but of itself no guarantee that '1992', however one looks at it, will actually have a major impact on Welsh politics. The debate is there for those who are aware of the implications, and the growing confidence and assertiveness of Welsh organizations gives an extra vitality to the argument, but the salience of European affairs as a Welsh electoral issue is a matter of doubt, and dependent on any number of variables. It should be noted that, despite great public support for the ideal of devolution, only a tiny minority puts the matter at the top of its list of priorities in opinion polls. Many still lack the knowledge of European affairs to make the link between integration and Welsh interests, however hard politicians may try. The relationship between Wales and the EC is likely to remain largely an elite preoccupation, although its effects at the ballot box may be felt in many subtle ways. Integration will act as a stimulus to the ongoing discussion about Wales's identity, and broaden that discussion beyond the national perspective. Whether this will be a decisive influence remains to be seen.

This is not, however, to underestimate the significance of current developments. There can be little doubt that the coincidence of interests in integration and devolution is likely to exert a very powerful – if indirect – pull on Welsh politics in the medium- to long-term. The spillover predicted by Neofunctionalism seeps into, rather than deluges, the political system. In innumerable ways European and Welsh political issues are certain to become ever more intricately intertwined.

NOTES

1   The EC's 'co-operation procedure' gives certain legislation relating to the Single Market a second reading. The EP may accept legislative proposals after the Council's first reading, or propose amendment or rejection of the measure. The 'assent procedure' refers to the accession of new member states or association agreements between the EC and third countries, over which the EP has a veto.
2   The main Neofunctionalist works are Haas (1958) and Lindberg (1963). Recent reappraisals of Neofunctionalism include George (1991), Mutimer (1989) and Tranholm-Mikkelsen (1991).
3   Speech at Hambach Castle, 24 September 1991.
4   The agreement with Baden-Württemberg was signed in March 1990; that with Catalonia in October 1991.

REFERENCES

Cecchini, P. (1988) *The European Challenge: 1992 – the Benefits of a Single Market*, Aldershot, Wildwood.

Centre for Local Economic Strategies (1991) *Local Work*, no. 24, March 1991.

Commission of the EC (1986) *Single European Act*, Luxemburg.

Commission of the EC (1991), *Bulletin of the EC*, Supplement 2/1991, Luxemburg.

Cutler, T., Haslam, C., Williams, J. and Williams, C. (1989) *1992: The Struggle for Europe*, Oxford, Berg.

Emerson, M. (1989) '1992 – the Bicycle Theory Rides Again', *Political Quarterly*, 59, pp. 289–99.

George, S. (1991) *Politics and Policy in the European Community*, 2nd edn, Oxford, OUP.

Grahl, J. and Teague, P. (1989) 'The Cost of Neo-Liberal Europe', *New Left Review*, no. 174 (March–April), pp. 33–51.

Haas, E. (1958) *The Uniting of Europe: Political, Social and Economic Forces, 1950–57*, London, Stevens.

Haas, E. (1976) 'Turbulent Fields and the Theory of Regional Integration', *International Organisation*, 30, pp. 173–212.

Hennessy, P. (1989) *Whitehall*, London, Fontana.

HTV Cymru Wales (1990) *The Wales Yearbook 1991*, Cardiff, HTV Cymru Wales.

Jones, B. (1985) 'Wales in the European Community', in B. Jones and M. Keating (eds), *Regions in the European Community*, Oxford, Clarendon Press.

Jones, B. and Keating, M. (1991), *Nations, Regions and Europe: The UK Experience* (unpublished paper).

Kellas, J. (1991) 'European Integration and the Regions', *Parliamentary Affairs*, 44, pp. 226–39.

Leonardi, R. and Nanetti, R. (eds) (1990) *The Regions and European Integration: The Case of Emilia-Romagna*, London, Pinter.

Lindberg, L. (1963) *The Political Dynamics of European Economic Integration*, London, OUP.

Lodge, J. (1989) 'The Political Implications of 1992', *Politics*, 9, pp. 34–40.

Marques-Mendes, A. (1990) 'Economic Cohesion in Europe: The Impact of the Delors Plan', *Journal of Common Market Studies*, 29, pp. 17–36.

Millar, D. (1991) *European Council, 9–10 December 1991, Maastricht Draft Treaty on European Union: Synopsis of Section on European Political Union*, Edinburgh, Europa Institute (University of Edinburgh).

Municipal Journal (1991) *Municipal Yearbook 1991*, London, Municipal Journal.

Mutimer, D. (1989) '1992 and the Political Integration of Europe: Neofunctionalism Reconsidered', *Journal of European Integration*, 13, pp. 75–101.

Neuburger, H. (1989), *The Economics of 1992* (Report commissioned by the British Labour Group of Euro MPs).

Paterson, W. and Southern, D. (1991) *Governing Germany*, Oxford, Blackwell.

Plaid Cymru, *Wales in Europe: A Community of Communities*, Cardiff, Plaid Cymru.

Tranholm-Mikkelsen, J. (1991) 'Neofunctionalism: Obstinate or Obsolete? A Re-appraisal in the Light of the New Dynamism of the EC', *Millennium*, 20, pp. 1–22.

Wales TUC (1991) *Annual Report*, Cardiff, WTUC.

Wallace, W. (1990) *The Transformation of Western Europe*, London, Pinter.
Wilke, M. and Wallace, H. (1990) *Subsidiarity: Approaches to Power-Sharing in the European Community*, London, RIIA.

2. WALES AS A PLURAL SOCIETY

John Giggs and Charles Pattie

INTRODUCTION

> Instead of arguing that the population [of Britain] is culturally homo-
> geneous and admitting a few 'special cases', it seems to be more realistic to
> recognise that our society is in fact plural, with clear differences of class,
> ethnicity and sense of nationhood. Furthermore, this plurality has not
> appeared suddenly but is deeply embedded in our history – most notably
> the differences between Scotland, Wales and Ireland, the Protestant/
> Catholic division, and the divisions by class. Postwar immigration has
> added a new dimension, with the advent of coloured minorities. (Chisholm,
> 1990, pp. 42–3)

The views expressed in the quotation cited above will surely elicit a fervent
'Amen!' from most Celtic historians and social scientists. For far too long
British history and British social science have, in fact, meant English history
and English social science, with only cursory attention given to matters in the
'Celtic Fringe' (G. Williams, 1977, 1978, 1983; Rees and Rees, 1980; Frame,
1990). However, the past 25 years have witnessed an exponential increase in
research into both Celtic and British topics. There are now simply too many
publications to attempt a complete bibliography here, but a few truly *British*
analyses merit citation (e.g. Hechter, 1975; Massey, 1984; Kearney, 1989;
Champion and Townsend, 1990; Davies, 1990; Frame, 1990).

There are, of course, many important subjects which remain as yet largely
unresearched. Thus there have been remarkably few geographical studies of
the Irish, Scots and Welsh who have settled in England, when one considers
the *longue durée* of the links between the four nations. In the postwar period in
particular it has been the settlement of New Commonwealth and Pakistani
(NCWP) immigrants which has captured the attention of scholars. The
Transactions of the Institute of British Geographers for example have, since
1968 (M. Williams, 1988 and updated to 1991) included five papers on the

NCWP-born, two on the Irish, one on the Scots and none on the Welsh. Yet, in 1981, there were 731,472 Scots and 573,045 Welsh-born persons resident in England, and they were, respectively, the first and second largest 'foreign-born' minorities.

In contrast to the dearth of studies of England's Scots and Welsh minorities (and, indeed of the Irish, especially in the postwar period), there have been numerous analyses of the pervasive effects of England upon her Celtic neighbours. Historians in particular have shown that Wales, by virtue of her location, has long had a plural society (e.g. K.O. Morgan, 1981; Davies, 1987, 1990; Jenkins, 1987; Walker, 1990; Williams, 1987; G.A. Williams, 1982, 1985). Although this social reality has also been studied by social scientists, there has been a tendency for researchers to work within the narrow confines imposed by their specific disciplinary perspectives, and also to be preoccupied with certain themes, notably ethnicity and the Welsh language, especially in the western rural heartland (C.H. Williams, 1986). It is only comparatively recently that researchers have broadened both their interests and analytical perspectives. Thus Glyn Williams (1978, p. 12) recognized that 'the strength and multi-dimensionality of the Welsh identity seems in many cases to be independent of language.' Similarly Day (1986, p. 159) in a review of the sociology of Wales observed that:

> Insofar as any society consists of numerous competing groups, engaged in processes of conflict, struggle, competition, employing whatever means come to hand to further their particular interests and goals, making and breaking alliances, but doing so normally within boundaries set by broad and deepseated constraints of social location, then Wales is exceptionally rich in possibilities, since alongside the normal relations of class, and town and country, there exist divisions between the 'Welsh Welsh' (Cymry Cymraeg), 'Anglo-Welsh', and the English. How alignments develop along these axes is of great interest, but these need to be seen against the adage that politics (and group relations) concern 'who gets what, when, how'.

The adage, should, of course, properly be: 'who gets what, when, how, *and where*', for, as Day (1986, pp. 158–9) himself showed earlier in his essay:

> In some respects, which are as awkward for nationalists as they are for sociologists, the problems and orientations of different sections of Welsh society are widely diverse. Thus the everyday concerns of people in Mid-Wales – depopulation, decay of social provision, tourism, second homes, the struggle to preserve a language – do not find straightforward

correspondences in the valleys and cities of South Wales, or, indeed, on Deeside where issues of decision-making in nationalised industries, the role of multi-nationals and large-scale movements of capital, urbanization and suburbanization, bulk larger.

It would clearly be both presumptuous and premature to attempt to provide here a comprehensive analysis of all the important structural and spatial cleavages which now characterize Welsh society. Instead, attention is focused upon three of the key 'axes' identified by Day – ethnicity, language, and social class. These three axes have been the subjects of much attention during the past twenty years. Even so, important gaps remain in our knowledge, not least the ways in which they intersect, and their varying significance in the social fabric of different parts of Wales.

WELSH SOCIETY: THE ETHNIC CLEAVAGE

Wales has received four 'tidal waves' of English and other foreign settlers. The first took place in the early Middle Ages, and its effects were limited mainly to the eastern lowlands (Davies, 1987, 1990; Walker, 1990). The second wave started in the late eleventh century and lasted for 200 years, extending foreign settlement chiefly in the borderland and the coastal lowlands of South Wales (G.A. Williams, 1985; Carter, 1986; Davies, 1987, 1990). The third – and greatest – tidal wave of immigration began after 1750 and accelerated massively to a peak between 1870 and 1911. In just over a hundred years the population quintupled and was sucked into the south-eastern corner of the country. By 1911 62 per cent of the population lived in Glamorgan and Monmouthshire, compared with only 20 per cent in 1801 (G.A. Williams, 1985; Carter, 1986). The fourth immigrant wave started in the early postwar years and has not yet dissipated. Some 250,000 new people, mainly English, have settled in Wales (Carter, 1986; C.H. Williams, 1987, 1990; Day, 1989; OPCS, 1990).

Most of these latest incomers have settled in the scenically attractive rural parts of the country (figure 2.1). Although the greatest numerical gains have occurred in the borderland districts the numbers moving to the more thinly settled western areas (i.e. 'Inner Wales') have had a perceivable impact in proportional terms. During the decade 1971–81 there have been modest losses in the numbers of English-born residents in most of the South Wales coalfield communities and in just two neighbouring districts in North Wales (Aberconwy and Arfon). The greatest losses, though, were in Cardiff and Swansea. All these localized losses can be attributed to intercensal mortality

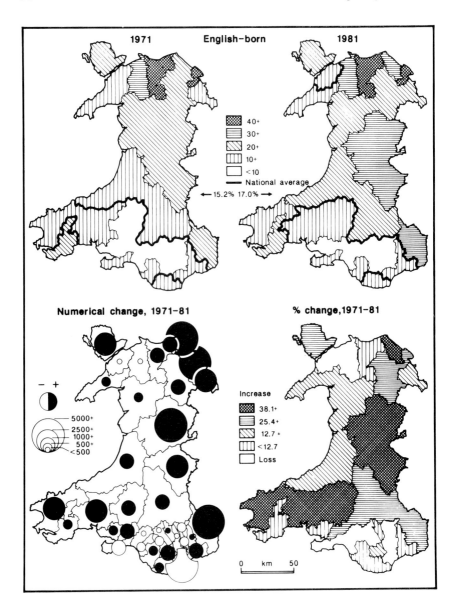

FIGURE 2.1
English-born residents of Wales, 1971 and 1981

TABLE 2.1

**Country of Birth of the resident population of the countries of Great Britain,[1]
1981**

	1,000 persons			
	Great Britain	**England**	**Scotland**	**Wales**
Total	53,557	45,772	5,035	2,750
England	41,850	41,085	298	468
Scotland	5,301	731	4,549	21
Wales	2,771	573	13	2,185
Rest of UK	275	232	35	8
Eire	607	567	27	13
NCWP	1,513	1,454	40	20
Other	1,240	1,130	73	35

	Per Cent			
	Great Britain	**England**	**Scotland**	**Wales**
Total	100.0	100.0	100.0	100.0
England	78.1	89.8	5.9	17.0
Scotland	9.9	1.6	90.3	0.8
Wales	5.2	1.3	0.3	79.4
Rest of UK	0.5	0.5	0.7	0.3
Eire	1.1	1.2	0.5	0.5
NCWP	2.8	3.2	0.8	0.7
Other	2.4	2.4	1.5	1.3

[1] 92% of the resident population of Northern Ireland was born in Northern Ireland.

and to migration – primarily from the coalfield communities and the cities to neighbouring suburban and rural districts, or back to England.

The cumulative impact of these four waves of in-migration upon Welsh society has been profound. In purely demographic terms it has meant that Wales now has the most cosmopolitan society among the four home countries, for it has much the lowest proportion of residents who are native-born (i.e. Welsh-born). Table 2.1 shows that in 1981, only 79.4 per cent were born in Wales. Among the immigrant groups, though, the English are overwhelmingly the largest minority, now accounting for 17 per cent of all residents. The spatial impact of immigration upon Welsh society has been dramatic. There are now profound regional variations in the proportions of the population which are native- (i.e. Welsh-) born. Of the 19 districts in Wales having native-born proportions greater than the national average in 1981 (i.e.

79.4 per cent) only three were predominantly rural in character (Arfon, Carmarthen and Dinefwr – see figure 2.2). The rest pick out the coalfield and metropolitan communities of South Wales. Rhondda district had the highest proportion of Welsh-born residents in Wales (92.9 per cent).

If these findings are set in the wider context of the entire United Kingdom (figure 2.3) the special status of Wales in the context of ethnicity is even more dramatically highlighted. In 1981 a mere 48 of the 483 local government districts in the United Kingdom had foreign-born minorities greater than 20 per cent of their resident populations. In this context foreign-born persons are defined as those born outside the UK and, in the case of England, for example, in other parts of the UK. Of the 364 districts in England only 28 had foreign-born (i.e. non-English-born) rates in excess of 20 per cent, and 23 of these were in Greater London. In contrast, 18 of the 37 districts in Wales had foreign-born (i.e. non-Welsh-born) rates in excess of 20 per cent. Both Scotland and Northern Ireland each had only one district with a foreign-born rate greater than 20 per cent.

WELSH SOCIETY: THE LINGUISTIC CLEAVAGE

The impact of immigrants upon Welsh society extends far beyond both their numbers and their uneven distribution within the country. Their presence is but one aspect of the progressive and seemingly inexorable anglicization of Wales (Davies, 1987, 1990; G.A. Williams, 1982, 1985; C.H. Williams, 1990). This phenomenon is most strongly evidenced in the catastrophic decline in the ubiquity of the Welsh language within the country. During the present century the numbers of resident Welsh-speakers has almost halved and, in proportional terms, has fallen from almost 50 per cent of the total in 1901 to just 19 per cent in 1981. Furthermore, by 1981, 99.2 per cent of Welsh-speakers were bilingual and 20.1 per cent of the adults could not read and write in the language (OPCS, 1983, pp. 48–9). The decline in the numbers of Welsh-speakers has been paralleled by the substantial contraction and fragmentation of the territory within which the language is dominant (Bowen and Carter, 1975; C.H. Williams, 1980, 1990; Aitchison and Carter, 1985; Carter and Aitchison, 1986). By 1981 Welsh speakers constituted over 60 per cent of the resident populations in just seven of the 37 Welsh districts (figure 2.4). Moreover, comparison with figure 2.3 shows that only two of these seven districts (Carmarthenshire and Dinefwr) also had Welsh-born populations exceeding the national average.

The early initiation and progressive extension of the 'dominant-subservient' relationship between England and Wales has, therefore, clearly had

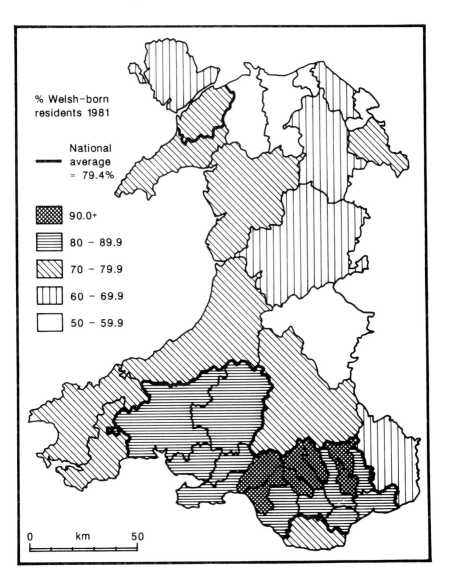

FIGURE 2.2
Welsh-born residents of Wales, 1981

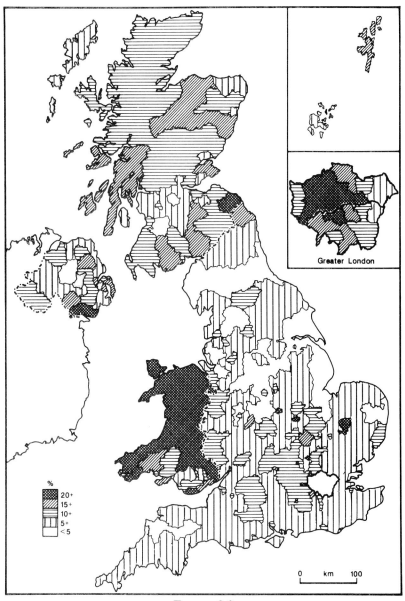

FIGURE 2.3
'Foreign-born' residents of the four home countries, 1981

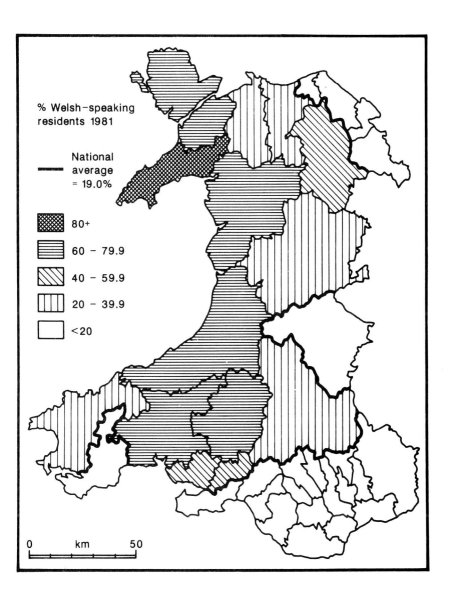

% Welsh–speaking residents 1981

National average = 19.0%

80+

60 – 79.9

40 – 59.9

20 – 39.9

<20

0   km   50

FIGURE 2.4
Wales: Percent Welsh-speaking residents, 1981

deleterious effects upon native Welsh society and culture. The impact of progressive anglicization upon the Welsh language has been devastating and is crucial, for

> The character and vitality of a culture is to a large extent language-dependent. Language helps to preserve traditions, shapes modes of perception, and profoundly influences patterns of social intercourse and behaviour...For a minority culture in particular, the absolute and relative strength of its language serves as a diagnostic and tangible indicator of that culture's general well-being and long-term viability. (Carter and Aitchison, 1986, p. 1)

However, 'Welshness' is not solely a matter of language:

> The role played by language in the structuring of Welsh society is a crucial one. For many, the Welsh language is a critical marker of ethnic identity; now, as in the past, therefore, its survival and even growth is a necessary condition of a distinctive national existence for Wales. This particular construction of 'Welshness' is not universally shared, of course, and alternatives exist which not only mobilise different cultural resources, but may actually be antipathetic to Welsh-language culture. (Day and Rees, 1989, p. 1)

This divergence of opinions concerning the role and status of the Welsh language in the construction and maintenance of a distinctively Welsh identity highlights the problems which have, increasingly, beset Welsh society since the 1950s. Although these matters have been extensively documented elsewhere, the key issues need to be reviewed briefly here, because they are germane to the interpretation of our own analyses, presented below. During the past 40 years the struggle to save the Welsh language has become increasingly politicized (Adamson, 1991). As a result of sustained pressure the Welsh-speaking minority (who comprised only 22.4 per cent of the Welsh-born population in 1981, see OPCS, 1983, pp. 48–9) has been successful in wringing substantial concessions from the British government (Delamont, 1987; B. Jones, 1988; G.E. Jones, 1988; P.E. Jones, 1988; C.H. Williams, 1986, 1987, 1989).

The policy of sustained governmental support of a hitherto threatened minority language and culture has much to commend it. Unfortunately, however, that policy has also generated tensions between the Welsh-speaking community and the English-speaking majority, who comprised 77.6 per cent of the Welsh-born population in 1981 (OPCS, 1983, pp. 48–9). These tensions have been graphically described in debates in the media, in novels and in academic works (e.g. *South Wales Echo*, 18 September 1991; *The Independent*, 1 August 1991; G. Thomas, 1964, 1984; Richards, 1973; K.O. Morgan, 1981; G.A. Williams, 1982, 1985; D. Smith, 1984; Denney et al., 1991). Williams (1985, p. 293) in particular, has provided an emotional account of the Anglo-Welsh viewpoint:

> An English-speaking working-class, neglected and treated with shoddiness, its necessities, not only social but cultural, scorned, not least by a British state subsidising the Welsh language reproduction of what is to them a middle-class minority. They see bilingual language qualification shutting off areas of employment for their children. They perceive Welsh-language schools as nurseries of a new order of privileged beings who employ Welsh and particularly the new language of Cymraeg Byw much as the Irish middle class has used official Gaelic and the medieval clergy used Latin, to manufacture a new oligarchy. They see subsidies going everywhere except to their culture.
>   In this litany of complaint there is much mythology which spokespersons for the Welsh language movement can rebut with statistics. It is, however, evidence of a much deeper malaise which is much more ominous: the denial of Welshness to the English-speaking Welsh.

This latter point was brought home forcibly to one of us (JG) in 1991. During the course of a conversation with a young Welsh-speaking academic, he ventured the opinion that 'Aneurin Bevan wasn't *really* Welsh.'

The relations between some of the Welsh-speaking community and the English-speaking majority are therefore matters for concern. However, those between Welsh-speakers and the incomers, who are settling in rural Wales, are becoming even more acrimonious. The spectacular flood of settlers into rural Wales during the 1970s and 1980s has revived the economies of localities hitherto characterized by decay and depopulation. Unfortunately, the speed, scale and sheer diversity of the in-migrating wave has also generated substantial social changes in many of these areas. 'One of the correlates of increased diversity is heightened disagreement' (Day, 1989, p. 155). In its most extreme form this disagreement has been expressed in the destruction (by arson) of many 'second homes' by a clandestine organization, the 'Sons of Glendower' (Meibion Glyndŵr) (Aitchison and Carter, 1990). The language issue has also reared its head. In 1989 Gwynedd and Dyfed County Councils decreed that all children living in predominantly Welsh-speaking areas should be taught entirely in Welsh, at least until they were seven. Several English-speaking parents have recently successfully challenged this decision in the High Court in London (*The Independent*, 25, 26 November 1991).

WELSH SOCIETY: SOCIAL CLASS CLEAVAGES

During the past 20 years historians and social scientists have argued that, for Wales, the socio-economic consequences of integration with England have been profound and generally negative. It has been claimed that, instead of evolving as an independent nation state with a developed social formation and a balanced economic base, Wales has, since the thirteenth century, become a peripheral region whose development has been both uneven and dependent upon decisions taken in England or abroad. The social and economic impact of this relationship has been cogently summarized by Day (1986, p. 163):

> This is the legacy of an economic history during which the main role of Wales has been to act as supplier of raw materials, basic products, and labour to the wider system. The resulting pattern has been one in which a succession of industries has been intensively exploited and then abandoned in the face of falling demand, rising costs or growing competition, producing a series of transformations of social and community structures. Usually, though not invariably, this has involved external investment and control, and the profits have been creamed off and realised elsewhere.

But, Wales is not unique within the UK in these respects, for several studies have shown that Scotland, Northern Ireland and, indeed, several parts of England can also be typified as subordinate and dependent regions. Indeed, for centuries the central fact of the economic history of the UK has been the dominance of London with respect to capital formation and decision-making (Massey, 1984). This metropolitan-based control intensified during and after the Second World War, when state intervention in manufacturing (via nationalization, subsidies and directive planning) attempted to redress the profound regional imbalances in employment opportunities. Moreover, in recent decades, there has been an increase in 'external control' within both manufacturing and public sectors. Thus Marquand (1979), Kirwan (1981), and Massey (1984) have shown that for most large manufacturing and service firms:

> There is broadly, within these industries a division of labour between on the one hand high-status, highly paid, non-routine jobs in the upper echelons of control and professional functions, and on the other hand routine

clerical work. Increasingly within the larger firms this technical division is taking on a geographical form, with the high-status jobs remaining in London and/or the south-east and the more routine work, providing only low-status and low-income jobs, being decentralised. Nor is it only private firms. A number of departments of central government have adopted a similar pattern. (Massey, 1984, p. 186)

The impact of these profound socio-economic and spatial changes can be confirmed by analysing the appropriate 1981 census tabulations. For illustrative purposes the 17 socio-economic groups (SEGs) identified in the census have been grouped into the four sets used by Fielding (1989), namely:

(1) Service class – professional, technical and managerial workers (i.e. SEGs 1, 2.2, 3, 4, and 5.1)
(2) Petite bourgeoisie = small employers and self-employed (i.e. SEGs 2.1, 12.12 and 14)
(3) White-collar proletariat = lower level white-collar workers (i.e. SEGs 5.2, 6 and 7)
(4) Blue-collar proletariat = blue-collar employees (i.e. SEGs 8,9,10,11 and 15)

In selecting these four 'social classes' Fielding (1989, p. 25) argued that:

any grouping of socio-economic groups (SEGs) is to some extent arbitrary, and no great claims are made for the classes produced by the grouping used here. However, this grouping does have the merit of distinguishing the upper level white collar workers from the lower level ones, and between employees on the one hand and employers and the self-employed on the other. The service class and the petite bourgeoisie are regarded for the purposes of this paper as constituting the 'middle class', while the white collar and blue collar proletariates [*sic*] constitute the 'working class'.

The geographical distributions of these social classes across the 10 regions of Great Britain (GB) are given in table 2.2 and figure 2.5. In addition, the south-east region has been subdivided because it contained 31.8 per cent of GB's economically active population. The results partially confirm the findings of the studies cited above, in that the high-status service class was over-represented throughout the south-east, whereas the low-status blue-collar proletariat were over-represented in the dependent 'provinces'. However, the white-collar proletariat were also over-represented in southern

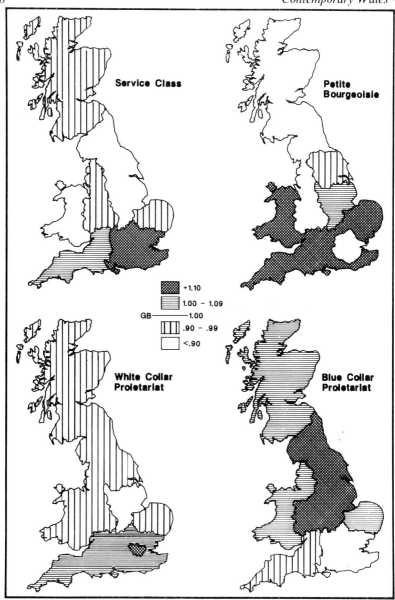

FIGURE 2.5
Location quotients for the four SEG-based social classes in Great Britain,
1981

TABLE 2.2

SEG-based location quotients for social classes 1981 (GB = 1.00)

	Service class	Petite bourgeoisie	White-collar proletariat	Blue-collar proletariat
South East	1.16	1.01	1.13	0.82
Greater London	1.17	0.87	1.22	0.78
Outer Metro. Area	1.18	0.97	1.09	0.84
Outer South East	1.12	1.30	1.03	0.86
South West	1.00	1.53	1.00	0.91
East Anglia	0.95	1.34	0.93	1.01
West Midlands	0.90	0.87	0.91	1.14
East Midlands	0.89	1.02	0.86	1.15
Yorks-Humberside	0.87	0.94	0.91	1.14
North West	0.96	0.77	0.97	1.08
North	0.80	0.75	0.95	1.18
Scotland	0.90	0.79	0.99	1.10
Wales	0.88	1.42	0.91	1.06
Gwynedd	0.91	2.09	0.91	0.92
Dyfed	0.84	2.39	0.80	0.98
Powys	0.78	3.21	0.73	0.92
Clwyd	0.87	1.47	0.91	1.05
West Glam	0.82	0.74	0.96	1.18
Mid Glam	0.79	0.79	0.83	1.27
Gwent	0.86	0.83	0.88	1.19
S. Glam	1.11	0.87	1.13	0.88
Great Britain	1.00	1.00	1.00	1.00

England, peaking markedly in Greater London. The petite bourgeoisie, in contrast, were over-represented in those regions possessing numerous small employers and self-employed persons, namely southern and eastern England, and Wales. For Wales, a large proportion of the petite bourgeoisie are, in fact, small farmers.

In 1981 the position of Wales in the national 'league table' of regions differed markedly across the four social classes (table 2.2). For the high-status service class and their lower-status counterparts (i.e. white-collar proletariat) Wales ranked only 10th and 11th respectively among the 13 regions. In contrast, for the petite bourgeoisie and blue-collar proletariat classes, Wales ranked 4th and 5th respectively. These findings confirm the underdeveloped and dependent nature of the Principality's social formation. Even so, viewed in the wider national context, it is evident that there were several other regions in which the condition of dependency was even more profound.

When viewed in this comparative contemporary context, Hechter's (1975) thesis concerning 'internal colonialism' (i.e. the cultural oppression of Wales by England) finds little support. Indeed, one of the major criticisms of Hechter's thesis was that:

Wales is treated as an unproblematic, homogeneous reality, the problems of which are reducible to the imposition of external power. Questions about the distribution and use of power within Welsh society are shelved, along with examination of its internal structure, in favour of a crude opposition between 'Anglo-Saxons' and 'Celts'. (Day, 1986, pp. 170–1)

The analyses of the ethnic and linguistic cleavages found in Welsh society presented above showed that Wales is manifestly *not* a 'homogeneous reality'. In both social and economic terms too, Wales has long been characterized by marked internal structural and spatial diversity (e.g. Thomas, 1977; K.O. Morgan, 1981; Morgan and Thomas, 1984; G. Williams, 1978; G.A. Williams, 1985; Hume and Pryce, 1986). Analysis of the contemporary social class cleavages found within the country confirms this fact. Table 2.2 and figure 2.6 show the distributions of Fielding's (1989) four social classes for the eight Welsh counties in 1981. These particular administrative units were employed because they bound reasonably well the major historical, cultural, social, and economic regions within Wales and have consequently been used extensively by other researchers (e.g. George and Mainwaring, 1987; D. Thomas, 1988, 1989, 1991; C.H. Williams, 1990). The results of this brief analysis (table 2.2 and figure 2.6) show that Wales is a mosaic of distinctive regions in which the contemporary social class divisions still strongly reflect the inheritance of past cycles of economic and social development. Thus the petite bourgeoisie were massively over-represented (in respect of the GB average) in rural Wales. Here the farming communities and the many small businesses located in both the countryside and in the region's small towns represent continuity from Wales's first economic cycle, triggered initially by the Anglo-Norman conquest, and subsequently sustained during succeeding cycles, notably the so-called industrial revolution, state involvement in rural areas (Murdoch, 1988) and the huge influx of foreign-born immigrants in the postwar years (Day, 1989).

The blue-collar proletariat, in contrast, were quite strongly over-represented in the three counties which straddle the South Wales coalfield (i.e. West Glamorgan, Mid Glamorgan and Gwent) and slightly over-represented in Clwyd, which embraces the much smaller North Wales coalfield. These two regions of low-status over-representation were generated during the second, industrial, development cycle in Wales, described as 'colonial' by some Welsh academics (e.g. Carter and Wheatley, 1982) and as 'semi-colonial' by some of

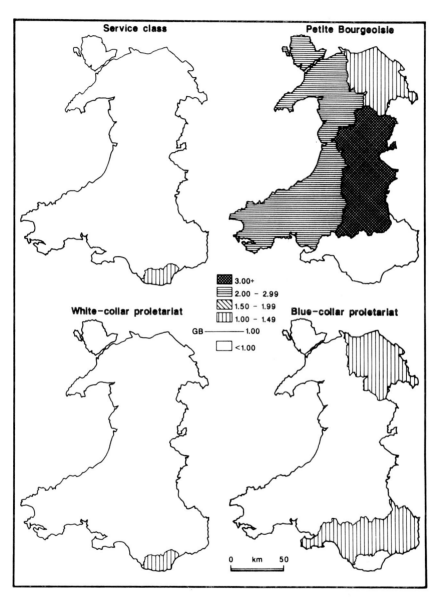

FIGURE 2.6
Location quotients for the four SEG-based social classes in Wales, 1981

their non-Welsh colleagues (e.g. Massey, 1984, p. 200). The solidly traditional masculine and manual working-class character of these areas has, though, been considerably diluted and increasingly differentiated since their heyday (*c.* 1921) by massive emigration (especially during the Great Depression), industrial decline and restructuring, and by the postwar development of new state-sponsored and private sector manufacturing and service industries (K.O. Morgan, 1981; G.A. Williams, 1985; K. Morgan, 1987; Adamson, 1988; Morris and Mansfield, 1988; Wass and Mainwaring, 1989). By 1981 about a fifth (19.3 per cent) of the employment in manufacturing industries in Wales was found in foreign-owned (chiefly American) firms, and these were concentrated mainly in South and north-east Wales (George and Mainwaring, 1987). In recent decades too, in both regions, there had been substantial in-migration of English settlers, many of them long-distance commuters (Day, 1986; *The Guardian*, 30 June 1989; see also figure 2.1).

South Glamorgan is the youngest major socio-economic region in Wales. It is also the country's only region in which, in 1981, both the high-status service class and the lower-status white-collar proletariat were over-represented with respect to the rates for Great Britain as a whole. Cardiff, the country's focus, grew slowly during the nineteenth century, only surpassing Merthyr Tydfil as the largest Welsh town by the 1881 census. Similarly the neighbouring towns of Barry and Penarth were late nineteenth-century developments. All three towns grew almost exclusively as ports for the burgeoning international coal trade from South Wales. Manufacturing consequently never figured prominently in their economies. Indeed:

> In 1971 of the 53 countries in England and Wales outside Greater London, South Glamorgan was ranked 42nd in the proportion of its resident workforce employed in manufacturing with 24.8 per cent, immediately below Surrey and the Isle of Wight. Similarly of the 18 towns and cities in England and Wales outside London with populations of over 200,000 Cardiff ranks last in the proportion of its workforce employed in manufacturing with 25.7 per cent, below Southampton and Plymouth. (H.R. Morgan, 1976, p. 6, cited in Carter, 1983, p. 56)

This evidence for Cardiff led Carter (1983, p. 57) to conclude that 'the parallels that have to be sought are not with the other long established capitals of the nations of the British Isles but with those of former British colonial territories.' In fact, Cardiff was only formally declared the capital of Wales in 1956. Since then it has rapidly become a 'transactional city' (Aitchison and Carter, 1987, p. 490), the hub of Wales's 'Costa Bureaucratica' (G.A. Williams, 1985, p.

303). This clustering of the Principality's new middle and working classes (Adamson, 1988) into the south-eastern coastlands has drained the rest of the country, creating a 'core' and 'periphery' which, in microcosm, mimic the broader pattern of Great Britain as a whole (compare figures 2.5 and 2.6).

INTERNAL COLONIALISM REVISITED: THE INTERSECTION OF ETHNICITY, CULTURE AND CLASS IN WELSH SOCIETY

Wales, then, is manifestly not 'an unproblematic, homogeneous reality' (Day, 1986, p. 170). This brief review has shown that Welsh society is a veritable kaleidoscope within which the key ethnic, linguistic, cultural and social class ingredients combine in contrasting proportions and combinations which change in character, across both time and space. Given these facts it is clearly impracticable to test the reality of Hechter's thesis of 'internal colonialism' (i.e. the cultural oppression of Wales by England) at the macro, national, level because the resident population of Wales is remarkably diverse, in both the structural and spatial senses.

More importantly, Hechter's thesis cannot really be proved as objective fact at *any* spatial scale because the *routinely* published census statistics which provided the evidence for his case are aggregated for administrative areas. Consequently, however sophisticated the statistical methods employed in analysing the relationships between the relevant variables, one is faced with the well-known geographical problem of the 'ecological fallacy' (i.e. that the results of analyses of *rates* for *areas* can be interpreted as being the same as analyses of individuals – see Stimson, 1983). In more recent papers Hechter (1978, 1983) himself recognized that aggregated socio-demographic statistics provided only indirect measures of the cultural division of labour. He further argued that 'Any direct measure of the cultural division of labour must be based on cross-tabulations of the relevant cultural categories with detailed occupational classifications, but such data are rarely published by governments for obvious political reasons' (Hechter, 1983, p. 34). Although such data are indeed rarely published, Glyn Williams (1986, pp. 186–8) has shown that, in Britain at least, OPCS are willing to provide the relevant cross-tabulations of census data. Thus Williams was able to compare the distributions of the Welsh-speakers and the immigrant population across the 16 socio-economic groups for Gwynedd. His analysis led him to conclude that:

The argument focusing on the cultural division of labour can be substantiated by looking, for example, at an area such as the county of

Gwynedd where there have been profound developments of branch plant and new manufacturing industries. The most obvious feature of such development is that if the employment decisions for both manufacturing and retail are made outside Wales, at head office , then most of the higher-level managerial or professional posts will be held by in-migrants. On the other hand, if the objective is the search for cheap labour, the proletarian labour will be local. That is, we envisage two different labour markets for different class locations...A comparison of Welsh speakers and residents born outside Wales in Gwynedd indicates clearly that this line of argument is correct. There is heavy under-representation of Welsh speakers in the top four official socio-economic groups used in the census tabulations. (Williams, 1986, p. 187)

These findings are exciting but they need to be treated with caution for several reasons. Firstly, the two groups selected for the analysis (i.e. the Welsh-speakers and the population born outside Wales) are not entirely mutually exclusive. Specifically, not all the resident Welsh-speakers in Wales are Welsh-born. In 1981 6.4 per cent of the Welsh-speakers aged 15–64 were born outside Wales (OPCS, 1983, pp. 48–9). Unfortunately the published data were not disaggregated for regions *within* Wales. However it is likely that most of the 'foreign-born' Welsh-speaking residents lived in the counties where native-born Welsh-speakers predominated, including Gwynedd. Secondly, the 1981 census socio-economic groups (SEGs) tabulation was only a 10 per cent sample. Cross-tabulation of 16 SEGs × two population sub-groups may consequently have generated small numbers in several of the cells, for the total *enumerated* economically active population of Gwynedd was only 8,904 persons. Some of the apparently important status differences between the two groups chosen by Williams *may* therefore be attributed simply to sampling error (OPCS, 1982). Thirdly, given that the data provided by Williams (1986, figure 21, p. 186) do not include the raw figures, we are unable to establish whether the in-migrants are *absolutely* or only *relatively* over-represented in specific socio-economic groups. Finally, the dominance (whether absolute or relative) of in-migrants in the more prestigious and powerful occupational strata within one county need not necessarily be interpreted solely as evidence of a cultural division of labour for, as Day (1986, pp. 169–70) has observed:

It is perfectly possible to argue that the industrialisation of Wales meant the importation of technical and managerial labour, indeed that such labour is still imported, and that many controlling interests lie outside Wales, without thereby committing oneself to the view that Wales is a colony or

TABLE 2.3

Economically active resident population of Wales and its Counties, by birthplace and linguistic groups: 1981

	EB	OFB	WB	SW	LW	IW	AW
			Per cent total (rows)				
Gwynedd	26.1	4.3	69.6	62.3	55.9	6.4	7.3
Dyfed	18.2	3.9	77.9	45.7	38.9	6.8	32.2
Powys	27.9	3.4	68.7	20.9	16.4	4.5	47.8
Clwyd	34.3	4.2	61.5	17.0	13.7	3.3	44.5
W. Glam	10.7	3.7	85.6	14.2	10.2	4.0	71.4
Mid Glam	9.6	2.5	87.9	5.5	3.9	1.6	82.4
Gwent	14.8	3.8	81.4	2.3	1.2	1.1	79.1
S. Glam	15.4	6.6	80.0	4.9	3.6	1.3	73.1
Wales	17.7	4.0	78.3	17.1	14.0	3.1	61.2

	EB	OFB	WB	SW	LW	IW	AW
			Ratios of national rates (columns)				
Gwynedd	147.5	107.5	88.9	364.3	399.3	206.5	11.9
Dyfed	102.8	97.5	99.5	267.3	277.9	219.4	52.6
Powys	157.6	85.0	87.7	122.2	117.1	145.2	78.1
Clwyd	193.8	105.0	78.5	99.4	97.9	106.5	72.7
W. Glam	60.5	92.5	109.3	83.0	72.0	129.0	116.7
Mid Glam	54.2	62.5	112.3	32.2	27.9	51.6	134.6
Gwent	83.6	95.0	104.0	13.5	8.6	35.5	129.2
S.Glam	87.0	165.0	102.2	28.7	25.7	41.9	119.4
Wales	100.0	100.0	100.0	100.0	100.0	100.0	100.0

even that Welshness is a main consideration in recruitment to roles. An adequate explanation would be provided by the general association of elite positions with geographical mobility, or 'spiralism'.

To further the analysis, then, we need the *national* picture. It would then be possible to put Williams's (1986) results into a wider context: was the under-representation of Welsh-speakers among the service class in Gwynedd the result of internal colonialism (in which case, the same result would be repeated throughout the Principality), or was it a consequence of 'spiralism' (which would lead us to expect greater 'success' for Welsh-speakers outside North Wales)? In order to investigate this, we have commissioned special tabulations from the 1981 Census, of class, ethnicity and language for the whole of Wales. We have differentiated between the Welsh-born (WB), the English-born (EB),

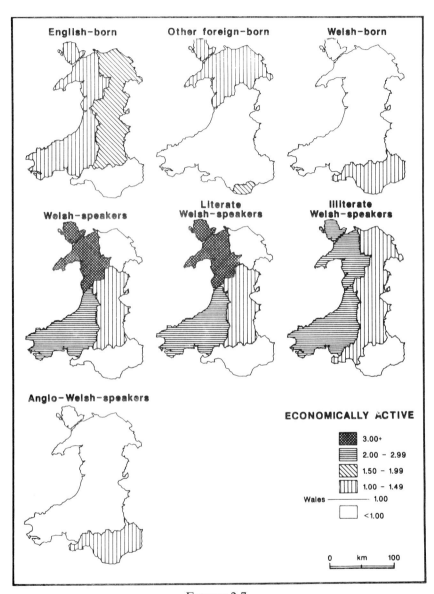

FIGURE 2.7
Location quotients for the ethnic and linguistic divisions of the economically active population in Wales, 1981

TABLE 2.4
SEG-based location quotients for social classes: 1981

	Service class	Petite bourgeoisie	White collar proletariat	Blue collar proletariat
South East	1.16	1.01	1.13	0.82
Great London	1.17	0.87	1.22	0.78
Outer Metro. Area	1.18	0.97	1.09	0.84
Outer South East	1.12	1.30	1.03	0.86
South West	1.00	1.53	1.00	0.91
East Anglia	0.95	1.34	0.93	1.01
West Midlands	0.90	0.87	0.91	1.14
East Midlands	0.89	1.02	0.86	1.15
Yorks-Humberside	0.87	0.94	0.91	1.14
North West	0.96	0.77	0.97	1.08
North	0.80	0.75	0.95	1.18
Scotland	0.90	0.79	0.99	1.10
Wales	0.88	1.27	0.91	1.08
English-born	1.32	1.56	0.92	0.78
Other foreign	1.21	1.57	0.78	0.93
Welsh-born	0.76	1.19	0.91	1.16
Welsh-speakers	0.99	2.01	0.83	0.94
Literate	1.07	2.11	0.76	0.87
Illiterate	0.63	1.59	0.73	1.28
Anglo-Welsh	0.70	0.96	0.93	1.22

and other foreign born (OFB). The Welsh-born are further divided between the monoglot English-speakers, and the Welsh-speakers (SW). The latter, Welsh-speaking group is further divided into those who *were* literate in Welsh (LW), and those who were not (IW) (table 2.3 and figure 2.7). The Welsh-born were the largest single group at both national and county levels. However, they were only over-represented relative to the national figure (78.3 per cent) in industrial and metropolitan South Wales, as were the Anglo-Welsh (61.2 per cent of the total workforce). By contrast, Welsh-speakers (17.1 per cent) were over-represented in the rural counties of Gwynedd, Dyfed and Powys, but only in Gwynedd did they comprise a majority of the workforce (62.3 per cent). The English-born were the second largest group in Wales (17.1 per cent), but they were over-represented only in rural Wales, especially in the border areas.

Further disaggregation of the data by social class shows that there are clear status divisions within Welsh society, which heighten ethnic cleavages (table 2.4). English-born residents were most heavily over-represented in the service class in Wales, with a location quotient of 1.32. In addition, they were also over-represented in the Welsh petite bourgeoisie, and were the second most important group in Wales's relatively weak white-collar proletariat. However, they were the most *under*-represented group among Wales's blue-collar workers.

Substantial differences in social status are also apparent among Welsh-born residents in 1981. Those literate in Welsh were relatively well represented in the higher-status classes, but the illiterate Welsh-speakers and the Anglo-Welsh were best represented in the lower-status petite bourgeoisie and proletariat. Clearly, for those born in Wales, the ability to read, write, and speak Welsh was closely associated with higher social status (cf. Carter, 1983, 1989; Carter and Wheatley, 1982).

However, the interpretation of the precise meaning of the evidence presented here is still fraught with difficulties. Thus the marked over-representation of the two non-Welsh-born groups in both of the high-status social strata could be construed either as confirming the 'internal colonialism' thesis, or simply as further evidence of 'spiralism'. Until we know the precise location of the substantial Welsh workforce in *England's* hierarchy of social status, we would suggest that the issue cannot be resolved. Among the native-born majority, though, it is the literate Welsh-speakers who are now the most fortunate group, for it is they, who, in 1981 were most heavily over-represented in both the high-status service class and the petite bourgeoisie.

On closer inspection this broad generalization is, of course, subject to considerable qualification: the social fabric of Wales is characterized by marked regional diversity. Indeed, the truth of the adage 'who gets what, when, how and where' within Wales can be demonstrated (given the constraints imposed by the particular data used here) by disaggregating the facts for Wales as a whole into their major regional components. The detailed statistics are given in tables 2.5–2.8 and mapped in figures 2.8–2.11.

In the wider context of Great Britain as a whole the high-status service class in Wales was over-represented only in metropolitan South Glamorgan (table 2.2 and figure 2.6). However, when this elite stratum is disaggregated into its major ethnic and linguistic components for the eight counties the structural and spatial patterns generally become much more complex. Thus figure 2.8 shows that over-representation among both the English-born and other foreign born members of the service class was found throughout Wales (save only Dyfed for the other foreign-born). In contrast, the Anglo-Welsh were under-represented in every county. Among literate Welsh-speakers though, the over-representation found for Wales as a whole was turned, at the county

TABLE 2.5
Service class (ratios of GB % = 23.1)

	EB	OFB	WB	SW	LW	IW	AW	Total
WALES	1.32	1.21	0.76	0.99	1.07	0.63	0.70	0.88
Gwynedd	1.20	1.29	0.78	0.82	0.83	0.71	0.51	0·91
Dyfed	1.14	0.85	0.76	0.81	0.86	0.54	0.70	0.84
Powys	1.15	1.14	0.61	0.81	0.90	0.48	0.52	0.77
Clwyd	1.14	1.32	0.71	1.05	1.17	0.56	0.58	0.87
W. Glam	1.48	1.28	0.72	1.02	1.21	0.53	0.66	0.82
M. Glam	1.30	1.22	0.73	1.55	1.92	0.67	0.67	0.79
Gwent	1.44	1.29	0.73	1.50	2.25	0.72	0.71	0.85
S. Glam	1.83	1.21	0.96	2.27	2.64	1.25	0.88	1.11

(Ratios of Welsh % = 20.3)

	EB	OFB	WB	SW	LW	IW	AW	Total
WALES	1.50	1.38	0.88	1.13	1.60	0.72	0.79	1.00
Gwynedd	1.36	1.47	0.89	0.93	0.94	0.81	0.58	1.04
Dyfed	1.30	0.97	0.87	0.93	0.98	0.61	0.79	0.95
Powys	1.31	1.29	0.69	0.92	1.03	0.55	0.59	0.88
Clwyd	1.30	1.51	0.81	1.20	1.33	0.64	0.66	0.99
W. Glam	1.68	1.45	0.82	1.16	1.38	0.60	0.75	0.93
M. Glam	1.48	1.39	0.83	1.77	2.19	0.76	0.76	0.90
Gwent	1.64	1.47	0.83	1.71	2.56	0.82	0.81	0.98
S. Glam	2.08	1.37	1.10	2.58	3.00	1.42	1.00	1.27

level, into dominance only in South Wales and in Clwyd. Illiterate Welsh-speakers were over-represented only in South Glamorgan. Thus Welsh-speakers collectively were an important component of the elite service class chiefly in metropolitan South Wales and its industrial hinterland and secondarily in north-east Wales. In contrast, in the Welsh-speaking rural heartland of Wales (i.e. in Gwynedd, Dyfed and Powys), Welsh-speakers were actually under-represented in the service class.

Among the ethnic and linguistic subsets of the middle-class petite bourgeoisie, in contrast, there was comparative uniformity in terms of their geographical distributions (table 2.6 and figure 2.9). In every case this class was over-represented in rural Wales. The other foreign-born and illiterate Welsh-speakers were the only groups which were also over-represented in South Wales. Within this general picture there were local variations in the relative importance of specific groups (table 2.6). Thus in Gwynedd and

TABLE **2.6**

Petite bourgeoisie (ratios of GB % = 7.2)

	EB	OFB	WB	SW	LW	IW	AW	Total
WALES	1.56	1.57	2.01	2.11	1.59	0.96	0.96	1.42
Gwynedd	2.46	1.99	1.96	2.03	2.09	1.57	1.37	2.09
Dyfed	2.99	2.89	2.23	2.67	2.77	2.10	1.59	2.39
Powys	2.65	2.04	3.50	3.13	3.09	3.28	3.66	3.21
Clwyd	1.54	1.39	1.43	2.10	2.17	1.83	1.18	1.47
W. Glam	0.68	1.27	0.72	0.90	0.93	0.84	0.69	0.74
M. Glam	0.90	1.28	0.76	0.93	0.82	1.19	0.75	0.79
Gwent	0.99	1.28	0.83	0.79	0.75	0.83	0.83	0.87
S. Glam	0.62	1.36	0.82	0.63	0.50	0.99	0.84	0.83

(Ratios of Welsh % = 9.2)

	EB	OFB	WB	SW	LW	IW	AW	Total
WALES	1.22	1.24	0.94	1.59	1.49	1.26	0.76	1.00
Gwynedd	1.93	1.56	1.55	1.60	1.64	1.24	1.08	1.65
Dyfed	2.35	2.28	1.75	2.11	2.18	1.65	1.25	1.88
Powys	2.08	1.61	2.75	2.46	2.43	2.58	2.88	2.53
Clwyd	1.21	1.09	1.13	1.66	1.71	1.44	0.93	1.15
W. Glam	0.54	1.00	0.57	0.71	0.73	0.66	0.54	0.58
M. Glam	0.70	1.01	0.60	0.73	0.65	0.94	0.59	0.62
Gwent	0.78	1.01	0.65	0.62	0.59	0.66	0.65	0.68
S. Glam	0.49	1.07	0.65	0.50	0.39	0.78	0.66	0.65

Dyfed, the heartland of Welsh-speaking Wales, it was the English-born who were the most strongly over-represented. Indeed, the literate Welsh-speaking petite bourgeoisie ranked first in terms of over-representation only in Clwyd. Conversely, in south Wales the Anglo-Welsh ranked below several other ethnic and linguistic groups despite their absolute numerical dominance in this region's workforce.

The rapid postwar diversification of the Welsh economic base resulted in the emergence of a new working class (Morris and Mansfield, 1988). Even so, the growth of this white-collar proletariat in Wales has not kept pace with developments elsewhere in Great Britain. Moreover, growth within Wales has occurred primarily in Cardiff and its region and so only metropolitan South Glamorgan was over-represented in relation to the British rate in 1981 (table 2.7 and figure 2.10). Among the distinctive ethnic and linguistic groups identified in this study the Anglo-Welsh were over-represented only in South

TABLE 2.7

White collar proletariat (ratios of GB % = 28.0)

	EB	OFB	WB	SW	LW	IW	AW	Total
WALES	0.92	0.78	0.91	0.83	0.76	0.73	0.93	0.91
Gwynedd	0.92	0.89	0.90	0.87	0.87	0.87	1.19	0.91
Dyfed	0.75	0.70	0.82	0.77	0.80	0.62	0.89	0.80
Powys	0.79	0.73	0.70	0.69	0.71	0.62	0.71	0.73
Clwyd	0.97	0.76	0.89	0.84	0.85	0.78	0.91	0.91
W. Glam	0.98	0.68	0.96	0.95	1.01	0.78	0.97	0.96
M. Glam	0.87	0.77	0.83	0.80	0.85	0.66	0.83	0.83
Gwent	0.94	0.68	0.88	0.78	0.85	0.71	0.88	0.88
S. Glam	1.03	0.91	1.17	0.89	0.90	0.85	1.18	1.13

(Ratios of Welsh % — 25.4)

	EB	OFB	WB	SW	LW	IW	AW	Total
WALES	1.02	0.86	1.00	0.92	0.84	0.81	1.03	1.00
Gwynedd	1.01	0.99	0.99	0.96	0.96	0.96	1.32	1.00
Dyfed	0.83	0.77	0.91	0.85	0.88	0.69	0.98	0.89
Powys	0.87	0.81	0.78	0.76	0.78	0.68	0.78	0.81
Clwyd	1.08	0.84	0.98	0.92	0.94	0.86	1.00	1.01
W. Glam	1.09	0.75	1.06	1.05	1.12	0.86	1.07	1.05
M. Glam	0.96	0.85	0.91	0.88	0.90	0.73	0.92	0.92
Gwent	1.03	0.75	0.97	0.86	0.94	0.78	0.97	0.97
S. Glam	1.14	1.00	1.29	0.98	0.99	0.93	1.31	1.24

Glamorgan and Gwynedd, the English-born in South Glamorgan, and the literate Welsh-speakers slightly so in West Glamorgan, which includes Swansea, Wales's second city. In the greater part of Wales, then, the white-collar proletariat were under-represented, irrespective of ethnic and linguistic cleavages. Even so, there were consistent variations in the relative status of the various groups within Wales, with the English-born ranking first or second in seven counties and the Anglo-Welsh likewise in five.

The blue-collar proletariat constituted 45.2 per cent of the Welsh workforce in 1981. Moreover, the profound changes which have occurred in the Welsh economy since 1945 have not significantly reduced the traditional pre-eminence of this stratum in the mining and industrial regions of South and north-east Wales (table 2.8 and figure 2.11). The majority of the blue-collar workers were Anglo-Welsh and illiterate Welsh-speakers, and they were over-represented in every county except South Glamorgan. In contrast, the literate

TABLE 2.8
Blue collar proletariat (ratios of GB % = 41.7)

	EB	OFB	WB	SW	LW	IW	AW	Total
WALES	0.78	0.93	1.16	0.94	0.87	1.28	1.22	1.06
Gwynedd	0.69	0.74	1.02	1.01	1.00	1.15	1.08	0.92
Dyfed	0.75	0.96	1.04	0.97	0.90	1.32	1.14	0.98
Powys	0.77	0.93	0.98	0.95	0.89	1.15	1.00	0.92
Clwyd	0.85	0.91	1.16	0.89	0.80	1.25	1.27	1.05
W. Glam	0.80	1.01	1.23	1.04	0.89	1.44	1.27	1.18
M. Glam	0.94	0.98	1.31	0.84	0.62	1.38	1.34	1.27
Gwent	0.80	1.01	0.94	0.91	0.45	1.38	1.28	1.19
S. Glam	0.59	0.89	1.26	0.44	0.24	0.97	0.97	0.88

(Ratios of Welsh % = 45.1)

	EB	OFB	WB	SW	LW	IW	AW	Total
WALES	0.72	0.86	1.07	0.87	0.72	1.18	1.13	1.00
Gwynedd	0.64	0.68	0.94	0.94	0.92	1.06	1.00	0.85
Dyfed	0.69	0.89	0.96	0.89	0.84	1.22	1.05	0.91
Powys	0.71	0.85	0.91	0.87	0.82	1.06	0.92	0.85
Clwyd	0.78	0.84	1.07	0.82	0.74	1.15	1.17	0.96
W. Glam	0.74	0.94	1.14	0.96	0.82	1.33	1.17	1.09
M. Glam	0.87	0.90	1.21	0.78	0.57	1.27	1.24	1.17
Gwent	0.74	0.82	1.17	0.84	0.42	1.27	1.18	1.09
S. Glam	0.54	0.93	0.87	0.40	0.23	0.89	0.90	0.81

Welsh speakers and the incomers (i.e. the English and other foreign-born groups) were under-represented in this lower class stratum at both national and county levels.

Clearly, simple 'internal colonialist' notions of Welsh society as dominated by the English do not sit easily with the findings reported here. To some extent they do seem to fit the pattern. Thus, despite the transformation of the Welsh economy in the postwar period, it was still, in 1981, very much a blue-collar society, with heavy English over-representation in the 'commanding heights' of the national economy. However, closer inspection reveals significant social and regional divides within the ethnic Welsh community too, with the emergence of a distinct Welsh-speaking middle class in and around Cardiff, contrasted against the more traditionally proletarian Anglo-Welsh found there and the illiterate Welsh-speaking minority throughout the Principality.

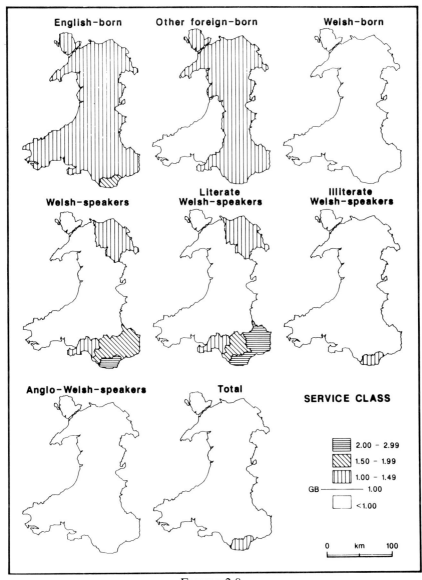

FIGURE 2.8

Location quotients for the ethnic and linguistic divisions of the service class in Wales, 1981

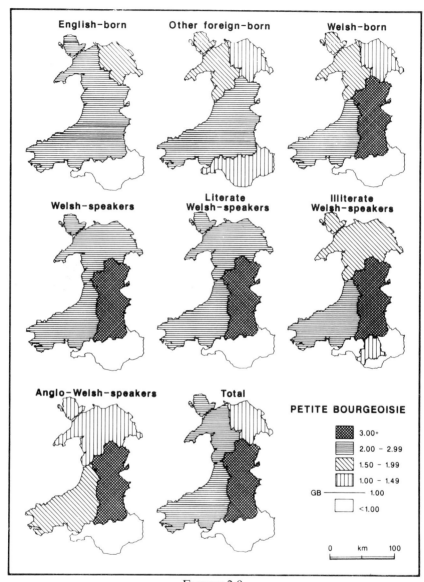

FIGURE 2.9
Location quotients for the ethnic and linguistic divisions of the petite bourgeoisie in Wales, 1981

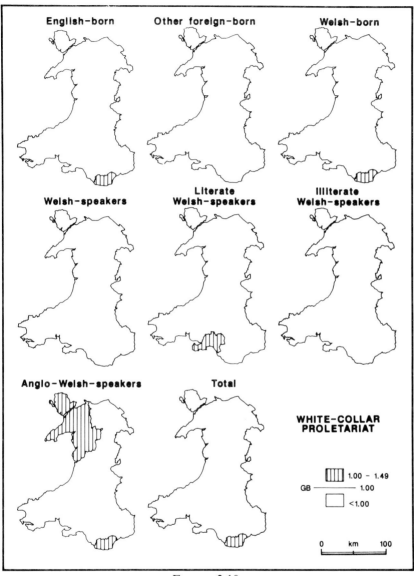

FIGURE 2.10
Location quotients for the ethnic and linguistic divisions of the white-collar
proletariat in Wales, 1981

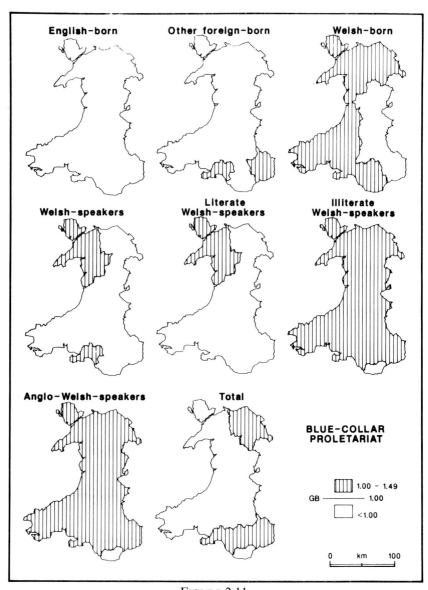

FIGURE 2.11
Location quotients for the ethnic and linguistic divisions of the blue-collar
proletariat in Wales, 1981

If Wales is an 'internal colony', then, the literate Welsh-speaking middle classes are increasingly its metropolitan administrators.

CONCLUSIONS

This study has shown that Wales had the most cosmopolitan society among the four home countries. Thus the brief survey of the ethnic composition of Welsh society revealed that, in 1981, one in five of the residents of Wales were not Welsh-born and that 83 per cent of these incomers were English. Furthermore, although they had settled in all parts of the country, their impact is greatest, in proportional terms, mainly in thinly peopled rural Wales. So it is the South Wales coalfield and Cardiff which now have the greatest absolute and relative numbers of native-born people in Wales. Secondly, analysis of the linguistic cleavage in Welsh society also affirmed the profound influence of the English state, English settlement (both past and present) in Wales, and of anglicization *per se*. These forces have, wittingly and unwittingly, engineered the progressive diminution in the numbers of Welsh-speakers in Wales and the erosion and fragmentation of the Welsh-speaking culture province. In turn, these trends have triggered a wide variety of responses from Welsh-speakers, notably the formation of a political party (Plaid Cymru), language societies, language education at all levels, and broadcasting in Welsh on both television and radio. Some Welsh organizations are now trying to 'build bridges between immigrants and local populations' (Aitchison and Carter, 1990) while others (e.g. Meibion Glyndŵr – the Sons of Glyndwr) have resorted to a campaign of arson, burning some 200 English holiday homes in rural Wales since 1983.

The postwar resurgence in Welsh language, culture and institutions, much of it sanctioned and financed by Parliament, has had some unforeseen negative repercussions. For a nation which has prided itself, justifiably, for its hospitality and, perhaps mythically, for its egalitarianism (Day, 1986) there seems to be evidence of a disquieting preoccupation with cultural elitism among some Welsh-speaking Welsh people. It is heartening that proficiency in Britain's oldest language (hitherto long derided and neglected) now provides dignity, social prestige and economic opportunity within Wales. At the same time it is also profoundly disheartening that a few zealots can seriously assert that the English-speaking majority, who constituted 77.6 per cent of the Welsh-born residents of Wales in 1981, are 'not *really* Welsh'. Moreover, the problems are not simply those of proficiency in the Welsh language being touted as the essential qualification for Welsh nationality, rather than mere nativity, which is deemed a sufficient qualification in the majority of countries:

there are attendant cultural, political and economic implications. Thus Alan Watkins (born in a mining village in what used to be Carmarthenshire) observed that the South Welsh majority

> have had myths forced upon them, not only by the English, who have created a romantic yet oddly unattractive stereotype, but also by their own leaders, who have imposed national characteristics to serve their own purposes.
> Thus the Welsh Establishment is still Welsh-speaking, literary but philistine, Nonconformist (with a bias towards Calvinism), hostile towards Labour and, above all, essentially pacifist. So it is that Welsh school children are asked to admire the works of some second-rate versifier while remaining ignorant of the fact that, in the Great War, Wales proportionately sacrificed more men than any other part of the UK. Likewise, children will be told about the exploits, largely made-up, of Owain Glyndwr but not about the very real achievements of the South Wales Borderers and the Welsh Regiment...
> The Labour Establishment co-exists uneasily with the other, which looks back to old Liberalism, with a few Nationalist flirtations. It is still powerful, not only in Wales but in the party at large. It is not entirely accidental that the three most recent leaders all represented Welsh constituencies, though only one of them, Mr Neil Kinnock, was a Welshman. (*The Observer*, 19 February 1989)

More recently it was reported in the press (i.e. *The Observer*, 17 February 1991) that the Welsh Language Board has just drafted a Parliamentary Bill promoting the Welsh language. One of the proposals was an amendment of Clause 9 of the 1976 Race Relations Act so that it 'becomes lawful for employers to make an ability to speak Welsh a qualification for employment'. Prior to drafting this proposal the Welsh Language Board consulted some 200 organizations, but the Commission for Racial Equality was somehow overlooked. In response the CRE has stated that 'people's job prospects should be looked at on the grounds of merit, not language alone, whether Urdu, Gujerati or Welsh'. The motives of the Welsh Language Board were understandable, given its terms of reference, for this attempt to introduce a form of 'positive discrimination' into the Welsh labour market probably reflects a desire to rectify past constraints on the economic advance of Welsh-speakers in their own country. Unfortunately, though, such initiatives now only serve to exacerbate the fears of the Anglo-Welsh majority, who regard it as yet another marker of the burgeoning exclusivity of the Welsh-speaking minority. There are striking parallels here with the American experience:

As these situations demonstrate, there is a fundamental tension between pluralism and democracy. That is to say, our society in principle sanctions the rights of ethnic groups to maintain their separate cultures and communities, but it also guarantees individual freedoms and specifically proscribes various forms of discrimination. The problem is that the two sets of rights are often in conflict. This is because ethnic groups in a position of social and economic advantage, when exercising their prerogatives of associating with their own ethnic kind deprive outsiders of rights and opportunities protected by democratic norms . . .

Just as ethnic groups have class reasons for tearing down ethnic barriers ahead of them, they also have class reasons for raising ethnic barriers behind them. Thus, it is not uncommon for ethnic groups to invoke democratic principles to combat the ethnic exclusivity of more privileged groups, but to turn around and cite pluralistic principles in defense of their own discriminatory practices. (Steinberg, 1982, p. 258)

Our analyses of the relative social class positions of the key ethnic and linguistic groups within Welsh society confirm the verity of Steinberg's assertions. Most importantly, among the elite service class, the in-migrant minorities are the most strongly over-represented groups, followed in turn by the indigenous literate Welsh-speakers the illiterate Welsh-speakers, and the Anglo-Welsh majority.

The animosities created in Welsh society by these aggregate 'structural' inequalities also have an important spatial dimension, for there are within Wales significant geographical variations in the relative status of these ethnic and linguistic groups within the four national (i.e. GB-wide) social classes. These geographical variations are especially marked in the case of the prestigious and influential service class. Thus in 'Inner Wales' (i.e. Gwynedd and Dyfed), where Welsh-speakers constitute the largest group, the literate Welsh-speakers are socially inferior to the English-born group, and further, are also under-represented with respect to the average for the whole of Great Britain. In South Wales, in contrast, the Anglo-Welsh majority is the only group which is everywhere under-represented in terms of the GB average for the service class. Moreover, in the south-east especially (i.e. Mid Glamorgan, Gwent, and South Glamorgan) it is the literate Welsh-speaking minority which is the most heavily over-represented group.

This evidence suggests that Welsh society has been slow to learn the lessons of history. For centuries, and certainly from the accession of Henry VII onwards, Welsh people have left Wales, lured especially by the economic and social attractions of London. Of all these varied emigrants the gentry have been vilified for abandoning their roles as leaders of their home communities (G.A. Williams, 1985). Since the 1950s, however, the Welsh (or more specifically, their relevant decision-makers) have created their own London, namely Cardiff. Here they have concentrated most of the nations's burgeoning administrative and cultural agencies, with their attendant service and white-collar employment opportunities. In Wales therefore, as in England, the capital city and its suburbs are draining the rest of the country of its best-qualified workers. For Wales, though, these developments have been particularly ironic because Cardiff, which is the core of the least Welsh-speaking region of Wales has, *pace* its role as the nation's capital, become the focus for most of the agencies and institutions which have been established to service the needs of the Welsh-speaking population. Given the lack of suitable employment opportunities in the rural Welsh-speaking heartland, many well-qualified Welsh-speakers have settled in Cardiff, thereby contributing to the decay of the language in Mid and North Wales. Their dilemma has long been recognized, and was poignantly described by Ned Thomas (1973). It would seem to us that the viability of the few remaining predominantly Welsh-speaking communities in Mid and North Wales would be considerably enhanced if they were to receive at least some of the relevant agencies which are currently located in Cardiff.

REFERENCES

Adamson, D. (1988) 'The New Working Class and Political Change in Wales', *Contemporary Wales*, 2, pp. 7–28.

Adamson, D. (1991) *Class, Ideology and Nation: A Theory of Welsh Nationalism*, Cardiff, University of Wales Press.

Aitchison, J. and Carter, H. (1985) *The Welsh Language 1961–1981: An Interpretative Atlas*, Cardiff, University of Wales Press.

Aitchison, J. and Carter, H. (1987) 'The Welsh Language in Cardiff: A Quiet Revolution', *Transactions, Institute of British Geographers*, n.s. 12(4), pp. 482–92.

Aitchison, J. and Carter, H. (1990) 'Battle for a Language', *Geographical Magazine*, pp. 44–6.

Bowen, E.G. and Carter, H. (1975) 'The Distribution of the Welsh Language in 1971: An Analysis', *Geography*, 60, pp. 1–15.

Carter, H. (1983) 'Internal Colonialism and the Interpretation of Aspects of the Urban Geography of Wales'. in D. Drakakis-Smith and S.W. Williams (eds), *Internal Colonialism: Essays round a Theme*, DARG, Geography Department, Edinburgh University, pp. 53–66.

Carter, H. (1986) 'Population Movements into Wales: An Historical Review', in P.S. Harper and E. Sunderland (eds) *Genetic and Population Studies in Wales*, Cardiff, University of Wales Press.

Carter, H. (1989) 'Whole City? A View from the Periphery', *Trans. Inst. Br. Geogr.*, n.s. 14, pp. 4–23.

Carter, H. and Aitchison, J. (1986) 'Language Areas and Language Change in Wales: 1961 and 1981', in I. Hume and W.T.R. Pryce (eds), *The Welsh and their Country: Selected Readings in the Social Sciences*, Llandysul, Gomer Press, pp. 1–25.

Carter, H. and Wheatley, S. (1982) *Merthyr Tudful in 1851: A Study of the Spatial Structure of a Welsh Industrial Town*, Cardiff, University of Wales Press.

Champion, A.G. and Townsend, A.R. (1990) *Contemporary Britain: A Geographical Perspective*, London Edward Arnold.

Chisholm, M. (1990) 'Britain as a Plural Society', in M. Chisholm and D.M. Smith (eds), *Shared Space: Divided Space*, London, Unwin Hyman, pp. 22–45.

Chisholm, M. and Smith, D.M. (eds) (1990) *Shared Space: Divided Space*, London, Unwin Hyman.

Davies, R.R. (1987) *Conquest, Coexistence and Change: Wales 1063–1415*, Oxford, Clarendon Press and Cardiff, University of Wales Press.

Davies, R.R. (1990) *Domination and Conquest: The Experience of Ireland, Scotland and Wales 1100–1300*, Cambridge, Cambridge University Press.

Day, G. (1986) 'The Sociology of Wales: Issues and Prospects 1979 and 1985', in I. Hume and W.T.R. Pryce (eds), *The Welsh and their Country: Selected Readings in the Social Sciences*, Llandysul, Gomer Press, pp. 153–75.

Day, G. (1989) 'A Million on the Move? Population Change and Rural Wales.', *Contemporary Wales*, 3, pp. 137–59.

Day, G. and Rees, G. (eds) (1989) 'Editorial', in *Contemporary Wales*, 3, p. 1.

Delamont, S. (1987) 'S4C and the Grassroots? A Review of Past and Future Research on the Mass Media and the Welsh Language', *Contemporary Wales*, 1, pp. 91–106.

Denney, D., Borland, B. and Fevre, R. (1991) 'The Social Construction of Nationalism: Racism and Conflict in Wales', *Contemporary Wales*, 4, pp. 149–65.

Fielding, A.J. (1989) 'Interregional Migration and Social Change: A Study of South East England based upon data from the Longitudinal Study', *Transactions, Institute of British Geographers* n.s. 14, pp. 24–36.

Frame, R. (1990) *The Political Development of the British Isles, 1100–1400*, Oxford, Oxford University Press.

George, K. and Mainwaring, L. (1987) 'The Welsh Economy in the 1980s', *Contemporary Wales* 1, pp. 7–37.

Hechter, M. (1975) *Internal Colonialism: The Celtic Fringe in British National Development, 1536–1966*, London, Routledge & Kegan Paul.

Hechter, M. (1978) 'Group Formation and the Cultural Division of Labour', *American Journal of Sociology*, 84, pp. 293–318.

Hechter, M. (1983) 'Internal Colonialism Revisited', in D. Drakakis-Smith and S.W. Williams (eds), *Internal Colonialism: Essays around a Theme*, Monograph no. 3., Developing Areas Research Group, Institute of British Geographers, Edinburgh, Edinburgh University, pp. 29–41.

Hume, I. and Pryce, W.T.R. (eds) (1986) *The Welsh and their Country*, Llandysul, Gomer Press.

Jenkins, G.H. (1987) *The Foundation of Modern Wales: 1642–1780*, Oxford, Clarendon Press and Cardiff, University of Wales Press.

Jones, B. (1988) 'The Development of Welsh Territorial Institutions: Modernisation Theory Revisited', *Contemporary Wales*, 2, pp. 47–61.

Jones, G.E. (1988) 'What are Schools in Wales for? Wales and the Education Reform Act', *Contemporary Wales*, 2, pp. 83–97.

Jones, P.E. (1988) 'Some Trends in Welsh Secondary Education', *Contemporary Wales*, 2, pp. 99–118.

Kearney, H. (1989) *The British Isles: A History of Four Nations*, Cambridge, Cambridge University Press.

Kirwan, R.M. (1981) 'A Note on Regional Economic Structure and Occupational Change in Britain 1973–1980' (mimeo, Department of Land Economy, University of Cambridge).

Marquand, J. (1979) 'The Service Sector and Regional Policy in the United Kingdom', *Research Series no. 29*, Centre for Environmental Studies.

Marshall, G. et al. (1988) *Social Class in Modern Britain*, London, Hutchinson Education.

Massey, D. (1984) *Spatial Divisions of Labour*, London, Macmillan.

Mingione, E. (1991) *Fragmented Societies*, Oxford, Basil Blackwell.

Morgan, H.R. (1976) *Development of Land at Wentloog, Cardiff*, General proof of evidence of H.R. Morgan, Industrial Development Officer, County Council of South Glamorgan (Cardiff).

Morgan, K. (1987) 'High Technology Industry and Regional Development: For Wales, see Greater Boston?' *Contemporary Wales*, 1, pp. 39–51.

Morgan, K.O. (1981) *Rebirth of a Nation. Wales 1880–1980*. Oxford, Oxford University Press and Cardiff, University of Wales Press.

Morgan, P. and Thomas D. (1984) *Wales: The Shaping of a Nation'*, Newton Abbot, David & Charles.

Morris, J. and Mansfield R. (1988). 'Economic Regeneration in Industrial South Wales: An Empirical Analysis', *Contemporary Wales*, 2, pp. 63–82.

Murdoch, J. (1988) 'State Institutions and Rural Policy in Wales', *Contemporary Wales*, 2, pp. 29–45.

OPCS (1982) *User guide 51*, Titchfield, Fareham, OPCS.

OPCS (1983) *Welsh Language in Wales*, London, HMSO.

OPCS (1990) *Population Trends 60*, London, HMSO.

Rees, G. and Rees, T.L. (eds) (1980) *Poverty and Social Inequality in Wales*, London, Croom Helm.

Richards, A. (1973) *Dai Country*, London, Michael Joseph.

Smith, A.D. (1991) *National Identity*, Harmondsworth, Penguin.

Smith, D. (1984) *Wales! Wales?* London, Allen & Unwin.

Steinberg, S. (1982) *The Ethnic Myth: Race, Ethnicity, and Class in America*, New York, Atheneum.

Stimson, R.J. (1983) 'Research Design and Methodological Problems in the Geography of Health', in N.D. McGlashan and J.R. Blunden (eds), *Geographical Aspects of Health*, London, Academic Press, pp. 321–34.

Thomas, D. (ed.) (1977) *Wales: A New Study*, Newton Abbot, David & Charles.

Thomas, D. (1988) 'Wales in 1987: An Economic Survey', *Contemporary Wales*, 2, pp. 131–72.

Thomas, D. (1989) 'Wales in 1988: An Economic Survey', *Contemporary Wales*, 3, pp. 199–243.

Thomas, D. (1991) 'Wales in 1989: An Economic Survey', *Contemporary Wales*, 4, pp. 189–245.

Thomas, G. (1964 and 1984) *A Welsh Eye*, London, Hutchinson.

Thomas, N. (1973) 'The Black Cloud', from 'Six Characters in Search of Tomorrow', in M. Stephens (ed.), *The Welsh Language Today*, Llandysul, Gomer Press.

Walker, D. (1990) *Medieval Wales*, Cambridge, Cambridge University Press.

Wass, V. and Mainwaring, L. (1989) 'Economic and Social Consequences of Rationalisation in the South Wales Coal Industry', *Contemporary Wales*, 3, pp. 161–85.

Williams, C.H. (1980) 'Language Contact and Language Change in Wales 1901–1971: A Study in Historical Geolinguistics', *The Welsh History Review*, 10(2), 207–38.

Williams, C.H. (1986) 'Bilingual Education as an Agent in Cultural Reproduction: Spatial Variations in Wales', *Cambria*, 13(1), pp. 111–30.

Williams, C.H. (1987) 'Location and Context in Welsh Language Reproduction: A Geographic Interpretation', *International Journal of the Sociology of Language*, 66, pp. 61–83.

Williams, C.H. (1989) 'New Domains of the Welsh Language: Education, Planning and the Law', *Contemporary Wales*, 3, pp. 41–70.

Williams, C.H. (1990) 'The Anglicisation of Wales', in N. Coupland (ed.), *English in Wales: Diversity, Conflict and Change*, Clevedon, Multilingual Matters.

Williams, Glanmor (1987) *Recovery, Reorientation and Reformation: Wales c.1415–1642*, Oxford, Clarendon Press and Cardiff, University of Wales Press.

Williams, G. (1977) 'Towards a Sociology of Wales', *Planet*, 40, pp. 30–7.

Williams, G. (ed.) (1978) *Social and Cultural Change in Contemporary Wales*, London, Routledge and Kegan Paul.

Williams, G. (ed.) (1983) *Crisis of Economy and Ideology: Essays on Welsh Society*, Bangor, Sociology of Wales Study Group.

Williams, G. (1986) 'Recent Trends in the Sociology of Wales', in I. Hume and W.T.R. Pryce (eds), *The Welsh and their Country*, Llandysul, Gomer Press, pp. 176–92.

Williams, G.A. (1982) *The Welsh in their History*, London, Croom Helm.

Williams, G.A. (1985) *When was Wales? A History of the Welsh*, London, Black Raven Press.

Williams, M. (hon. ed.) (1988) *Keyword Index*, London, *Transactions, Institute of British Geographers*.

3. THE POLITICAL CONSEQUENCES OF MIGRATION INTO WALES

Dylan Griffiths

United Kingdom . . . a national society affected by class divisions but not by the regional, ethnic or cultural conflicts that scarred political life in less fortunate countries. (Birch, 1977, p. 13)

This rosy view of Britain as a modern society where socio-economic conflicts between classes and class-based parties have supplanted ethnic or cultural conflict has informed much of the debate on political behaviour in Britain (for example Butler and Stokes, 1974, p. 121). Yet it has been claimed that Wales provides an exception to what Balsom (1984) terms the British homogeneity thesis. Balsom et al. (1983) found that attributes such as being able to speak Welsh and possessing a Welsh identity influenced political behaviour in Wales. Arguably, the reaction by some groups in Wales to migration into Wales from England shows that cultural issues can still play a major role, even in a 'modern' society such as Britain, contrary to the expectations of modernization theorists (for example: Birch, 1977, p. 33). Jones et al. (1983) noted a process of acculturation in Wales whereby Wales was acquiring the 'politico-cultural characteristics of the wider, English political and social system' (p. 226). One element in this process that they identified is demographic change, through in-migration from England. 'Such diffusion can occasion culture conflict', they warn (p. 226), and I will examine evidence for this by considering the political reactions to in-migration by local and central government, among linguistic and cultural nationalist groups, and also the reactions of in-migrants (and others) to the issues raised by in-migration. Finally I examine whether and to what degree in-migration may have hastened the process of acculturation in Wales.

The British homogeneity thesis was perhaps captured most concisely by Pulzer (1968, p. 98) when he stated that 'Class is the basis of British party politics, all else is embellishment and detail.' A great deal of evidence could be found to support this notion; the near-monopoly of parliamentary representation and votes by two class-based parties for most of the postwar period, the high predictive value of a person's class in predicting partisanship (Bogdanor, 1983, p. 53) and the uniformity of the electoral swing between regions (Crewe, 1985, pp. 101–2). However, there were dissenting voices. From a study of Scottish political behaviour which had shown that non-class issues such as religion, Scottish issues and a sense of Scottish identity affected political behaviour in Scotland Budge and Urwin (1965) concluded that 'the theory of British political homogeneity has been proved to be defective.' Richard Rose found that such differences also existed in Northern Ireland and Wales, and from this, concluded that Britain was a 'multi-national state' (Rose, 1970).

Politically, Wales exhibits certain particular characteristics. Miller (1977, p. 89) identifies a 'Welsh effect' which depresses the share of the vote gained by the Conservative party below what would be expected from the socio-economic structure in Wales. Earlier Blondel (1974) had found that the Labour party in Wales gained a larger share of the votes of both the working and the middle classes than it did in England. This finding was repeated in the Welsh Election Study of 1979 which found that the Welsh middle class was twice as likely to vote Labour as the British middle class, and that 84 per cent of Welsh working-class respondents had voted Labour, as against 70 per cent of working-class respondents in the British Election survey of the same year. In explaining this anomaly Balsom et al. draw on the concept of an 'ethnic sentiment which relates to and affects partisanship' (1983, p. 311). They found that a sense of Welsh identity could act as a substitute for attachment to the working class, and where Welsh identity was absent, then class pressures, including middle- or cross-class pressures, were more influential. Thus, they found (p. 304) that 'the behaviour of British identifiers in Wales is very similar to those of identical class in Britain as a whole.' Elsewhere Balsom et al. have written that 'divisions about national identity are a significant factor in assessing Wales' peculiar status within the United Kingdom, being both politically highly integrated and yet highly distinctive' (1982, Summary).

If the pattern of political behaviour found in Wales in 1979 was partly shaped by Welsh culture and a widespread sense of Welsh identity, the factors that go to produce and reproduce these things become important matters politically. G.A. Williams makes clear that Welsh history and Welsh culture are the products of the Welsh themselves: 'Wales is an artefact which the Welsh produce' (1985, p. 304). It thus becomes important who the inhabitants of Wales are. Referring to English politics, Rose and McAllister (1984, p. 80) make this point clear:

Discussions of electoral divisions in territorial terms usually imply that there are distinctive political cultures or sub-cultures associated with given areas. People who live in a given place, because they live in a given place, are expected to have certain attitudes and behaviour, differentiating them from people that live elsewhere. Just as people who are born or raised in Lancashire will be socialized to support Lancashire at cricket, so people raised in County Durham will be socialized to support Labour at general elections. Territorial divisions can persist, since most people living in a region will have been born there. Newcomers to the area will usually arrive in sufficiently small numbers at any one time so that they (or their children) will adapt to local outlooks. Regional differences . . . are not derived from physical geography such as height above sea level or the climate but from the social consequences of people living together, thereby tending to acquire outlooks in common that also differentiate them from people in other regions. (Rose and McAllister, 1984, p.80)

Demographic change can alter the character of a community, as D. Keri Rosser (1989) shows in his study of the decline of a Welsh-speaking street community in the face of continuous population turnover and, later on, an increasing number of English-speaking in-migrants. The process of 'gentrification', the movement of wealthy incomers into working-class areas, has been observed to have political consequences, and Denver (1989 p. 20) notes that population movements can change the character of a constituency or ward over time.

During the 1980s, especially the end of the 1980s, Wales received considerable numbers of in-migrants from England. Many of the statistics are by now familiar; they have been rehearsed in Day (1989), Carter (1988), *Western Mail*, 7 August 1991, and a detailed analysis of migration into rural Wales is contained in the Institute of Welsh Affairs study of *Rural Wales* in 1988. Briefly, during the 1970s and 1980s the population of Wales, in particular rural Wales, increased because of an in-migration of population from outside Wales. Aggregate statistical data from the Office of Population Censuses and Surveys can tell us a good deal about in-migration and in-migrants. OPCS statistics show that the population of Wales rose by 68,000 between 1981 and 1990, 47,400 of this increase as a result of in-migration. OPCS data also showed that the rate of migration into Wales was increasing during the late 1980s, which, together with the cumulative effect of migration in the past, may have increased the visibility of in-migration and concern about its consequences. Rural districts in Wales gained population through in-migration whereas urban districts continued to lose population. An indication of this divergence between urban and rural Wales is the fact that 85 per cent of the population of urban Wales were born in Wales, whereas only 70 per cent of the population of rural Wales were born within Wales. Thus it is in rural Wales that any political consequences of in-migration will be found.

OPCS data also shows that the popular impression of migration being a form of 'geriatic infill' is mistaken. Net migration was positive for all age groups save the 15–24 age groups where a small net out-migration was seen. Figures from Gwynedd County Council's Planning Department indicate that this net out-migration amongst 15–24-year-olds is due to a very large out-migration by local people in this age group. This may in turn be partly due to the effects of in-migration on the local housing market, driving prices beyond the reach of local people, many of whom are on low incomes. Groups protesting against in-migration into Wales have seized upon these consequences to further their campaigns.

OPCS data also reveal that most in-migrants come from England and particularly the south-east, the north-west and West Midlands regions of England. It is possible therefore that in-migrants may bring with them a different language and different attitudes to religion and politics for example, in short, a different culture.

Studies of areas where in-migration has taken place, in particular survey data, can reveal more about the cultural, linguistic, social and economic characteristics of in-migrants, their differences from the native inhabitants and some of the consequences that in-migration has brought for these communities in its wake.

The Anglesey Population Survey conducted by Anglesey Borough Council in 1977 found that two thirds of the migrants to Anglesey between 1971 and 1977 had come from outside Wales and only some 18 per cent of migrants could speak Welsh. Unsurprisingly, the areas of the island experiencing the greatest influx of persons from outside Anglesey were also those areas that showed the steepest declines in Welsh speaking (Anglesey Borough Council, 1977, p. 199). A study of Tregaron in 1989 by Aitchison et al. revealed the same picture of linguistic decline despite a growth in the total population of the area following in-migration from outside Wales.

Another source of official statistics that can show the changes wrought by in-migration are school rolls. A report by school inspectors found that less than half the pupils at Ysgol Bodedern on Anglesey came from Welsh-speaking homes. The report commented that 'In recent years there has been a decline in student numbers and a change in their linguistic and social backgrounds' (quoted in *Herald Mon*, 17 April 1990, my translation). In 1984 the register of

Ysgol Rhoshirwaun, Llidiardau on the Lleyn peninsula contained 15 names; all the children came from Welsh-speaking homes. By 1989 there were 26 pupils, half from English-speaking homes. The president of UCAC, the Welsh teachers' union, stated that 'due to migration into Welsh-speaking areas, the linguistic nature of these areas changes very quickly, and the number of Welsh-speakers in a . . . school can decline substantially, almost overnight' (reported in *Herald Mon*, 28 April 1990, my translation). Not since the evacuation of English children into rural Wales during the Second World War has the linguistic character of rural Welsh schools changed so drastically, so quickly.

An extrapolation of these trends into the future paints an even more disturbing picture of the consequences of in-migration for the Welsh language. Professor John Aitchison has forecast that if present trends continue then Welsh speaking communities will have virtually ceased to exist in twenty years' time and the numbers of Welsh-speakers in North and west Wales, the traditional heartlands of the language, will have declined dramatically (*Week In Week Out*, BBC 1, 9 January 1990).

Population movements and linguistic change may be of intrinsic interest to demographers and socio-linguists but such matters do not become the concern of political scientists until migration or language decline enter the political domain. A necessary condition for this is that people are aware of in-migration and have some orientation towards it. The Institute of Welsh Affairs survey into *Rural Wales: Population Change and Current Attitudes* found that a majority of local people are aware that 'lots of new people are coming to this area' and that 'amongst "locals" the perception is that too many people are moving into the area from outside Wales, and this is more noticeable amongst fluent Welsh speakers and the lower social classes.' The survey also found that a majority of 'locals' believed that in-migrants got the best jobs and that 'there are tensions between in-movers and longer established residents, between Welsh and English people and between Welsh speakers and non-Welsh speakers' (IWA 1988). Delyth Morris (1989) found that there was little interaction between Welsh- and English-speaking migrants in a village on Anglesey and attributed this partly to the fact that 'several of the Welsh speakers interviewed said they felt the in-migrant English posed a threat to their livelihoods and to that of their children, and hence they "did not have much to say to any of them" ' (1989, p. 117). Thus, if politics is the 'mobilization of bias', the basic ingredients for in-migration to become the focus of political action are present.

Another definition of politics, however, relates political activity to attempts to influence the policies of government. Carter (1988, p. 12) urges an enhanced status for the Welsh language, greater educational facilities to learn Welsh and an examination of planning policies to combat in-migration and its consequences. These are the concerns of government, in particular education and planning are responsibilities of local government. Thus, it is in the activities of local government in rural Wales that some of the political consequences of in-migration can be observed.

Gwynedd County Council in north-west Wales is aware of the responsibility it holds for the maintenance of the Welsh language. Clive James of Gwynedd's Planning Department wrote in a paper given to a conference on 'Language, Planning and Housing in Gwynedd' that:

> The linguistic heritage of Gwynedd is unique. Within its borders live the most intensely Welsh speaking communities that exist today. It is the policy of the County Council to foster its linguistic heritage and to encourage the use of the language in the day to day life of the County's inhabitants.

In-migration is identified as a threat to the Welsh language in Gwynedd, and James states, 'it is now recognized that land use planning can affect the fate of the language in a community.' It follows from this that planning measures can be taken to foster and maintain the Welsh language in Gwynedd. He recommends that three measures specifically related to planning should be incorporated into the county's structure plan to achieve this goal. Firstly, the impact of any development on the Welsh language and culture in an area should be considered when assessing planning applications; secondly, new housing should be restricted to local community requirements with due regard to what happens to the existing housing stock, and finally communities should be encouraged 'to develop at a pace and in a form which reflect the individual character of the community' (James, 1987). He also points to the contribution that housing policies, particularly those related to retirement or second homes in an area, can make to the well-being of the Welsh language. Anglesey Borough Council explicitly stated that 'the decision to inhibit migration growth by regulation of land supply is, in essence, a political one' (Anglesey Borough Council, 1978, p. 119).

Many of these recommendations were included in the memorandum presented to the Secretary of State for Wales in 1988 by Gwynedd Council and three district councils. The title, 'Language, Planning and Housing' suggests the general direction of the recommendations. The planning process is seen as an integral part of any policy to stem the tide of in-migration and thus to help preserve the Welsh language in Gwynedd. The memorandum quotes with approval the sentiments expressed in the original National Park Plan of the Lake District National Park Planning Board:

> Planning is not only about the physical appearance of the landscape but also about people and their community life, and when community life is threatened it seems reasonable to the Board that steps should be taken by the planning authority to defend it. The Board is not content to play a passive role in exercising its development control powers; it believes that there is a need for more positive planning, and that discrimination between the needs of local people and wishes of retirement or second home owners is justified.

The councils expressed concern at the number of extant planning permissions that existed for very substantial developments granted before 1974, when circumstances were different but which now undermine the councils' local structure plans.

The councils wished to control the occupancy of houses which were built to meet the needs of the local community, and not see them used to satisfy the demands of people from outside. To do this, changes in housing legislation would be necessary, and they recommended in the memorandum that the law should be changed so that planning permission would be required before a property could be turned from a main residence to a second home, and so that a planning permission limiting the use of a dwelling to local persons or to persons using it as a main residence would be acceptable on both policy and legal grounds. The councils suggested that Section 52 of the 1971 Town and Country Planning Act, which allowed councils to impose conditions restricting the occupation of new dwellings to local people by agreement, would be a suitable, if unwieldy, device to achieve this. Similar requests were contained in a memorandum to the Secretary of State in 1981.

The councils also wished to see the Welsh language accepted as a material consideration when assessing the suitability of new developments. They noted with approval the statement made by Sir Wyn Roberts on 27 October 1986 that it is appropriate for local planning authorities when considering applications for planning permission to have regard to policies which reflect the needs and interests of the Welsh language.

The memorandum contained a number of other proposals not related to planning but also directed at the problems of migration and the (perceived) threat it posed to the Welsh language. The need to promote the local economy was stressed. Out-migration by young locals has as serious a consequence for the language as in-migration from outside. Greater prosperity, the councils argue would stem this flow, providing more job opportunities locally, and by raising the level of local incomes, local people would be enabled to compete more effectively with wealthy outsiders in the housing market. Economic hardship does undoubtedly contribute to the problems identified by the councils. In December 1987 Lleyn had an unemployment rate of almost 25 per cent, and the 1986 Welsh Inter Censal Survey found that 43 per cent of households in Gwynedd had an annual income of less than £4,000.

Education is also seen as a vital tool to cope with the consequences of in-migration. Gwynedd County Council has a fully bilingual education policy, and a large influx of monolingual English-speaking children imposes a heavy burden on this policy. To address the problems of in-migration Gwynedd education authority has employed a number of *athrawon bro*, peripatetic teachers, who give additional teaching to Welsh learners and set up a number of latecomers' centres to give additional instruction to recent in-migrants of school age. These policies have had some success, but between September 1988 and March 1989 the numbers of in-migrants aged 7–11 were such that over half of them did not attend such a centre, either because there was no centre for them or because their local centre was full (Gwynedd County Council, 1989). Like Harold Carter (1988) they also call for a new Welsh Language Act, as this might have the advantage of allowing the Welsh language to be made a material consideration when considering applications for planning permission (see above). However, they acknowledge that new legislation is a central government matter and devote more time to the difficult issue of housing. As elsewhere, the numbers of council dwellings in Gwynedd are declining as a result of the government's 'right to buy' scheme. The councillors argue that because of the poverty of many households in Gwynedd the provision of housing at an affordable rent is a priority and call on the government to provide housing authorities with the necessary powers and finance to buy houses which come on the market to sell or rent to local people. Given the house price boom of the late 1980s in the south-east of England, they note that it is impossible for local people to compete in the market. Gwynedd County Council's 1989 supplementary memorandum quotes the retiring chairman of Mid Wales Development:

It is a fact that a couple selling a house in the South East can buy an attractive house in Mid Wales and still be left with a balance large enough to live the rest of their lives on the interest. This is causing special problems by creating powerful competition for housing at a time when the supply of rented accommodation is much reduced. I see this as unhelpful to . . . retaining our young people, and creating a self-sustaining population structure.

The second memorandum just mentioned rehearses many of the same points but is stronger in tone, and this is because the councils note that, since the publication of the first memorandum, 'house prices have been escalating, the scale of in-migration has been increasing and the Welsh language has been declining as a community language' (Gwynedd County Council, June 1989, p. 1)

The response of central government is crucial if local authorities are to put some of these policies into effect, as in many cases they require new powers, new money and sometimes new legislation which central government alone can provide. In a letter to the chief executive of Gwynedd County Council the Welsh Office responded to the specific proposals in the memoranda and outlined what steps the Welsh Office was already taking to cope with the consequences of in-migration.

The Welsh Office Circular 53/88, 'The Welsh Language: Development Plans and Planning Control' states that 'Where the use of the Welsh language is a component of the social fabric of a community it is, clearly, appropriate that the implications of this be taken into account in the formation of land use policies.' This went some way to meet the councils' demands. The Welsh Office also set aside £1m in 1989–90 for local authorities to buy up properties for rent or resale to local people where the incidence of second homes was high. This at least went in the same direction as the councils' proposals, as did the researches of Tai Cymru (Housing for Wales) and its pilot projects into the provision of affordable village housing in rural areas (Welsh Office response to the Gwynedd County Council memoranda, September 1989).

However, the Welsh Office could not commit itself to uphold the 'local need' policies of local authorities when considering appeals against their refusals to consider planing applications. Nor did it wish to intervene in the matter of dealing with planning permission given to substantial developments before 1974. This was seen as a local authority matter. Neither did the government feel that amending legislation to require planning permission before a dwelling could be turned from a main residence to a second home was appropriate, as this would create administrative difficulties, be arbitrary, could substantially affect the local housing market, be inequitable and lessen the freedom of some householders. Neither did the Welsh Office consider appropriate the imposition of conditions restricting tenure of property to local inhabitants through Section 52 agreements. Recently Nicholas Bennett, Welsh Office Under-Secretary, warned that 'I cannot see that it would be appropriate to use Section 106 [formerly Section 52] in blanket fashion or to skew an entire local market' (*Western Mail*, 16 April 1991).

Not surprisingly, in the light of the limited political response, in-migration has also drawn a response from cultural and linguistic groups and from nationalist groups. More worryingly for Plaid Cymru, it has also divided nationalist opinion in Wales, over aims and methods. Established groups such as Cymdeithas Yr Iaith Gymraeg and Plaid Cymru have sought a legislative response to the problems posed by in-migration. Others, however, have sought to mobilize opinion against in-migration without making clear demands on government for action. Such groups include the Covenanters of the Free Welsh, who decided to field a candidate against Plaid Cymru's then president, Dafydd Elis Thomas, because of his alleged 'reluctance to discuss the problem of migration into Wales' according to Owain Clynnog, the Covenanters' chairman (*Herald Mon*, 22 September 1990). Other groups fall off the edge of the scale of conventional politics altogether, Meibion Glyndŵr's activities may be directed against what they have termed 'white settlers' but they have not sought to mobilize local opinion or make specific demands to the government. Such a passion for anonymity is understandable amongst a secret army, and the poet R.S. Thomas, who has spoken in robust fashion against English in-migration, reflected this when he recently warned 'Whoever thinks in terms of violence, do not publicize it' (*Western Mail*, 6 August 1991). Such secrecy, however, is not compatible with accepted definitions of politics and, in any case, makes the study of such groups remarkably difficult.

Plaid Cymru has responded to in-migration by producing a paper on the issue. It is the only major party in Wales to have done so. In 'Migration into Wales: A Positive Response' (1988) it states that it believes that 'In-migration is a political issue', and claims that its proposals are 'based on the principles of development, control and assimilation aimed at tackling the in-migration phenomenon in a positive and constructive spirit' (p. 26). Plaid Cymru does not regard in-migration as harmful in itself and accepts that some is inevitable and that a new Wales would have to combine the cultures of natives and in-migrants in a new synthesis. However, it sees the impact of in-migration, especially in the rural heartlands of the Welsh language, as a threat to 'the maintenance of Welsh nationality and the development in progressive directions of our people's sense of national identity' (p. 10). Its measures address the need to preserve and foster this sense of Welsh nationality.

As a long-term solution, Plaid Cymru argues that only the creation of a democratic Welsh state can transform Wales's role in the British polity and economy. It argues, 'The in-migration crisis underlines in dramatic fashion the need for this fundamental change in the relationship of Wales with the British state' (p. 14). However, as it is unlikely that Wales will gain her statehood in the near future, it is the short term remedies proffered that are of most interest to us.

Short-term solutions address the need for economic development in the poorer regions of Wales and call for development bodies like the Welsh Development Agency, Mid Wales Development or the Wales Tourist Board to incorporate 'the protection and reinforcement of Welsh nationality' in their strategies and activities. Greater funding for such bodies is urged along with the demand that the reintegration of the Welsh economy should figure more highly in their plans.

Housing and planning policies are also seen as a vital cornerstone of coping with the consequences of in-migration. Many of the recommendations echo those made by Gwynedd County Council and include the granting of low-interest finance to native people to enable them to compete with potential in-migrants in the housing market, adequate finance for district councils to enable effective intervention in the housing market, including the renovation of existing properties. Numerous alterations to the planning process are proposed; for example, it is recommended that new development is directed towards the needs of the local community, the Welsh language is made a material consideration in assessing applications for planning permission, restrictions on the change of a dwelling to a second home or for a non-local to reside there (as supported by Gwynedd County Council) are commended, as is an enhanced role for community councils in judging applications for planning permission.

Finally, in addition to these measures, the document addresses itself to measures to protect the Welsh language including adequate funding for a system of language centres for the children of in-migrants and the designation of primary and secondary schools as Welsh/bilingual schools with a clear definition of their language policy. Adequate provision for adult in-migrants wishing to learn Welsh should also be made available and, again an ambitious measure, a new Welsh Language Act is seen as essential in the longer term.

Both Gwynedd County Council and Plaid Cymru explicitly accept that certain restrictions on the property market are necessary to stem the tide of in-migrants. Neither however, go as far as Cymdeithas Yr Iaith Gymraeg in their campaign for a Property Act regulating the sale of dwellings in areas where in-migration is threatening the way of life of the local community. Their proposed Act would regulate the sale of all properties, old and new, farms and businesses as well as homes in a local community according to a structure plan devised by local district and community councils. The structure plans would consider such factors as the number of second homes in the area and whether the community could absorb and assimilate more English-speaking in-migrants without harming the Welsh language locally. By these radical (and in a free market society, revolutionary) measures they aim to create 'a market that services the needs of the local community' (Cymdeithas Yr Iaith, 1989, p. 4, translation mine).

Cymdeithas Yr Iaith have also brought their direct campaigning methods to bear on the controversy surrounding in-migration. In September 1988 they launched a campaign under the title *Nid Yw Cymru Ar Werth* ('Wales is not for sale') to draw attention to the problem of in-migration. A series of rallies have been held, as well as other actions including the painting of slogans on estate agents' offices and the gluing of their locks. Two leading members of Y Gymdeithas, Alun Llwyd and Branwen Nicholas, were sentenced to six months in prison after causing £6,500 of damage to a government office. Their actions have brought forth a sympathetic response in some quarters. The editorial in the *Herald Mon* on 7 September 1991 declared boldly, 'Now is the time to speak plainly against in-migration', and said of the two defendants, 'At least they did something to draw attention to the curse of in-migration.'

Cymdeithas Yr Iaith were also heavily involved in opposing in-migration at a local level in their opposition to Anglesey Borough Council's Structure Plan, *Mon 2000*, which included proposals to build many more houses in villages throughout the island. Alun Lloyd, who writes a column for the *Herald Mon,* described the plan as 'an immigrants' charter' (*Herald Mon*, 16 June 1990, translation mine). The Cymdeithas were active in opposition to proposed developments in several villages, drew attention to what they claimed was a housing crisis on the island, and finally forced the council to reconsider the *Mon 2000* plan.

Thus it is clear that in-migration has emerged as a political issue amongst some groups within the native Welsh community. It has led to many political initiatives and also significant divisions amongst nationalist opinion. How-ever, some of the policies pursued by local authorities to preserve the Welsh language in the face of in-migration have, in their turn, drawn a political response. For example, Dyfed County Council has designated 188 of its primary schools as Category A schools where the bulk of the teaching takes place through the medium of Welsh. This policy is intended to preserve the

Welsh character of these schools and their mainly rural surrounding communities. Some parents however, worry that teaching in a language unfamiliar to many of the children now attending these schools will inhibit their children's progress. Fears that this policy is more concerned with social engineering than education is shared by some native people as well as in-migrants, and a pressure group, Education First, has been formed to persuade Dyfed to alter its Welsh-medium policy. They have claimed that Dyfed imposed its new policy without consulting parents. Blodwen Griffiths, a teacher who spoke no English until she was ten, said, 'it seems incredible, but the first many knew about the change was when their kids stopped coming home with English books and English written work' (*Guardian*, 31 July 1990). Education First wishes to see each child educated in its mother tongue, an aim that has the support of Dr Alan Williams, the Labour MP for Carmarthen, a fluent Welsh-speaker and Eisteddfod adjudicator. In a series of test cases, Education First sought to have Dyfed's categorization policy overturned on the grounds that the policy represented a 'substantial change' in the nature of the schools involved, contrary to the 1944 Education Act (*Western Mail*, 10 October 1991). However, the Welsh Secretary recently pronounced that the policy did not contravene the Act and could stand (*Times Educational Supplement*, 16 August 1991). Undaunted, Education First have threatened to take their case to the High Court (*Western Mail*, 30 July 1991). This episode certainly bears out the view that in-migration can give rise to new issues and conflicts.

It is clear that in-migration has become a political issue in parts of Wales at least, and that it exercises the minds of some, virtually to the exclusion of all else. Cynog Dafis, now a prospective parliamentary candidate for Plaid Cymru, declared as long ago as 1979 that 'in-migration by the English is now the most important political issue in Wales today – by a long way if you consider the survival of Wales's distinctiveness and identity to be an important matter that is' (Cymdeithas Yr Iaith, 1979). However, the migration of English people into Wales is a highly visible (or audible matter); the permeation of English values is a much more intangible/ephemeral matter. Nevertheless it may have far-reaching consequences and transform Wales politically as well as linguistically.

Historically anglicization in Wales has been associated with support for the Conservative party. At least since the latter half the nineteenth century the Conservatives have fared best in the most anglicized, least Cymric parts of Wales (Morgan, 1981, p. 45). An examination of Welsh electoral history yields the intriguing fact that in 1945 the Conservatives made only one gain in Wales,

Caernarfon Boroughs, Lloyd George's old seat, and Morgan attributes Conservative success there to 'the influx of English civil servants and academics' (p. 302).

Also, as was mentioned above, national identity was found to be a significant variable in determining partisanship in the 1979 election in Wales (Balsom et al., 1983). British identifiers had a weaker attachment to the Labour party than did Welsh identifiers. Balsom et al. also found that one-third of Conservative voters in Wales in 1979 were born outside Wales, adding further weight to the expectation that in-migration may have considerable political consequences. Where the Conservatives performed best, capturing the seat of Anglesey on a 12.5 per cent swing for example, in-migration had also been heaviest. This may partly explain why the Conservatives increased their vote in rural Welsh Wales, an area not usually favourable to the Conservatives. Balsom et al. (1983, p. 324) note that 'extensive immigration has concentrated the non-indigeneous population in these areas. Thus intense Welshness, with a high degree of cultural attachment, is to be found alongside substantial non-Welsh populations. Such coexistence may polarize attitudes to the advantage of the Conservative Party.'

Statistical analysis gives further support to the hypothesis that high Conservative support is associated with a large non-Welsh-born population. Balsom and Burch (1980) provide statistics for the percentage of the population in each constituency born in Wales according to the 1971 census. Correlating this with the percentage share of the vote gained by the Conservatives in each constituency in Wales in 1979 gives a score of − .604, a fairly high result. Regression analysis gives R-square of 0.59. Using counties as the unit of analysis the relationship between Conservative support and the percentage born in Wales remained significant during the 1980s. Correlating the percentage born in Wales according to the 1981 census and the percentage share of the vote gained by the Conservatives in 1987 the R-square score remains about the same at 0.59, but the correlation result rises to − .760, a high statistical relationship.

Not too much should be made of these results however. Firstly, the percentage born outside Wales includes many Welsh people: English maternity hospitals, Shrewsbury for example, are often the nearest hospital for many areas of Wales. Secondly, the 1980s were a very successful period for the Conservatives, and many of the factors that contributed to their success generally, for example a perceived economic miracle, the Falklands factor or Labour disunity will have been felt in Wales too. It must be remembered, though, that these factors did not save the Conservatives in Scotland and this perhaps indicates that Wales is more closely integrated with England than Scotland. Integration is due partly to in-migration as it erodes the cultural basis of a Welsh political identity and has continued apace during the 1980s. The Institute of Welsh Affairs survey (1988) found that 74 per cent of in-migrants regarded themselves as British or English and only 21 per cent considered themselves to be Welsh. With the native population this proportion is almost exactly reversed, 78 per cent of non in-migrants identified themselves as Welsh and only 20 per cent as either British or English.

These facts seem to indicate that in-migration has hastened the process of acculturation and that, despite the best efforts of local government, nationalist politicians and language groups, Wales will become increasingly closely integrated in the wider British political system.

REFERENCES

Aitchison, J., Carter, H and Roger, D, (1989) 'Immigration and the Welsh Language: A Case Study of Tregaron', Rural Survey Research Unit, UCW Aberystwyth, Monograph no. 3.

Anglesey Borough Council (1977) 'Anglesey Population Survey', Llangefni, Anglesey Borough Council Planning Department.

Anglesey Borough Council (1978) 'Employment and Unemployment in Anglesey', Llangefni, Anglesey Borough Council Planning Department.

Balsom, D. (1984) 'An Analysis of Recent Voting Behaviour in Wales with particular reference to Socio-economic Factors Derived from the Census in Wales', Aberystwyth, unpublished PhD thesis.

Balsom D. and Burch, M. (1980) *A Political and Electoral Handbook for Wales*, Farnborough, Gower.

Balsom D., Madgwick, P. J. and Van Mechelen, D. (1982) 'The Political Consequences of Welsh Identity', *Studies in Public Policy*, no. 97, University of Strathclyde.

Balsom, D., Madgwick, P. J. and Van Mechelen, D. (1983) 'The Red and the Green: Patterns of Partisan Choice in Wales', *British Journal of Political Science*, 13, pp. 299–325.

Birch, A.H. (1977) *Political Integration and Disintegration in the British Isles*, London, Allen & Unwin.

Blondel, J. (1974) *Voters, Parties and Leaders*, Harmondsworth, Penguin.

Bogdanor, V. (1983) *Democracy and Elections*, Cambridge, Cambridge University Press.

Budge I. and Urwin, D.W. (1965) *Scottish Political Behaviour: A Case Study in British Homogeneity*, London, Longmans.

Butler, D. and Stokes D, (1974) *Political Change in Britain*. London, Macmillan.

Carter, H, (1988) 'Immigration and the Welsh Language', National Eisteddfod.

Crewe, I. (1985) 'Great Britain', in I. Crewe, and D. Denver, (eds), *Electoral Change in Western Democracies*, London, Croom Helm.

Cymdeithas Yr Iaith Gymraeg (1979) 'Mewnlifiad, Iaith a Chymdeithas', Aberystwyth.

Cymdeithas Yr Iaith Gymraeg (1989) 'Cartrefi, Mudo, Prisiau: Rheolaeth Gymunedol as y Farchnad Eiddo', Aberystwyth.

Day, G. (1989) ' "A million on the Move"?: Population Change and Rural Wales', *Contemporary Wales*, 3, pp. 137–59.

Denver, D. (1989) *Elections and Voting Behaviour in Britain*, Hemel Hempstead, Philip Allen.

Gwynedd County Council (July 1988) 'Language, Planning and Housing in Gwynedd: A Memorandum to the Secretary of State for Wales', Caernarfon.

Gwynedd County Council (June 1989) 'Language, Planning and Housing: A Supplementary Memorandum', Caernarfon.

Gwynedd County Council (1989) 'Report on the Development of the Welsh Language Policy in the Primary and Secondary Schools of Gwynedd 1988–90', Caernarfon.

Institute of Welsh Affairs (IWA) (1988) *Rural Wales: Population Change and Current Attitudes*.

Morgan, K. O. (1981) *Wales 1880–1980: Rebirth of a Nation*, Oxford, Oxford University Press.

Morris, D, (1989) 'A Study of Language Contact and Social Networks in Ynys Mon', *Contemporary Wales*, 3, pp. 99–117.

Plaid Cymru (1988) 'Migration into Wales: A Positive Response'. Cardiff, Plaid Cymru Publications.

Pulzer, P. (1968) *Political Representation and Elections in Britain*, London, Allen & Unwin.

Rose, R. (1970), 'Britain as a Multi-National State', in R. Rose (ed.), *Studies in British Politics*. (1976), London, Macmillan.

Rose, R. and McAllister, I (1984) *The Nationwide Competition for Votes*, London, Pinter.

Rosser, D. K. (1989) 'The Decay of a Welsh Speaking Street Community: Migration and its Residual Effects', *Contemporary Wales*, 3, pp. 119–36.

Williams, G. A. (1985) *When Was Wales?* Harmondsworth Penguin.

4. REDEVELOPMENT IN CARDIFF BAY: STATE INTERVENTION AND THE SECURING OF CONSENT

Huw Thomas

The actual character of land use change cannot be deduced from global economic forces; rather it depends on previous usage and the local political situation...

...The particular outcome of conflicting actors and objectives inevitably reflects the unique history of a city, even while the forces at work may be generally similar from place to place. (Fainstein and Fainstein, 1988, p. 156)

INTRODUCTION

At a recent conference on urban policy held in Cardiff, a stranger to the city expressed astonishment at the extravagance of Cardiff Bay Development Corporation's (CBDC) proposal to construct an almost ceremonial mall from Cardiff's city centre to the waterfront, demolishing an established industrial area in the process. However, to those who are familiar with the development of Cardiff perhaps the most striking aspect of the proposal is not its scale, or likely effects, for good or ill, but its echoes of other attempts physically to restructure the city in order to create a more 'fitting' built environment for whatever role or status was being claimed for it. In each case, the particular form that the urban development proposals took can be fully understood only if due account is taken of the city and region's politics.

In the early twentieth century, for example, the laying out of a civic centre in Cathays Park (the ceremonial aspects of which have parallels in the CBDC plan) was both an expression of the civic pride of the liberal bourgeoisie which had successfully challenged the Bute family's political hegemony in the city, and was also an important element in a political strategy designed to buttress Cardiff's demographic significance in Wales with administrative and cultural leadership (Evans, 1984/5). The project was to have its successes – (e.g. the achievement of city status in 1905, and securing the National Museum of

Wales on a site in Cathays Park) – and failures (e.g. losing the National Library of Wales to Aberystwyth).

More recently, the major reorganization and redevelopment of the city centre in the 1970s and 1980s was sponsored and co-ordinated by the local authorities and supported by the Welsh Office as, in large measure, a project to create a 'fitting' capital city and regional centre. Rees and Lambert (1981) show how the development of Cardiff as a 'true' capital city, as required by 'Wales: The Way Ahead' (Welsh Office, 1967), fitted into a politically dominant analysis of the region's problems and the appropriate solutions to them. Indeed, the regional aim of the central state had been concerned since the 1950s that the urban structure of Cardiff, and, in particular, its centre was inappropriate for the modern capital city (in a modernizing region) at which it was aiming. Locally, the idea of city centre redevelopment had broad-based political support and was a long-standing element of the postwar planning agenda in the city (Roberts, 1966) – in part, no doubt because it exploited that strand of civic pride which had been significant in local politics since the late nineteenth century. Though the vagaries of the redevelopment process reflected the state of the property market nationally and internationally (Cooke, 1980; Hamilton, 1988), the persistence of the state, centrally and locally, in pursuing the project, and the mix of uses which was deemed appropriate can be fully understood only within the local and regional political context.

The designation of an urban development corporation in 1987 to initiate and manage the physical, social and economic transformation of Cardiff Bay undoubtedly fits into the view of Cardiff as a city which needs to modernize to fulfil its role both nationally and (now) internationally. CBDC's aim is 'to establish Cardiff internationally as a superlative city, which will stand comparison with any similar city in the world, enhancing the image and economic well being of Cardiff and of Wales as a whole' (CBDC, 1988, p. 2). The suggestion is that having established itself as the capital of Wales, with all that that entails, Cardiff is now ready to make its mark on a wider stage (pp. 3– 4).

One might expect that the broad-based political support enjoyed by city centre development would now shift behind Cardiff Bay. On the face of it, that support exists – politicians of all political parties, and from all the local authorities in the area are represented on CBDC's board. There is, it is true, well-publicized opposition to a specific feature of CBDC's strategy – namely, the 1.2 km barrage across Cardiff Bay - but this does not extend to questioning the fundamental nature of what is proposed for the Bay (Brookes, 1989a).

However, this paper will argue that the history of an earlier dockland redevelopment in Cardiff provides a basis for speculating that the lack of overt political opposition to the general thrust of CBDC's policies may mask local tensions which have yet to be resolved. Their examination shows how important it is to analyse the local politics of urban redevelopment for a complete understanding of the forces at work in shaping it.

The redevelopment episode in question is the Atlantic Wharf development of 1983 onwards. It is significant because it marked a major department in planning policy for the city, inasmuch as the docklands area, previously seen as an industrial belt with associated working-class housing, was now viewed as having potential for up-market housing, and a variety of commercial uses. Not only did this idea raise questions about the future of industry in the docklands, it also identified the possibility that the city centre might no longer be the sole location for major new commercial development, an idea which had previously been regarded as potentially subversive of the concerted efforts to establish the city centre as a significant regional commercial centre. The Atlantic Wharf episode can fairly be represented, therefore, as a forerunner of the Cardiff Bay initiative, and its examination throws an important light on the tensions surrounding the Cardiff Bay project.

THE REDEVELOPMENT OF ATLANTIC WHARF, CARDIFF

Atlantic Wharf is an area of some 100 acres in the south of Cardiff, sandwiched between the redundant Bute East dock (opened, 1855–9; closed, 1970) and an area of mixed industry and warehousing called Collingdon Road (see figure 4.1). In the second half of the nineteenth century and the first half of the twentieth century the area was an important part of Cardiff docks (indeed a substantial proportion of the developable land at Atlantic Wharf consists of the filled Bute West dock (opened, 1838; closed, 1964). At that time the area was identified by reference to these working docks; the name 'Atlantic Wharf' is a coinage of the developers who helped transform the area's physical and socio-economic characteristics in the 1980s.

The outline of what happened at Atlantic Wharf is straightforward. Until the early 1980s, in line with the dominant state and private sector perspective described earlier, every local planning policy document which referred to the area at all saw its future as largely one of accommodating heavy industry. The south of Cardiff, the docks and their hinterland, contained by far the largest single concentration of heavy industry in the city. Until the late 1970s the area hardly featured explicitly in local authority planning policies, but the closure of the East Moors steelworks in 1978, as part of a national programme of

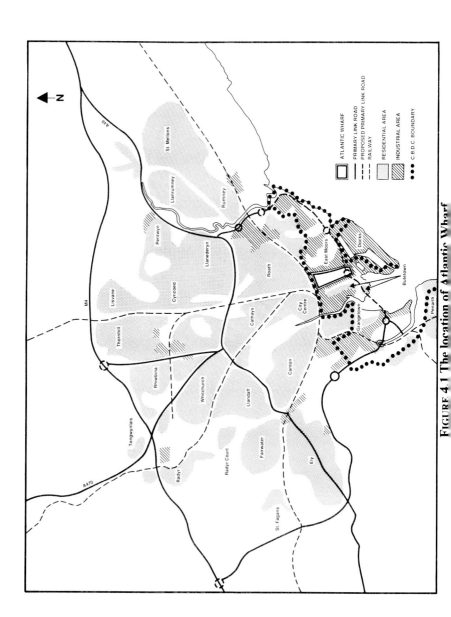

FIGURE 4.1 The location of Atlantic Wharf

rationalization by the British Steel Corporation, focused the minds of local and national politicians on the area and its prospects. With thousands of jobs lost, and knock-on effects in the local economy expected to be severe, it was politically essential for the state at all levels to be seen to be doing something to address the problems of South Cardiff. There followed concerted action by local authorities and the Welsh Development Agency with Welsh Office support. In effect, this sought to turn a nineteenth-century industrial area into something resembling a twentieth-century industrial estate: infrastructure was upgraded, large areas of dereliction (including the closed steelworks) were cleared, and factories built in advance of demand. The activity, over a five-year period, 1978–83, was impressive. Underlying it, however, was the shared policy position that the dockland area of the city would remain largely industrial, a home for large and small firms (Cardiff City Council, 1982). It might need modernizing, but its essential character would remain the same.

Atlantic Wharf was largely by-passed by the initial input of public investment, but of its future there seemed little doubt. It was surrounded by industry, and industrial access roads into it were being promoted by the County Council up to and including 1982. Yet by 1990 most of Atlantic Wharf has been developed for housing, offices and leisure facilities. Major shopping developments are planned (though it is unlikely that these will come to fruition in the present investment climate), and the humble industrial access road has been replaced by a major highway connecting the area directly with the city centre. This physical transformation has been undertaken by private developers, with the support of a range of regional and local state agencies, and minimal private sector opposition. It has involved a complete reversal of both private and public sector expectations and policies for the area. However, the consensus about the new shape of the area's future has not been complete, and such support as has existed has been the result of careful organizing.

A major redevelopment involves a number of strands:

(1) Land acquisition/site assembly.
(2) Planning permission.
(3) Commitment from developer(s).
(4) Finance.

Table 4.1 summarizes the chronology of the way these elements were put in place at Atlantic Wharf, and identifies public agencies which played especially important roles in securing them. What it does not bring out is the varying commitments and attitudes of those involved in, and affected by, the development.

TABLE 4.1
Schedule of main events in redevelopment of Atlantic Wharf (principal actors given in parentheses)

Application for planning permission (SGCC/CCC)	Site assembly: compulsory purchase order (LAW/WO)	Commitment from developer (SGCC/Tarmac)	Finance (SGCC/WO/Tarmac)	Notes
SGCC lodged planning application with CCC (August 1983)		Costed schemes invited from private sector by SGCC (September–November 1983). Tarmac chosen (November 1983); endorsed by ABP (January 1984).		ABP = Associated British Ports; CCC = Cardiff City Council; LAW = Land Authority for Wales (public sector body)
	Compulsory purchase orders lodged by LAW (May/September 1984)		Urban development grant appn. submitted (March 1984).	Tarmac = Tarmac Properties Ltd (developers). WO = Welsh Office (central government)
Planning permission granted (March 1985)	Public inquiry (April 1985). Compulsory purchase order confirmed by WO (July 1985).	Final development costings and content agreed by SGCC/Tarmac/WO and grant agreed in principle (February 1985)		
Final legal agreements between CCC and Tarmac signed (September–November 1985)			Final amount of urban development grant agreed by WO (October 1985)	This table contains only the broad outline of events. See Thomas and Imrie (1989), for further details of some elements.

Some indication of the variety is provided by simply listing the ways in which agencies were involved. South Glamorgan County Council played a number of key roles in facilitating development – it made an early application for planning permission in its own name in order to set the formal policy review process in motion; it invited developers to put forward proposals for the area and sponsored one of them for an Urban Development Grant application to central government (the Welsh Office); it was prepared to contribute some £2m itself in grant aid; and it developed its own headquarters in the area, at a cost of around £20m.

The City Council, on the other hand, played a largely reactive role. It considered the planning application(s) before it and (eventually) gave planning permission. Before doing so it undertook a revision to the local plan for the area, which was certainly not legally necessary and resulted in a document which, while formally endorsing a mixed use redevelopment, was ambivalent enough in its discussion of details for City Council evidence not to be called as 'expert' support at a public inquiry into the compulsory purchase order (CPO) by the Land Authority for Wales: some of the areas which fell within the CPO's boundary were simply outside the area identified by the council as suitable for redevelopment (Cardiff City Council, 1984a).

These subtle, but significant differences appear to stem from differences in policy trajectories and policy constituencies. Throughout the 1970s the major focus of the City Council's planning efforts had been initiating and co-ordinating a series of major redevelopments and highway improvements in the city centre and, simultaneously, identifying (and developing) sites for public and private housing on the city's periphery. The broad-based political support for the principle of modernization, of which city centre redevelopment was one example, has been mentioned above. In addition, in a city dominated by service sector employment there was always likely to be a basis of support in the business sector for the Council's strategy of compulsory land acquisition as a way of assembling sites for redevelopment. This was exemplified by the bipartisan political support the redevelopment programme received and the close liaison which occurred between the City Council and the Chamber of Trade on matters relating to the centre. This commitment to the centre had, as its corollary, explicit planning policies limiting peripheral commercial and retailing developments. Opposition to 'out of town' major office and shopping developments was consistent in the City Council, with apparent support from planning officers and politicians.

The severe recession of the late 1970s, and the locally significant closure of the East Moors steelworks in 1978, added a new dimension to the City

Council's concerns – namely, the future of manufacturing industry and, more generally, the poor environment and infrastructure of the south of the city. Its response was to prepare land use plans for the area – the East Moors Plan, 1981; South Bute Town Local Plan, 1981; North Butetown Local Plan 1981 – and to institute regimes of grants for industrial and commercial firms wishing to improve or extend their premises. The focus of its activity was local small firms; the future of south Cardiff was to be one of an expanding number of small firms in a more functional and pleasant environment. This 'small firm' focus won the support of Labour politicians, who were pleased to see something being done to improve the area, and Conservative politicians, many of whom were small businessmen (albeit typically in the service sector) themselves.

The evolution of the County Council's concern for south Cardiff was different, and seemed to have two strands. The first was a straightforward concern that south Cardiff had been neglected, that its population had, in general, the worst living conditions in the county. This concern was especially strong when Labour controlled the County Council, as it did from 1981, particularly as the Labour group contained some influential members of long standing from the south of the city. These concerns found their way into the County Structure Plan as strengthened and sharpened commitments to promoting investment in this part of the county, and to improving highway access into it (South Glamorgan County Council, 1985).

The second strand in the County's policy evolution stemmed from its increasing involvement in economic development and, in particular, the attraction of inward investment to the county. This seems to have sensitized officers (and later councillors) to national and international economic trends (in particular, the collapse of British manufacturing industry in the late 1970s and early 1980s) and persuaded them that the future of the southern part of the city might not be as an industrial enclave. The County Council continued to support city centre redevelopment and restraints on decentralization of shops and offices into the 1980s, but interview evidence suggests that senior councillors and officers involved in economic development were increasingly sceptical about the necessity or practicality of such policies.

Against this background it is, perhaps, not surprising that the two local authorities responded very differently to initial soundings about the possibility of a major mixed use redevelopment at Atlantic Wharf. In the summer of 1982 a local architect/property developer who apparently had already received some encouragement from senior Welsh Office civil servants (interview evidence) approached both City and County Councils with ideas for such a redevelopment, details of which do not seem to have survived. The response of the City Council, with Planning as lead department, was cautious. Internal memoranda suggest that from the outset there was officer concern that large-scale commercial development in Atlantic Wharf would create an area which was competing for investment with the city centre, a concern which was to be articulated at a political level almost a year later, when the Conservative leader of the council stated that 'Offices are not on and that is the end of the story' (quoted in Thomas, 1983e). When the City Council undertook its own planning study of Atlantic Wharf, in November 1982, it did so without any commitment to a re-evaluation of the plans for the area (Cardiff City Council, 1982).

The County Council, by way of contrast, was already working with the local architect/entrepreneur to produce a joint report and proposal for the Welsh Office in January 1983 (South Glamorgan County Council, 1983).

This document was a major departure from the ideas of the East Moors Plan:

(1) The dock was to be reopened to the sea, instead of being partially filled.
(2) Only two small sites were identified for industrial and workshop use.
(3) Most of the remainder of the land north and west of the dock was designated for housing, commercial uses (hotel and shopping), and various leisure uses. A large site at the southern end of the dock was reserved for 'special projects' – this site was roughly the location of the site later identified for County Hall.

Over the next two years there were to be a number of proposals for the redevelopment of Atlantic Wharf, but all included a mixture of land uses with housing as the major element (but little or no industry), the creation of a major recreational facility around the dock, and varying amounts of shops and offices. It was over the latter that haggling was to take place to create a broad level of support for the proposals. But on 10 February 1983 a House of Commons statement by Nicholas Edwards, the Secretary of State for Wales, showed that pressure was about to be brought to bear on all those involved with the redevelopment to co-operate in implementing it.

Edwards (1983) took the opportunity of a debate on Welsh Affairs to speak at length and in some specificity about the urban renewal prospects in Cardiff. He stated: 'In my view the time is now ripe...to initiate measures which could lead to the rebirth and rapid growth of South Cardiff.' He indicated that an initial review of prospects had already been undertaken (presumably a reference to the meeting between his ministers and/or senior civil servants and the County Council about their submission, and he identified a priority, namely 'to develop...the area that lies between the Hayes and Bute Town...the fundamental feature of the area and the key to our future success must surely lie in the Bute East Dock. The land that matters is in the area around the head of the dock and the broad belt from its western bank. This is the land that should provide the link between the present city centre and the sea.' He went on to suggest suitable uses: 'a mix of housing, offices, space for small modern industry and cultural and sporting facilities'. He said that he had been assured that in future ABP would be taking a more flexible attitude towards its land holdings, and he asked the local authorities 'to consider what I am now suggesting to pursue discussions with ABP and potential developers'. He ended by holding out the prospect of money: 'While I can at this stage make no specific developing commitment, I have made it clear that I will consider sympathetically for inclusion in any future performance any project which commands the support of the local and planning authorities, which attracts investment by the private sector, and which offers a good prospect of viability.'

The significance of this statement is difficult to overestimate. Welsh Office support – in confirming compulsory purchase orders, in grant-aiding development and in making appropriate planning decisions – had been and would continue to be the essential underpinning for both City and County Council planning and development policies. It was virtually unthinkable, therefore, that either authority should directly oppose such a clear expression of Welsh Office aims.

The specificity of the February statement indicates that the Welsh Office was not only convinced of the general land use mix adopted by the January 1983 plan, but also saw it as a potential exemplar of the leverage planning (private/ public partnership) approach then being promoted by central government nationally (Brindley et al., 1989). The statement also made it perfectly plain that such a flagship project was not to be marred by inter-authority bickering – consensus, a coalition of support, was a prerequisite for the essential central government financial underpinning (cf. Morgan, 1985, on the West Midlands). The reference to Associated British Ports (ABP) is also significant. ABP, the operator of the docks, was the major landowner on the site; however, for a number of years the organization had adopted a policy laid down centrally – of protecting its land holdings close to operational docks in case of future operational need (Nicholson, 1982). Bute East Dock was one such 'operational' site, and as late as January 1983 the local ABP office still emphasized its operational significance. This view was to change dramatically following privatization of ABP in stages from 1983, after which likely trends in future operational needs were balanced against the opportunity costs of holding land idle.

Securing the support of the various public sector agencies for the change of policy was in many respects more difficult than securing private sector acquiescence. Businesses which had a direct interest in the scheme fall into two categories: (1) large companies with major interests in the area, of which there were two – Associated British Ports (a landowner) and Allied Steel and Wire (whose steel mill stood opposite Atlantic Wharf); (2) the dozens of smaller firms, employing between two and a hundred or so employees, which were based on Atlantic Wharf.

Associated British Ports fell in behind the principle of a high-value development at Atlantic Wharf very quickly once it had been privatized, and its major concern thereafter appears to have been to maximize its own return from any development. Allied Steel and Wire (ASW), which employed thousands, chose to make its views know exclusively through the normal planning consultation procedures (interview evidence). It was concerned that in the medium term residents of new houses at Atlantic Wharf would complain about the noise and general nuisance of having a rolling mill within half a mile, but it was hopeful that its high economic profile in the city would ensure that any development of Atlantic Wharf did not affect its operations directly. It was proved correct about the latter point – great care has been taken, in undertaking redevelopment, to consult regularly with ASW. However, it was unable to influence the mix of land uses in the development, though to date it has not suffered from complaints about its operations. Any such complaints will, in any event, be of a nuisance value rather than a fundamental threat to the company, which is convinced by its treatment to date that its value to the economy of Cardiff is recognized by the state at local and national level.

The same cannot be said about the smaller firms in the Atlantic Wharf area. The formal amendment of the local plan for the area by the City Council was the first and only formal invitation they had to consider the general principles of the policy changes proposed for Atlantic Wharf. Most made no comment, but a few expressed grave concerns about the effects on their firms of any disruption and uncertainty that would be caused (Cardiff City Council, 1986).

As Table 4.1 indicates, it was to be three more years before land, finance, a developer and planning permission were all in place, and a start could be made on site. It was a period of regular, sometimes intense, discussions between the various parties involved, with formal inter-agency officer working parties (on which the Welsh Office, local authorities, ABP, LAW and Tarmac, the chosen developer, were represented), and joint members' working parties convened by the local authorities to break occasional impasses in negotiations. Having set down a pretty clear idea of what was wanted in the February 1983 statement, the Secretary of State seems to have left it largely to the local authorities and agencies on the ground to work out how the redevelopment could be made consistent with existing policy or financial commitments. By September 1984, when a City Council local planning document for Atlantic Wharf was endorsed by both City and County Councils, a broad measure of agreement had been reached. The City Council's concerns about commercial development, which were, indeed, forerunners of the Chamber of Trade's own concerns (Cardiff City Council, 1984b), were, in effect, ignored, though the city found a form of words which preserved the appearance of policy consistency. With respect to small firms in the dockland area, however, on paper the City Council was less accommodating to the promoters of the redevelopment. However, the lack of any statements by councillors on the issue suggests that it was at officer level that there was a strong desire to exclude a strip of small-scale industry (much of it already grant-aided) from the Atlantic Wharf redevelopment. This supposition is also supported by the lack of political fall-out from the somewhat brusque way in which these small firms were subsequently dealt with by the Land Authority for Wales in pursuing its (successful) compulsory purchase order (Thomas and Imrie, 1989).

A similar conclusion can be reached about the influence of the local population in nearby Butetown; but its response, and, indeed, that of minor private capital, is best understood against the background of the public face of policy change, as presented in the local newspaper.

THE PUBLIC PRESENTATION OF THE REDEVELOPMENT: THE LOCAL PRESS

Analysis of the role of local newspapers in Britain has suggested that they generally support those council policies, such as the promotion of major redevelopments, which can be presented as contributing to the civic standing of a locality (Cox and Morgan, 1973). The coverage of Atlantic Wharf by the *South Wales Echo* bears out such a view, and must be taken into account, as one factor, in understanding the lack of popular opposition to a redevelopment which seemed to offer little to existing businesses or residents in Butetown.

A considerable amount of the early discussion in governmental circles was not public knowledge and so went unreported, and significant early pointers to there being change in the air were not picked up by the paper – for example, the report of Nicholas Edwards's February statement devoted its headline and most of its content to the granting of a substantial Urban Development Grant for the development of a city centre Holiday Inn, rather than to his ruminations about the future of the docks (Anon, 1983a).

But in May 1983 the story of developer interest in a massive docklands scheme broke. The two whole pages devoted to artists' impressions suggest that one of the principals (probably South Glamorgan County Council, had 'fed' the story to the newspaper. There was also a speculative résumé of a scheme's content, and reactions from local councillors and Council officers (Thomas, 1983a, b). The positive tone of the description of the proposals was confirmed as an explicit editorial line less than a week later: 'The ambitious and imaginative South Glamorgan County Council scheme to transform the Butetown Dock at a cost of £100m represents a renewal of interest in the water and the enormous potential it represents' (Anon, 1983b, p. 8). This uncritical tone was to remain throughout the paper's coverage of the next eighteen months or so, during which the Atlantic Wharf scheme moved from being an opportunistic bright idea to being established local planning policy, with a substantial measure of area and central government support. Some notable features of this coverage were, first, its lack of detail about the technicalities of the administrative processes involved. The complexity of table 4.1 above (itself a simplification of reality) was not even hinted at in the unfolding drama reported in the *Echo*. Interesting as the newspaper's coverage might be, it provided an inadequate guide to anyone – such as local residents or businesses – who might feel a need for an understanding of the processes by which important policy changes were coming about, and which agency was responsible for what.

A second feature of the reporting was related to this glossing over of administrative technicalities, namely the hyperbolic headlines and editorial copy which regularly found their way into accounts of Atlantic Wharf. In July 1983, it was suggested that 'Edwards Backs Cardiff Dockland Plans' (Thomas, 1983c), almost two years before the Secretary of State considered, in a quasi-judicial capacity, the compulsory purchase orders for land needed for the development; a few days later 'It's Full Speed on Docks Scheme' (Thomas, 1983d). Throughout 1983 and into 1984 similar headlines featured, with editorial copy regularly referring to 'an imaginative scheme', 'new Cardiff', 'catalysts' for change, and so on.

Interestingly, and significantly, the only notable exceptions to the 'All Systems Go for that Docks Scheme' (Thomas, 1983g) variety of headline were a few which focused on alleged threats to the scheme caused by a lack of consensus in support of it. In September 1983, for example, under a headline

'Fears over Docks Plan' (Thomas, 1983e) it was argued that potential developers of Atlantic Wharf 'could lose interest because they will not be allowed to build offices' (p. 1) by the City Council. Apparently, 'The County [Council] are very pleased with the support they have received from all organisations involved in the adventurous proposals' (pp. 1–2), and were looking for some flexibility from the City Council. The theme of *consensus* and, in particular, the alleged support of the Secretary of State, was a third prominent feature of the *Echo's* coverage.

On 8 October 1983, for example, a report of a County Council meeting to consider proposals from developers (Thomas, 1983f) also reported that the leader of the County Council 'paid tribute to the way in which everyone concerned – the county council, Cardiff City Council, Associated British Ports, the Land Authority for Wales, the Welsh Development Agency and the companies – had cooperated' (p. 4). The *Echo* regularly included references to the encouragement the County Council received from the Secretary of State in its reports about Atlantic Wharf.

The final feature of the *Echo's* coverage of Atlantic Wharf in these early years was the *failure* to develop further a theme which was prominent in its *first* editorial on the topic in May 1983, where it said that 'The plans are not yet finalised and some public input to the discussions is desirable...It is vitally important that the people of Cardiff also have their say in a more direct fashion and that this concept goes ahead with as much public support as possible.'

However, thereafter there was no attempt to encourage expressions of public opinion (though varied letters on the scheme were published up to September 1984), and no attempt to evaluate what benefits (or losses) might accrue to existing residents or firms. It was to be nearly a full year before some forthright reactions from Butetown were reported in the middle of a piece about a proposed monorail scheme. Two local women active in a residents' association were quoted as follows: 'I want people in other areas to be made aware of the fact that with all the millions of pounds that are being poured into Cardiff Dockland generally the people who actually live here are not really benefiting' and 'There seems to be a massive plan for the area that the community knew nothing about until the past few weeks and what we were trying to do or say is considered a nuisance to that plan.'

The latter quotation might reasonably be regarded as a prescient judgement on the City Council's proposed local plan amendments, which were exhibited in the area a month or so later. The amended plan, which in purely administrative and legal terms was quite distinct from the developers' plans for Atlantic Wharf, nevertheless coincided with the plans of the developers in almost all its details, the major exception, referred to above, being the reluctance to countenance the removal of small firms from the north end of the dock. The public exhibition, as part of a period of participation required by planning law for formal amendments of local plans, was regarded with suspicion as a delaying tactic by leading Labour councillors in the County Council (Thomas 1984a).

The credibility of the official City Council retort that it wished to give Butetown residents a say over what was proposed for the area was undermined somewhat by the fact that its protestations were coupled with a renewed commitment to fostering the redevelopment of Atlantic Wharf (Thomas, 1984b): clearly, any influence by Butetown residents world be marginal, at best. In the event, the comments received through public consultation seem to have changed nothing of significance (Cardiff City Council, 1984c) and it hardly seems overly cynical to see the whole consultation process as either a manipulative exercise to help boost the democratic credentials and legitimacy of the redevelopment proposals or part of an attempt by the City Council to carve a distinctive role for itself in the redevelopment (or, indeed, perhaps it was both).

RETROSPECT AND PROSPECT

The Atlantic Wharf redevelopment and, indeed, the current activity of the Cardiff Bay Development Corporation are, in general terms, fairly standard examples of state intervention to assist in, and underpin, spatial restructuring, largely (if not exclusively) for the benefit of finance capital. But the details of the process, the ways in which the idea of regeneration surfaced, was promoted and presented, reflect the particularities of the local context.

The tensions derived from actual or anticipated clashes of material interest in the Atlantic Wharf episode have not subsided with the designation of a development corporation. Indeed, they have been sharpened by the greater scale of the operation and the imposition of new institutional rivalries between the local authorities. While the rhetoric of civic and national pride remains an essential, and potent, component of the ideological packaging of the Regeneration Strategy, it is accompanied by an effort to be seen to be addressing some of the problems of displaced indigenous small firms, local residential communities and even city centre businesses, though with questionable effect (Anon, 1991).

The two local authorities (both now Labour-controlled) have continued to be sensitive to these constituencies, which tempers their working relationship with a formal commitment to the activities of the Development Corporation.

Yet each, in its own way, and with broad political support, is also operating within a conception of the future of Cardiff which equates progress with the 'continued development of Cardiff as an administrative, commercial and cultural centre' (Rees and Lambert, 1981, p. 126), and all that entails in terms of physical redevelopment. This conception apparently remains as powerful now as it was 25 years ago.

REFERENCES

Anon (1983a) '£2½m Aid for Prestige Hotel', *South Wales Echo*, 11 February, p. 1.

Anon (1983b) 'Cardiff on the Up and Up', *South Wales Echo*, 18 May, p. 8.

Anon (1991) 'Get Moving!' *Cardiff Independent*, 23 October, p. 1.

Bassett, K. and Harloe, M. (1990) 'Swindon: The Rise and Decline of a Growth Coalition', in M. Harloe et al., *Place, Policy and Politics*, London, Unwin Hyman, pp. 42–61.

Brindley, T., Rydin, Y. and Stoker, G. (1989) *Re-making Planning* (London, Unwin Hyman).

Brookes, J. (1989a) The Living Waterfront Scheme: Landuse Proposals. Preliminary Report to Royal Society for the Protection of Birds.

Brookes, J. (1989) 'Cardiff Bay Renewal Strategy - Another Hole in the Democratic System', *The Planner* 75(1), pp. 38–40.

Cardiff Bay Development Corporation (1988) *Cardiff Bay Regeneration Strategy: The Summary* Cardiff, CBDC.

Cardiff City Council (1982) 'East Moors District Plan, Implementation 1978–1982', Report of the City Planning Officer to Planning and Development Committee, 12 November.

Cardiff City Council (1984a) *East Moors Local Plan: Proposed Amendment No. 1*, Cardiff, Cardiff City Council.

Cardiff City Council (1984b) 'East Moors Local Plan: Proposed Amendment No. 1. Public Consultation and Comments Received', Report by City Planning and Development Officer to Planning and Development Committee, 13 July 1984.

Cardiff City Council (1984c) 'East Moors Local Plan. Proposed Amendment No 1. Amendments following Public Consultation', Report by City Planning and Development Officer to Planning and Development Committee, 14 September 1984.

Cardiff City Council (1991) *City of Cardiff Local Plan: Draft Proposals for Consultation*, Cardiff, Cardiff City Council.

Carter, H. (1986) 'Cardiff: Local, Regional and National Capital', in G. Gordon (ed.), *Regional Cities in the UK, 1890–1980*, London, Harper and Row.

Cooke, P. (1980) 'Capital Relation and State Dependency: An Analysis of Urban Development Policy in Cardiff', in G. Rees and T. L. Rees (eds), *Poverty and Social Inequality in Wales*, London, Croom Helm.

Cox, H. and Morgan, D. (1973) *City Politics and the Press*, Cambridge, Cambridge University Press.

Edwards, N. (1983) Statement in the House of Commons, 10 February, *Hansard* cols 1176–8.

Evans, N. (1984/5) 'The Welsh Victorian City: The Middle Class and Civic and National Consciousness in Cardiff, 1850–1914', *Welsh History Review*, 12, pp.350–87.

Fainstein, N. I. and Fainstein, S. S. (1988) 'The Politics of Planning New York as a World City', in M. Parkinson, B. Foley and D. Judd (eds), *Regenerating the Cities*, Manchester, Manchester University Press.

Hamilton, N. (1988) 'The City Centre', in E. Evans and H. Thomas (eds), *Cardiff Capital Development*, Cardiff, Cardiff City Council.

Imrie, R. and Thomas, H. (1992) 'The Wrong Side of the Tracks: A Case of Local Economic Regeneration', *Policy and Politics* (forthcoming).

Llewelyn-Davies Planning (1988) *Cardiff Bay Regeneration Strategy*, Cardiff, Cardiff Bay Development Corporation.

Morgan, K. (1985) 'Regional Regeneration in Britain: The Territorial Imperative and the Conservative State', *Political Studies*, 33, pp. 560–77.

Nicholson, D. (1982), *Vacant Urban Land in South Wales*, PhD thesis, University of Wales (unpublished).

Rees, G. and Lambert, J. (1981) 'Nationalism as Legitimation? Notes towards a Political Economy of Regional Development in South Wales', in M. Harloe (ed.), *New Perspectives in Urban Change and Conflict*, London: Heinemann Educational.

Reeves, R. (1987) 'On the Waterfront', *Radical Wales*, 15, pp. 11–12.

South Glamorgan County Council (1983), *North Docks Redevelopment: A Proposal by South Glamorgan County Council and Project Management Wales Ltd*, Cardiff, SGCC.

South Glamorgan County Council (1984). Minute no. 1470, Policy (South Cardiff Redevelopment) Sub-Committee, 11 and 12 October.

South Glamorgan County Council (1985) *County of South Glamorgan Structure Plan: Proposed Alterations*, Cardiff, South Glamorgan County Council.

South Glamorgan County Council (1990a) *South Glamorgan Structure Plan: Proposals for Alteration No. 2, Draft Policies*, Cardiff, South Glamorgan County Council.

South Glamorgan County Council (1990b) *South Glamorgan Structure Plan: Proposals for Alteration No. 2, Draft Explanatory Memorandum*, Cardiff, South Glamorgan County Council.

Swanstrom, T. (1985) *The Crisis of Growth Politics*, Philadelphia, Temple University Press.

Thomas, H. and Imrie, R. (1989), 'Urban Redevelopment, Compulsory Purchase and the Regeneration of Local Economies: The Case of Cardiff's Docklands', *Planning Practice and Research*, 4(3), pp. 18–27.

Thomas, M. (1983a) 'Dockland to Get £100m Facelift', *South Wales Echo*, 13 May, p. 1.

Thomas, M. (1983b) 'Bringing Cardiff's Decaying Docklands Back to Life', *South Wales Echo*, 13 May, pp. 1 and 2.

Thomas, M. (1983c) 'Edwards Backs Cardiff Dockland Plans', *South Wales Echo*, 1 July, pp. 1 and 2.

Thomas, M. (1983d) 'It's Full Speed on Docks Scheme', *South Wales Echo*, 6 July, pp. 1 and 2.

Thomas, M. (1983e) 'Fears over Docks Plan', *South Wales Echo*, 14 September, pp. 1 and 2.

Thomas, M. (1983f) '700 Jobs Boost in Dockland', *South Wales Echo*, 8 October, pp. 1 and 4.

Thomas, M. (1983g) 'All Systems Go for that Docks Scheme', *South Wales Echo*, 4 November, pp. 1 and 2.

Thomas, M. (1984a) 'Is Red Tape Strangling Docks Bid?' *South Wales Echo*, 17 May, pp. 1 and 2.

Thomas, M. (1984b) 'City Council Deny Delaying Plan', *South Wales Echo*, 18 May, p. 3.

Welsh Office (1967) *Wales: The Way Ahead*, Cmnd. 3334, Cardiff, HMSO.

5. SMASHING THE DARK GLASS CEILING: WOMEN AT THE TOP IN WALES

Teresa Rees and Sarah Fielder

INTRODUCTION

In November 1991, Business in the Community launched Opportunity 2,000, a project backed by the Prime Minister, Mr John Major, where 61 leading companies pledged themselves to increase the quality and quantity of women's participation in the workforce, including providing better access to the upper echelons of their organizations. The initiative was designed to assist more women to 'smash the glass ceiling', which they can feel preventing their rise to the top, but cannot see. In January 1992, a consortium of employers in Wales led by the Welsh Development Agency with Business in the Community and the Equal Opportunities Commission launched *Chwarae Teg* (fair play), an initiative designed to focus attention on and encourage fair play for women in the workforce in Wales. At its launch, the Secretary of State for Wales, Mr David Hunt, challenged the consortium's steering committee and Business in the Community to find 20 key employers in the Principality willing to sign up to Opportunity 2,000 by the end of the year. In his own words:

> This challenge is really for the business world to stand up and be counted. Declare your commitment to the promotion of equal opportunities and spell out the steps that you intend to make this commitment a reality and I believe in due course all of Wales will reap the reward. (Hunt, 1991, p. 4)

It would appear that the interests of social justice and economic development are coinciding, and that the well-established patterns of gender segregation at work, so marked in Wales in particular, are now receiving the attention of major employers. But why do so few women reach the top - especially in Wales? And what real prospect is there for change, even in a favourable climate?

Gender segregation at work has received considerable academic attention in recent years (see Crompton and Sanderson, 1990; Walby, 1988); it is held largely responsible for the fact that women earn on average only about 72 per cent of men's wages (EOC, 1991a), that they have access to relatively poor terms and conditions of employment, and receive only restricted training and promotion prospects. However, most of the attention so far has been focused on horizontal segregation, that is the distribution of men and women into different industries and sectors. Figures on vertical segregation are more difficult to come by. Most organizations do not keep statistics on the distribution of the two genders in the hierarchy, although such monitoring is usually the first stage in any equal opportunities policy. A number of reports, such as that of the Hansard Society Commission on Women at the Top (1990) detailed, in the 'political arithmetic' tradition, just to what extent gender determined access to top jobs, despite anti-discriminatory legislation, the effects of decades of the women's movement, a new climate of 'social justice', and a more educated female workforce. The report was a landmark in drawing attention to the issue. It has been followed by a clutch of publications from organizations such as the Law Society (1990), Women in Management (1989), the Policy Studies Institute (Howe and McRae, 1991) and the Conference Board Europe (Rolfes, 1991), all producing similar pictures of different sectors, and making similar points, for example, that it is a criminal waste of human resources for women to be denied access to top jobs because of their gender. This chapter offers a snapshot of women at the top in Wales, it explores some of the explanations for the rather bleak picture which emerges and offers comments on the potential efficacy of positive action measures.[1] First of all, a brief section provides the context.

WOMEN AT WORK IN WALES

Female economic activity rates have traditionally been low in Wales, and they remain so despite patterns of industrial restructuring which have led to an increase in 'women's work'. In 1989, the rate was 63.9 per cent, lower than that for any English region, and comparing with an average of 70.5 per cent for Britain as a whole (Department of Employment, 1990a).

As elsewhere in Europe, women tend to be concentrated in occupations in education, welfare and health, clerical work, selling, catering and other personal services. Women are found in the manufacturing sector, particularly in Mid Glamorgan, but overwhelmingly in semi-skilled manual work. Compared with England, there are relatively few women professionals working in science, engineering and technology.

Nearly half the Welsh female workforce are in 'other services', an inadequate classification which covers public and private sector services.

Nearly a quarter are in the low-paid distribution, hotels and catering sector and a further 9 per cent in 'other manufacturing'. The financial services sector employs a small (12.4 per cent) but growing number of women in Wales.

Pay levels for women in Wales are lower than those for men in manual and non-manual work. The average weekly earnings for full-time workers was £180.30 for women, as opposed to £258.60 for men (Department of Employment 1990b).

Pay levels are related to occupations, and those jobs more or less exclusively done by women tend to be deemed low-skilled and are poorly remunerated accordingly. Equal pay for work of equal value cases are helping to break this association between the perceived skill level of a job and the gender of its incumbent.

Women in work in Wales, then, are in a worse position than those in English regions. They are more likely to be in a low-paid sector and less likely to be in highly paid professional and technical posts. Many are clustered in jobs seen as an extension of their work at home: catering, cleaning and caring.

WOMEN AT THE TOP IN WALES

Compared with either England or the UK, there are relatively few women at the top in Wales. It should be said that a fairer comparison would be with an English region of a similar industrial structure, but nevertheless it is striking that the picture portrayed by the Hansard Society Commission for Britain in such disparaging terms looks enlightened compared with figures for Wales.

Overall, the public sector has a rather better record than the private sector, and within the public sector, the Civil Service and some local authorities compare favourably with further and higher education, and with the NHS. Some employers, such as Cardiff City Council, South Glamorgan County Council and the Welsh Office, are making efforts to open more doors to women. Other employers do not recognize that there is a problem, or lack the commitment to tackle it effectively. They put the onus on women to fit into and succeed within an organization which is designed for men, rather than restructuring the organization of work to allow employees to accommodate their family responsibilities.

Civil Service

The Civil Service opened its doors to single women in 1920, but married women remained ineligible to join until 1946. Equal pay was granted in 1946. In 1984, a Programme of Action for Equal Opportunities was introduced

TABLE 5.1
Women in Top Management in the Civil Service, 1991

Grades	% Women Wales	GB
1–4	3	6
5	9	14
6	11	11
7	13	13

Source: Unpublished data from Cabinet Office.

which led to a series of initiatives on child-care, career break schemes, flexible working and so on (Cabinet Office, 1984).

Women comprise just under half the civil servants in Wales, but are found in diminishing numbers in the top grades. Nationally they make up 6 per cent of senior management (grades 1 to 4), but only 3 per cent in the Principality.

Within the Welsh Office, there are a higher proportion of women in grades 5 and 6 than in the country as a whole, which bodes well for the future, but the numbers are very small. And indeed, looked at another way, of the 1,042 female civil servants employed at the Welsh Office, only 4 per cent are on grades 1 to 7, compared with nearly a quarter of all the men: this is on a par with the national figures.

The Civil Service has sought to identify barriers to women's promotion, and there has been a slow growth in the number of women in senior management nationally, and increased numbers of women in the fast stream recruitment competition. A new programme of action is now being planned to consolidate this progress. Within Wales, the Welsh Office has introduced a number of policies, especially in the field of child-care.

Local Government

Local government compares badly with the Civil Service. Only 3.5 per cent of principal officers in county councils are women, compared with 4.2 per cent in county and metropolitan counties in England and Wales. In the highest grades, four counties have no women at all; the remaining four have one each. In district councils the situation is worse: women comprise only 1.6 per cent of principal officers.

There has been little attention paid to the barriers preventing women from reaching the top in local government in Wales, except notably in Cardiff City Council, which has an active equal opportunities policy, has introduced

TABLE 5.2
Local Government Principal Officers in Wales

County Councils	Total	Women
Clwyd	12	0
Dyfed	17	0
Gwent	17	1
Gwynedd	17	1
Mid Glamorgan	14	1
Powys	11	1
South Glamorgan	15	0
West Glamorgan	11	0
Wales	114	4

Source: Compiled from Municipal Journal (1991).

careers counselling for women and has widened the management band for which training is available. South Glamorgan County Council has a workplace nursery for employees and a Women's Committee, which among other activities has engaged in statistical monitoring of the County's workforce by gender.

More generally local authorities in Wales, as elsewhere, are relatively woman-friendly environments, in that they are more likely to offer flexible working hours and possibilities for part-time work at middle management grades. These help women to continue working, but do not necessarily by themselves assist women to reach the top.

Police

In the four Welsh police forces, there are no women at all in any of the top five grades, there is one in the sixth (superintendent), but then none again in the next rank, chief inspector. All the forces fall below the England and Wales average of 11.4 per cent female police officers, although it should be noted that none of the English forces can boast a woman in the top three grades either. In the fourth grade, assistant chief constable, there were two women out of 125 posts in England and Wales, all in English forces (*Hansard*, 25 October 1990).

Seniority is a major qualification for promotion in the police, and is one of the causes of women's failure to rise to the top. It is usual for superintendents to have 25 years' service or more, but there are relatively few women who fall into this category, because of career breaks. Indeed, in 1989, in the South Wales force, only four women satisfied this criterion.

TABLE 5.3
Men and Women in Welsh Police Forces, August 1990

	Dyfed/Powys		Gwent		N. Wales		S. Wales	
	Male	Female	Male	Female	Male	Female	Male	Female
Chief Constable	1	0	1	0	1	0	1	0
Deputy Chief Constable	1	0	1	0	1	0	1	0
Assistant Chief Constable	1	0	1	0	1	0	3	0
Chief Superintendent	7	0	5	0	7	0	14	0
Superintendent	13	0	14	0	24	0	42	1
Chief Inspector	21	0	17	0	27	0	64	0
Inspector	38	0	46	3	66	2	178	3
Sergeant	149	4	152	4	206	8	525	15
Constable	618	82	668	88	863	129	2028	249
Total	849	86	905	95	1196	139	2856	268
% Women	9.2%		9.5%		10.4%		8.6%	

Source: *Hansard Parliamentary Questions* 5 October 1990, cols 255–8.

Solicitors

Women were barred from entering the legal profession until 1919. In 1987, they comprised 54 per cent of students qualifying as solicitors in England and Wales. However, after ten years of admission to the Roll, over one-third of women solicitors cease practising, compared with only 12 per cent of men (Women in Management, 1989).

In Wales, women comprise less than 10 per cent of solicitors who are partners and sole practitioners, compared with 12.5 per cent in England and Wales as a whole (calculated from Butterworths, 1991; Law Society, 1990). Moreover, the pay differential between men and women assistant solicitors doing the same job is larger in Wales; men earn 18 per cent more than women compared with a national average differential of 9 per cent (Chambers and Partners, 1990). Within the legal profession, women tend to be segregated into family law. Senior members of the judiciary are drawn from practising barristers and solicitors. The fact that fewer women remain in the profession means that there are fewer to draw upon.

Private Sector Management

There are different estimates of the proportion of managers who are women in Britain, according to which definition is used, and reliable data are scarce. The

Hansard Society Commission on Women at the Top (1991) put the figure at 6.7 per cent. Women are 6 per cent of the members of the Institute of Directors. NEDO (1991) estimates the percentage of women middle and senior managers as 4 per cent, but those in top industrial management posts to be nearer 1–2 per cent

A survey of the top 100 companies revealed that less than 2 per cent of the 1,333 directors were women: given the small pool from which such women were found to be recruited, this is hardly surprising: 'The profile of the average woman board member is someone in her fifties with an international or traditional Oxbridge education and with a family connected to the company or a title' (Holten and Rabbetts, 1991, pp. 1–2).

In Wales, only 2.3 per cent of directors (executive and non-executive board members) of registered companies are women, yet the same source identifies 6.7 per cent of company directors nationally as being women (Thomas Skinner Directories, 1989). Within Wales, there are no women directors of Gwynedd- and Powys-based firms, and few in Mid Glamorgan, where far more companies are registered.

A Welsh Development Agency survey of employers in South Wales found that over 50 per cent had no women managers at all (Rees and Willox, 1991). Only 12 per cent of British managers have degrees (NEDO, 1991), so this is not an arena that women can enter through gaining the appropriate credentials, unlike accountancy and law. Barriers to women reaching top management posts include employers' demands for continuous employment, geographical mobility, and a high workload. However, other barriers, such as being the right 'age' (reaching senior management by the forties), and having a 'face that fits' are almost impossible to overcome, even if the first round of hurdles are successfully jumped. Further barriers are exclusion from the old boy network, and insistence on a corporate sector background.

Higher and Further Education

The number of female students has increased over the years, and by 1988 they comprised 43 per cent of all university undergraduates. However, this has not been matched by increases in women in the academic hierarchy. They tend to be clustered in short-term contract research posts (which have been expanding) and are relatively sparse among the non-clinical, tenured posts (which have been decreasing), particularly above lecturer level. Indeed the proportion of promoted women academics has been falling.

Nationally some 3 per cent of women are professors but in the University of Wales the figure is half that, 1.3 per cent. Only 1.6 per cent of readers, the next grade down, are women, compared with 6 per cent nationally. The figure for senior lecturers is rather better, at 4.2 per cent, compared with 3 per cent in the country as a whole (all figures from Universities Funding Committee, 1990, and University of Wales, 1990). In other higher and further education institutions, only 2.3 per cent of college principals and 4.6 per cent of vice-principals are women (Welsh Office, 1990b).

Education

In Wales, renowned for its teachers, the position of women at the top compares very unfavourably with the picture in England. Moreover, the proportion of head teachers who are women has declined. In 1989, women comprised 6.9 per cent of secondary school heads in Wales, compared with 16.3 per cent in England, and 23.7 per cent for England and Wales in 1965 (DES, 1991; Welsh Office, 1990a). There are no women heads at all in Dyfed and Powys, but 14.2 per cent of heads in South Glamorgan are women. In a numerically female-dominated profession, 3.3 per cent of all male teachers are heads, compared with 0.2 per cent of all female teachers.

In primary schools, women make up 41 per cent of heads in the Principality overall. But again, looked at another way, nearly 40 per cent of all male teachers in primary schools are heads, compared with only 8 per cent of women (1989/90). There are wide county variations: only 25 per cent of primary heads in Gwynedd are women,and only 31 per cent in Clwyd, but 48 per cent in South Glamorgan.

There are no women Directors or Deputy Directors of Education in Wales, although there have been, and are, women Assistant Directors (for example in Clwyd, Gwent and South Glamorgan).

National Health Service

Medical schools were obliged to admit women from 1948 (some did so before this) and women now constitute half of all medical students. Women constitute 75 per cent of NHS employees in Wales, but only 13.3 per cent of the consultants, just below the level in England. However, there are rather fewer women in the middle ranks (senior registrar, 17.3 per cent; registrar, 18.4 per cent), compared with England (25 and 22.8 per cent) (Department of Health, 1990), and rather more in the bottom grade of house officer. This suggests that in the medium term there will be relatively few women from whom future consultants may be drawn. It remains to be seen how many of the female housemen (*sic*) in Wales eventually reach consultant level.

In NHS administration overall women comprise 9.6 per cent of senior officers in health authorities in Wales, ranging from none in four health authorities to four in South Glamorgan (Institute of Health Services Management, 1991). At top management level, three of the nine district health authorities are chaired by women, and the management boards had one female member each in Mid Glamorgan, Powys, South Glamorgan and West Glamorgan. All nine district general managers and 29 of the 33 unit general managers in Welsh health authorities are men.

A recent study by the Equal Opportunities Commission revealed that despite the fact that the figures for women at the top in the NHS are worse than for the English regions, the Principality comes second from bottom of all the Regions in Britain for the number of its districts to have set up an equal opportunities committee or equivalent (EOC, 1991b). Health districts in Wales are singled out for being noticeably inadequate by not having an equal opportunities policy in which managers are trained: only one district in Wales does this (EOC, 1991b).

Financial Services

The Welsh Development Agency has adopted a policy of seeking to attract the relocation of financial services to Wales, with some success, although so far it is mostly 'back room' functions that have materialized. Although many women are employed in the sector, they have not fared particularly well in the upper echelons in Wales. Lloyds Bank is known to have a woman branch manager in Cardiff, 9.7 per cent of managers at the Midland Bank in Cardiff are women, 11.4 per cent in Swansea, 4 per cent in Wrexham and 5.1 per cent in north-west Wales. However, these figures include assistant managers, operations managers and lending managers within branches as well as branch managers.

In building societies, it has been argued that the effect of new technology has been to 'de-skill' assistant branch management posts (Crompton and Sanderson, 1990). They have become in effect 'women's jobs', as evidenced by the images of friendly, unintimidating women in television advertisements. Decisions about lending are made on the basis of a formula provided on computer print out. Difficult cases tend to be referred up the line to a more senior manager off the premises. In the Abbey National Building Society in Wales, it is telling that in 1989 there were no women branch managers, yet almost all assistant managers were women (Bricault et al., 1989).

Public Bodies

The Welsh Office comes close to the average of government departments for the proportion of public appointments given to women, at 20.6 per cent. However, public appointments vary in their power and remit. Executive bodies employ staff and have their own budgets: women's membership of these in Wales is relatively high, but the small numbers overall may distort the figures. Women are under-represented in Wales (compared with Britain) on Advisory Bodies (17.1 per cent) and Tribunals (10.6 per cent – half the national figure) (Women's National Commission, 1990).

The Public Appointments Unit in Cabinet Office maintains a list of names of people for active consideration for public appointments, which are vetted. In 1989, of the 5,800 names, about 30 per cent were women. While the list is not the only source of names for appointments, it is clearly an important one. The Welsh Office's list has 1,447 names, 440 of which are women (again around 30 per cent, as at October 1991). However, the Welsh Office has been actively soliciting women to put their names forward, and the Prime Minister has urged ministers to offer public appointments to women.

EXPLANATIONS

Gender clearly remains robust as a characteristic which divides people into those with access to top jobs and those without. Four main factors combine to exclude women from the top: the fact that women have a disproportionate share of responsibility for domestic work and child-care, their relative lack of educational qualifications and training, the use of 'old boy networks' for recruitment and promotion, and what has been described as the 'male-streamism' of top establishment. These are discussed briefly, in turn.

Domestic Work and Child-Care

Women shoulder the major burden of domestic responsibilities, they are more likely than men to have a career break, and for many years of their working life, many women are available to work only part-time. All these factors inhibit women's rise to the top.

Even when both partners are working, women still retain the lion's share of child-care and domestic responsibilities (Brannen and Moss, 1991; Gershuny et al., 1986). Men in the UK work more hours than those in any other EC member state (Eurostat, 1990). Management jobs are demanding, exacting a toll in health and family life; senior managers in particular are expected to put in long hours. Male managers may have wives to service their needs full-time, but women managers are much less likely to be married, and if married, to have children (NEDO, 1991 p. 33).

The UK has the lowest level of pre-school child-care provision of all the EC members states except Portugal. Two-thirds of three- and four-year-olds in Wales are in nursery schools and classes in infants' sections of primary schools, which compares favourably with both England and Scotland (EOC, 1990). However, finding suitable provision remains a lottery.

A study of would-be women returners in Gwent underlined the need for child-care after school, in half-terms, school holidays and when children are inconveniently ill, without giving advance notice (Honess, 1989). Moreover, a recent Welsh Development Agency study revealed that women working part-time would feel more comfortable about working full-time if arrangements for special child-sickness leave could be made (Rees and Willox, 1991).

The Career Break   Women in the professions are less likely to take a career break for domestic reasons than other women (Martin and Roberts, 1984). However, those who do take a break usually return to a different employer, and if they then work part-time, they tend to experience downward occupational mobility (Dex, 1987). Career break policies and 'Keeping in Touch' schemes are growing in popularity, but very few women have as yet returned to work through such schemes.

Part-time work   Few senior jobs are available on a part-time, job-split or job-share basis. Whereas 44 per cent of all women in employment work part-time, only 18 per cent of those employed in either managerial occupations or in professional and related occupations supporting management do so (EOC, 1991a). Senior women who work part-time have on the whole negotiated individual deals for themselves.

Training and Qualifications

Women are more likely to go on to further education and less likely to go on to higher education than men. They have fewer educational qualifications when they leave full-time education than men, and they are less likely to be sponsored by employers for training of more than three days' duration (Clarke, 1991; Training Agency, 1989). Nevertheless, more women have been pulling the 'qualifications lever' (Crompton and Sanderson, 1990) and hence securing access to the professions: the difficulty is remaining there without career break schemes, and getting sponsored for training for senior management, which is in the gift of line managers.

Old Boy Networks

Networks are important for the development of contacts, role models and mentors. Many men's networks specifically exclude women, for example freemasonry, golf clubs, and certain bars in clubs. Women find it less easy to engage in drinks after work, and chats in gents' washrooms where strategic pre-meeting decisions are rumoured to be taken!

With so few women at the top, female networks have hardly begun to develop effectively. In Wales, a number of professional and business women's clubs are now getting established, for example in Swansea, Cardiff and Ogwr. Women's groups are emerging among employees of South Glamorgan County Council, Midland Bank and the BBC.

Malestreamism of Establishment Work Cultures

Many arguments used as to why women are not suitable for top jobs are couched in terms of women 'failing' to reach some objective set of criteria. In fact, organizations are constructed around a set of working practices and criteria for success that are designed to suit men. Some corporations have begun the process of seeking to identify hidden barriers that stem from an organizational set of structures that have been built to fit the particular circumstances of men, to see if they can be changed to fit employees of both genders. 'Positive action' is often portrayed as giving women an unfair advantage, whereas it is more accurately viewed as compensating for the positive action which already exists in organizations that assists men; positive action 'levels the playing field'.

Elements of 'malestreamism' can be found not only in the organization of hours, shifts, promotion criteria and so on, but in the very language used to describe the characteristics of people suitable for the top. The discourse used to describe the characteristics of a good manager denotes masculinity: for example 'being able to command confidence', 'standing up for the department', 'lean, hungry and aggressive'. Such terms fit the stereotype of a man better than that of a woman (Skinner and Coyle, 1988). Women with such characteristics are viewed as 'dragons' and 'bossy' (Breakwell, 1985). Studies of women in engineering have found that they are either treated as 'one of the lads', their gender in effect denied, or they are treated as a special case.

Some of the companies signed up for Opportunity 2,000 pledged themselves to undertake cultural change of their organizations, to seek to identify structures, processes and attitudes which are restricting women's opportunities. If this can be done successfully, it is likely to be more effective than measures which simply make it easier for women to carry the double load, rather than move up the organization. Such cultural change, however, is extremely difficult to secure, and studies of organizations which have tried document a variety of forms of male backlash (Cockburn, 1991).

CONCLUSION: POSITIVE ACTION FOR CHANGE?

Women with ambitions in Wales face particular difficulties. Positive action measures, which attempt to identify and remove some of the barriers, such as insistence on geographical mobility, privileging seniority as a criterion for promotion and so on, have mainly been introduced by companies in the southeast of England, informed by the climate of a tight labour market. There is not such a labour supply imperative in Wales. Such measures are on the whole introduced by large national or multinational companies. Wales is overwhelmingly an economy made up of small- to medium-sized enterprises.

Nevertheless, the effect of the much-heralded demographic changes (NEDO/TA, 1989) (albeit currently tempered by the recession) means that much more reliance will need to be placed on women to fill vacancies in the future, including senior management grades. The challenge to employers issued by the Secretary of State for Wales is a formidable one: real success can be contemplated only if organizational changes are in tandem with cultural and attitudinal shifts. It is relatively straightforward to introduce a career break scheme or allow a senior manager to work from home or to job-split. It is another matter entirely to challenge the stereotypes of breadwinner and home-maker, to resist the pressure of male resistance, and to bring about cultural change which recognizes that the best man for the job may be a woman. If successful, however, it would remove the onus from women at the top to be either Superwoman, or be like a man.

NOTE

1   This paper draws on a study on women at the top undertaken for HTV Wales. The findings and full details of the statistics are available in Rees and Fielder (1991).

REFERENCES

Berry-Lound, D. (1990) 'Towards the Family Friendly Firm', *Employment Gazette,* vol. 98, no. 2, pp. 85–91.
Brannen J. and Moss, J. (1991) *Managing Mothers: Dual Earner Households,*London, Unwin Hyman.

Breakwell, G. (1985) *The Quiet Rebel: Women at Work in a Man's World*, London, Century.

Bricault, G. C., Isbell, P. and Carr, J. L. (eds) (1989) *Corporate Financial Services in Wales*, London, Graham and Trotman.

Butterworths (1991) *Law Directory*, London, Butterworths.

Cabinet Office (1984) 'Equal Opportunities for Women in the Civil Service, Programme of Action', London, Management and Personnel Office, Cabinet Office.

Chambers and Partners (1990) *Directory of the Legal Profession 1990*, London, Chambers and Partners.

Clarke, K. (1991) *Women and Training: A Review*, Manchester, Equal Opportunities Commission.

Cockburn, C. (1991) *In the Way of Women: Male Resistance to Equality in Organisations*, London, Macmillan.

Collinson, D., Knights, D., and Collinson, M. (1999) *Managing to Discriminate*, London, Routledge.

Crompton, R. and Sanderson, K. (1990) *Gendered Jobs and Social Change*, London, Unwin Hyman.

Department of Education and Science (1991) *1988 Secondary School Staffing Survey*, *Statistical Bulletin 18/91*, London, DES.

Department of Employment (1990a) *Employment Gazette*.

Department of Employment (1990b) *New Earnings Survey*, London, HMSO.

Department of Health (1990) *Health and Personal Social Services Statistics for England and Wales*, London, HMSO.

Department of Health (1991) 'Women Doctors and Their Careers', Report of the Joint Working Party, London, Department of Health.

Dex, S. (1987) *Women's Occupational Mobility: A Lifetime Perspective*, London, Macmillan.

Equal Opportunities Commission (1990) *Women and Men in Britain 1990: Comparative Gender-related Statistics for England, Scotland and Wales*, London, HMSO.

Equal Opportunities Commission (1991a) *Women and Men in Britain 1991*, Manchester, EOC.

Equal Opportunities Commission (1991b) *Equality Management: Women's Employment in the NHS*, Manchester, EOC.

Eurostat (1990) *Labour Force Survey*, Luxemburg, Office for Official Publications of the European Communities.

Gershuny, J., Miles, I., Jones, S., Mullings, C., Thomas, G. and Wyatt, S. (1986) 'Time Budgets: Preliminary Analyses of a National Survey', *Quarterly Journal of Social Affairs*, vol. 2, no. 1, pp. 13–39.

Hansard Society Commission on Women at the Top (1990) *Report of the Hansard Society Commission on Women at the Top*, London, Hansard Society.

Holten, V. and Rabbets, J. (1989) 'Pow(d)er in the Board Room: Report of a Survey of Women on the Boards of Top UK Companies', Berkhamsted, Ashridge Management Centre.

Honess, T. (1989) *Managing Recruitment Needs in Gwent: Retention and Career Development of Key Female Staff*, Report to the Training Agency in Gwent, Cardiff, Michael and Associates.

Howe, E. and McRae, S. (1991) *Women and the Board*, London, Policy Studies Institute.

Hunt, D., Secretary of State for Wales (1991) Keynote Address delivered at launch of *Chwarae Teg* at the Holiday Inn, Cardiff, January.

Institute of Health Services Management (1991) *The Hospital and Health Services Year Book 1991*, London, IHSM.

Law Society (1990) *Annual Statistical Report*, London, Law Society.

Martin, J. and Roberts, B. (1984) *Women and Employment, A Lifetime Perspective*, London, HMSO.

Municipal Journal (1991) *Municipal Year Book 1991*, London, Municipal Journal.

National Economic Development Office (1991) *Women Managers: The Untapped Resource*, London, NEDO/Royal Institute of Public Administration.

National Economic Development Office/Training Agency (1989) *The Demographic Time Bomb*, London, NEDO.

Rees, C. and Willox I. (1991) *Expanding the Role of Women in the South Wales Labour Force*, Sponsors' Summary Document, Cardiff, Welsh Development Agency

Rees, T. and Fielder, S. (1991) 'Women and Top Jobs in Wales', a report for HTV Wales, *Wales this Week*, Cardiff, Social Research Unit, School of Social and Administrative Studies, University of Wales College of Cardiff.

Rolfes, R. (1991) 'Europe's Glass Ceiling: Why Companies Profit From a Diverse Workforce', Brussels, The Conference Board Europe.

Skinner, J. and Coyle, A. (1988) 'Women at Work in Social Services', in A. Coyle and J. Skinner (eds), *Women and Work: Positive Action for Change*, London, Macmillan.

Thomas Skinner Directories (1989) *Directory of Directors*, London, Thomas Skinner Directories.

Training Agency (1989) *Training in Britain: A Study of Funding, Activity and Attitudes: The Main Report*, London, HMSO.

Universities Funding Committee (1990) *Universities Statistics*, vol. 1: *Students and Staff 1988–9*, London, UFC.

University of Wales (1991) *Calendar 1990/91*, Cardiff, University of Wales.

Walby, S. (1988) (ed.) *Gender Segregation at Work*, Milton Keynes, Open University.

Welsh Office (1990a) *Statistics on Education in Wales: Schools*, Cardiff, Welsh Office.

Welsh Office (1990b) *Statistics of Education in Wales: Further and Higher Education*, Cardiff, Welsh Office.

Welsh Office (1991) *Health and Personal Social Services Statistics for Wales*, Cardiff, Welsh Office.

Women in Management (1989) *The Female Resource: An Overview*, London, Women in Management.

Women's National Commission (1990) *Women into Public Appointments*, London, Women's National Commission, Cabinet Office.

6. TAILOR-MADE OCCUPATIONS: A STUDY OF GENDER AND SKILL IN THE WELSH CLOTHING INDUSTRY[1]

Caroline Lloyd

INTRODUCTION

There continue to be persistent differences in the way that women and men are treated in the labour market. The demand for female labour is linked to rigid patterns of sex segregation (Rubery, 1988). Work that is considered to be 'women's work' is generally characterized by low pay, weak union organization and lack of craft status, and is invariably defined as unskilled (Phillips and Taylor, 1986). Although the structure of segregation has largely persisted throughout the twentieth century (Bradley, 1989), during periods of change such as the introduction of new technology, opportunities exist to allow these patterns to be broken down and redefined (Bettio, 1988). Feminization, the process of replacing male workers with female workers, is considered as one strategy that firms may pursue in order to remain competitive.

This article examines gender and skill in relation to the process of restructuring and technical change in the Welsh clothing industry.[2] Over 85 per cent of the workforce are women, and jobs are very rigidly segregated. Women work mainly in low-paid, unskilled and semi-skilled areas of machining, and men work in higher management and the more 'craft' areas of pre-production work. However, the industry has faced a number of changes. The late 1970s and early 1980s was a period of considerable difficulty for the British clothing industry, as over 30 per cent of jobs were lost between 1978 and 1983 (Winterton and Winterton, 1990). A price war by high street retailers was followed by a number of retailers following competitive strategies based on design, quality and variety. This had a number of implications for manufacturers in the speed, quality and response rates that were being demanded, and led many firms to reconsider their organization of production in order to compete (Totterdill et al., 1989; Crewe, 1988). Computers were being suggested as an effective means to respond to these demands, and these were being introduced in an area of work traditionally occupied by 'skilled' men. Machining, where the majority of women work, has changed very little and still relies on low pay based on piece work. This chapter considers how particular jobs within clothing have been sex-typed as 'male' or 'female', and in what way definitions may be changing as a result of work reorganization and new technology.

The first section gives a brief outline to the structure of the industry in Wales and recent employment changes. Job segregation within the industry is then discussed, focusing on two areas of production. Firstly, assembly work is considered as an example of a job which almost exclusively involves women workers and effectively excludes men. Secondly, pre-assembly work is examined as an area of production which is facing considerable change with computerization. This discusses the way jobs are being reconstructed and redefined in terms of skill and gender. Finally I will consider some of the problems associated with organizing an industry on the basis of cheap labour.

BACKGROUND AND STRUCTURE OF THE INDUSTRY

Historically the Welsh clothing industry produced only for the local market, while the majority of clothes were brought in from London, Leeds and Manchester (Dobbs, 1926). Clothing manufacture, with its reliance on abundant supplies of cheap labour, tended to be based in areas with high populations and immigrant communities. This only changed significantly in the inter-war years, when many firms moved to longer production runs which required new production methods and larger factories. Some of these firms established plants in new areas, like Wales, where land was more easily available and where a labour force, with no experience in clothing, was prepared to accept the new production methods (Wray, 1957). This trend continued in the postwar period and was further encouraged by changes in grant structure and regional aid in the 1960s and 1970s, which benefited Development Areas, such as Wales.

Currently, the Welsh clothing industry consists of well over 100 firms, and employs at least 10,000 people. It consists of companies which have located a number of their plants in Wales, e.g. Courtaulds and Coates Viyella, the largely Welsh-based companies of Laura Ashley and Morris Cohen, and a large number of small independent firms. The plants are mainly concentrated in Gwent, Mid Glamorgan and Clwyd, although a number are located in rural areas. Clothing accounts for around 5 per cent of manufacturing jobs, and for women it is particularly important, representing 15 per cent of manufacturing jobs in Wales (Census of Employment, 1987).

The Welsh industry consists of a large variety of firms in terms of size, product and market (Short, 1987; Lloyd, 1990). The respondents of the survey varied from single-person firms to plants with 500 employees. The industry tended to divide up into the following three main sectors, although there were overlaps:

(1) Firms which produce clothing from their own designs and sell them under their own label, either in their own or other retailers' outlets.
(2) Firms which are purely 'Cut, make and trim' (CMT), i.e. both the cloth and design are supplied by the customer.
(3) Firms, often part of larger companies, which produce under contract to major retailers or mail order firms.

Their production methods varied from make-through, where one or two machinists assembly the whole garment, to section work, where up to 20 operators produce one garment. Production runs consisted of individual designs to lines of tens of thousands.

The Census of Employment shows the number of employees had increased in Wales by 7 per cent between 1984 and 1987 to just under 11,000. These figures are, though, generally considered to be on the low side because of the underestimation of the number of very small firms (Mitter, 1986). This growth represents a greater percentage increase than found in any other region in Britain, apart from the north of England. Indeed, many other areas lost jobs during this time. This might suggest that the Welsh industry was beginning to recover after the large job losses in the early 1980s, but it could also mean a redistribution of jobs around the UK. Just over half the plants in my survey of Welsh clothing plants reported an increase in employment from 1987 to 1990, a further one quarter saw no change, while the rest had seen a decline in employment, though these were not generally considered to be great losses. On the whole, more plants were gaining jobs than losing jobs. However, this survey was carried out during the last consumer boom, and it is uncertain how these firms fared during the recent recession. It is clear that a number of clothing companies in the UK have been closing plants and making redundancies since the survey was undertaken.

The clothing industry is one area of manufacturing with a very high proportion of women workers. In 1987 around 80 per cent of British clothing workers were women, while in Wales the proportion was higher at 86.4 per cent of the workforce (Census of Employment, 1987). However, despite this women are concentrated in particular occupational categories. Women predominate in unskilled and semi-skilled areas. Table 6.1 shows that nearly 90 per cent of the women in the survey were machinists, pressers, auxiliary or

TABLE 6.1
Distribution of Workforce by Job

Job	Women (%)	Men (%)	All workers (%)
Machining	70.5	2.6	60.6
Cutting	3.2	24.0	6.2
Pressing	6.3	8.6	6.6
Mechanical/technical	0.5	14.7	2.6
Management/supervisory	6.5	22.4	8.8
Design	0.7	0.7	0.7
Auxiliary e.g. clerical/packing	8.6	15.6	9.6
Other	3.6	11.1	4.7
Total workforce	85.4	14.6	100.0
Number of plants = 54			

other workers. This compares to 38 per cent of men who were employed in those jobs. Twenty-four percent of men were employed in cutting, 15 per cent in mechanical and technical work and 22 per cent were in management. Only 3 per cent of women were in cutting, 0.5 per cent in mechanical and technical jobs and 7 per cent in management. Women are still highly under-represented in higher-skilled jobs and management, and are still over-represented in semi- and unskilled work.

Despite women making-up over 85 per cent of the workforce, the Welsh industry does not rely heavily on part-time workers. Of the plants surveyed, 24 firms employed no part-timers, 29 firms replied that between 1 and 20 per cent of their workforce were part-timers and only four firms had over this amount. This suggests a very limited amount of part-time work in clothing firms in Wales. This is consistent with the recent data on the number of part-time workers in Wales compared to other regions in Great Britain. In the clothing industry the Census of Employment for 1987 shows that Wales had a lower proportion of part-time workers than any other region. Part-timers in the clothing industry represent less than 5 per cent of the workforce, compared to 11 per cent of workers in Britain. In many other areas part-time workers and homeworkers are integral to the clothing industry. They provide cost advantages in that they can either be paid less than wage council rates (in the case of homeworking) or there are lower costs in terms of National Insurance contributions and other benefits (Mitter, 1986). However, the use of particularly low-cost labour can cause problems with quality and reliability, and so the excessive use of these methods tends to be at the cheap end of the clothing market (Phizacklea, 1990).

TABLE 6.2
Percent of women and men in each job

Main Job	Women (%)	Men (%)
Machining	99.4	0.6
Cutting	43.9	56.1
Pressing	81.1	18.9
Mechanical/technical	17.3	82.7
Management/supervisory	63.0	37.0
Design	59.2	40.8
Auxiliary e.g. clerical/packing	76.4	23.6
Other	65.8	34.2
Total	85.4	14.6

Number of plants = 54

MACHINING

Machinists account for over 60 per cent of the workforce and they are virtually all women workers. In the survey only 0.6 per cent of machinists were men (table 6.2). The definition of sewing as 'women's work' seems to be persistent and unchanging, yet this sexual division of labour has developed over the last 200 years.

Pre-industrial clothing was produced by male tailors using handicraft methods. These tailors worked for themselves, often travelling around houses and villages for work, making up cloth which they or their customer bought. In the seventeenth century, a class of master tailors developed who owned their own shops and employed tailors to work for them. Gradually female members of the tailor's family, who had often helped the tailor to do some of the simpler tasks in the past, were employed directly by the master tailors in their workshops. But as Morris argues, 'these women were subordinate to the male workers' (1986, p. 103) and were used as cheap labour to undercut traditional working practices.

The market for clothing developed rapidly with the emergence of ready-made clothes, i.e. off the peg, rather than traditional made-to-measure garments. Subdivision of the production process had already occurred in tailoring, with women doing the simpler operations, and it was found to be much easier to break down tasks when producing many clothes which were exactly the same. Increasingly women were employed instead of men doing what was classified as 'unskilled' work. They were paid considerably less than the 'skilled' tailors who were organized into societies and clubs, and later trade unions. Women and Jews tended to be excluded from these organizations and were effectively unorganized for many years. The introduction of the sewing machine in the 1870s further reinforced the division of labour which had emerged, and increased the number of women in the industry (Schmiechen, 1984).

Women gradually came to be predominant in machining, while men almost exclusively worked in the more skilled, higher-paid and better-organized areas of pattern-making, cutting and the bespoke tailoring trades (Schmiechen, 1984; Bythell, 1978). The intense price competition within the clothing industry and the lack of barriers to new entrants led many manufacturers to rely heavily on cost cutting as a means to remain competitive. In a labour-intensive industry this could be most effectively achieved by the subdivision of the labour process and by employing women on significantly lower pay rates than skilled male workers. These women were effectively unorganized and were available in large quantities in inner city areas (Morris, 1986). This sexual division of labour has remained virtually unchanged, as women now make up almost all machinists and men dominate cutting, technical jobs and management.

The only major divergence from women machinists in Britain is amongst immigrant communities. From the 1960s the clothing trade in the East End of London, for example, relied heavily on male Bengalis for machinists. This occurred, it has been argued, because of the racism and lack of alternative opportunities available to these men, which forced them into low-paid jobs (Mitter, 1986). However, the persistent high levels of unemployment of men in the South Wales valleys and the problems firms have reported in attracting young women into the industry, have not impacted on the traditional division of labour within the Welsh clothing industry. At least two reasons for this can be identified. Firstly, the extreme rigidity of sex roles within the local economies; and secondly, the low levels of wages within the industry.

An official from the NUTGW told me how she was particularly keen to have men as operators: 'My attitude is that I have to fight with women who interview to get men on machines.' In cases of redundancy and redeployment the women were offered machine tests whereas the men were not. The typical reasons managers gave were: 'the boys haven't got the nimbleness of finger' or 'it's not been successful in the past.' Her response to this was, 'I could probably take you to a factory where you could see boys on machines and you would see that they do it quite well.'

Personnel managers were a major problem in breaking down sex segregation, but she acknowledged that the men could also suffer from harassment by women on the shopfloor. These attitudes appeared to be common among the managers of the firms visited. One plant manager of a large company stated that they had employed a few young men as machinists. This had not been successful and he would now be reluctant to try any more. He felt that the job was more suitable for women because it was an all-female environment and people felt that the jobs were 'cissy'. Two owners of a single-plant firm discussed this issue. 'We give them trials. We have had one or two people come in, but they have not passed our simple dexterity test.' When asked whether there was a reason for this, he said, 'probably because the tests and the supervisor are probably against having men in the factory.' His female partner stated: 'I am not saying that men aren't good at sewing, but I think what you will find is that women are more dexterous than men, so they probably do that job better.' They agreed that men did machine in other countries and in ethnic minority firms in London. 'It would have to be a really thick skinned one wouldn't it to do the same job as well as all these women here...We tried a couple of lads...in the early days. They weren't very good.'

Despite the historical pre-eminence of men within tailoring and current examples of their existence as machinists, women are still perceived to be more able. They could have some initial advantages, though not through any innate nimbleness. Cockburn states that women are important because through their 'unpaid and unrecognised apprenticeship of a domesticated girlhood, a woman has acquired the qualities which the employer can set to profitable work' (1985 pp. 90–1). In other words, they have already learnt basic sewing at home or school. Many men she spoke to felt that semi-skilled work 'was a woman's job'. 'I was told more than once: men will only come into the industry today when they can see their way to the top. It seems that women or more precisely female sex-typed jobs, now block that way' (ibid., p.73). This may be true to some extent, but there are still a significant number of men who are in management within the clothing industry.

In the Welsh industry the survey did find higher numbers of women than men in management and supervisory positions and design (table 6.2). However, as management and supervisors were grouped together it is impossible to know if women are predominantly found in lower levels of management, in particular in supervisory roles. In all the plants I visited, the machinists' supervisors, for example, were women. In the firms Cockburn (1985) surveyed, women made up 65 per cent of supervisory grades, 25 per cent of the next grade up and only 18 per cent of the grade above that. There was only one woman executive director. In Wales the position seems similar. The regional officer for the NUTGW said that women do become senior supervisors or factory managers, but there is always a production manager over them 'Very few factories, I think I know of three, in my area, whereby they (women) have got positions of authority, where they are either production directors or round about that level or factory manageress. But most of them are male.' This suggests that in the clothing industry women face both horizontal and vertical job segregation. Horizontally women are segregated through the job of machinist and vertically, they remain at the lower levels of the firm. This is similar to many other areas of British industry and has been associated with women's relative low pay (Rubery and Tarling, 1988).

CUTTING: A JOB IN TRANSITION

The introduction of microcomputers into the clothing industry is said to be having an impact on the gender composition of workers such as cutters, graders and markers (Cockburn, 1985). The survey of Welsh firms found almost equal numbers of male and female cutters (table 6.2). Cutting has historically been seen as a skilled occupation, dominated by men. The survey results, showing that nearly 44 per cent of workers in cutting are women, suggest that the old barriers are breaking down. However, it has been argued (Cockburn, 1986) that one of the reasons for an increase in the number of women is that these jobs are becoming less skilled. The cutters were traditionally apprenticed for a number of years and, when experienced, could move on to grading, marker-making and pattern construction. This latter job was considered the most skilled in the industry. These workers earned relatively high wages and had a large amount of control over their work. They were mainly men, although in some regions such as Barnsley only women were employed. This appeared to be because of the development of the local economy and the opportunities available to men in steel and coal. This raised male wages well above those in the clothing industry and created an environment in which clothing was considered to be exclusively women's work (Winterton and Winterton, 1990). However, despite the predominance of these industries in South Wales, the same developments did not occur.

Cockburn argues that the 'unitary craft occupations were gradually broken down' (1985, p. 48). Cutting was increasingly separated from pattern-making, and with lighter materials and new machinery the work became physically lighter. Women increasingly began to replace men on some of these lower occupations. As an NUTGW's full-time official stated,

It hasn't changed an awful lot as far as the main cutters are concerned, but you do tend to get more women going in and laying up and getting involved more with cutting...In general if I were to say have I ever seen a main cutter being a woman I don't think I have.

There is evidence that as women have entered into cutting and pattern room jobs, relative earnings have fallen (Cockburn, 1985).

Direct sex discrimination was still firmly apparent in one plant I visited, which was part of a large multinational. They did not employ any women in cutting. The cutting room manager agreed that some places did have women but 'I don't think that it is right because it is not really suitable for women. The work is quite heavy.' This plant does however, now appear to be in a minority, given that over half the plants employed women in cutting. There appears to be a longer-term change in the pre-assembly process, with the gradual dilution of skills and employment of women. This is in sharp contrast to the introduction of computerization in these areas, which is having a much more profound impact on work organization.

Computer-aided grading and marking making systems (CAD) can convert drawings, i.e. designs, into numerical co-ordinates and initial patterns, which can be used to make up a marker for cutting. Suppliers suggest that savings of up to 12 per cent in fabrics can be obtained. Although this might be the case for poorly made markers, for well-made manual markers the difference is much more marginal. Short (1987) suggests 2–3 per cent and Hoffman and Rush (1988) estimate savings of between 4 and 6 per cent. The main use of these systems is claimed to be in the speed, flexibility and quality of the marker. But it removes the need for most of the highly skilled graders and markers, and transfers the jobs to computer operators. It has been argued by Mitter (1986), that one of the main advantages of the system is that it can increase managerial control of the production process by reducing reliance on the 'moodiness' of skilled workers.

These machines are becoming fairly widespread, particularly among the larger, multi-plant firms. Of the plants surveyed, eight had installed CAD, a further eight planned to, and another eight had access to these computers elsewhere in the company. Thirty-two had no plans to install the equipment.

The new jobs created for computer operators are typically, although not always, filled by women. As Cockburn argues, the women 'are acceptable to employers as the operators of equipment'. This work is 'quickly learned, is not readily generalisable or transferable to other situations, and...above all is vulnerable to further technological change' (Cockburn, 1986, p. 181). It was typical that the role of computer technician was invariably male, and that these technicians were frequently employed outside the company by the supplying firm.

The job of computer operator does involve learning some new skills but this entails only limited training and, once learnt, the job requires little initiative. Some of the workers in the Welsh plants I visited were new to the industry, while others were retrained lay planners or graders. One woman said that she needed only very basic computer knowledge and that lay planning was 'quite quick to learn' and ultimately 'boring'. Another operator who had worked for many years as a marker-maker with manual tools found the new job very different. Previously she had more freedom in her manual work, which involved her moving around the factory, rather than remaining in front of a computer screen. Now she felt the job was 'more battery hen'. A computer manager stated that 'deskilling will always come with computers' and his firm were now training women to undertake grading and lay planning on the computer. Similarly, a technical manager described the jobs as 'up-market typewriter operators'. He regretted that people were no longer trained manually. 'The basic skills of grading manually are being lost.' In one sense these jobs have been de-skilled, but they are also being devalued. As the two managers implied, either the predominance of women doing the job has downgraded it to that of a typist (which again is assumed to involve little skill), or the job being less skilled means that women can now be employed. This therefore makes the notion of skill quite complex, particularly when dealing with gender. 'The equations – men/skilled, women/unskilled – are so powerful that the identification of a particular job with women ensured that the skill content of the work would be downgraded' (Phillips and Taylor, 1986, p. 63).

Computer-aided numerically controlled cutting (CAM) is linked to the pattern-making machines, which instructs a knife or laser to cut through the layers of fabric. This can allow considerable savings in labour cost and substantially speeds up the process. In one firm that was visited, they had reduced the number of cutters by half and increased their output from 25,000–30,000 garments a week to between 40,000 and 45,000. The cutters' job becomes that of watching the knife to make sure that it follows the paper marker and that there are no overlaps.

Computerized cutting is being more slowly implemented than CAD. It is considerably more expensive than a lay planner and grading machine, and therefore a firm needs large volumes to make it cost-effective. Four plants had installed the equipment, a further two planned to, while seven had access elsewhere within their company. Forty-three plants had no plans to use this equipment.

It would seem clear that the pre-assembly parts of the production process are in transition. As computerization is introduced skills are being replaced, and it would seem that de-skilling is being associated with feminization. Men were, however, still being employed on computerized cutting in some plants which were visited. It would seem likely that these changes will be slow, and occur through new recruitment policies rather than wholesale redundancy and replacement. With computerization, more women are entering cutting and grading, and there is evidence to suggest that wages are falling as a result. In a female-dominated industry, based on low wages and intense competition, pre-production is one area where wages can be cut. This is occurring through productivity increases, capital intensification, de-skilling and feminization. If pay continues to fall in these jobs and the work becomes more monotonous, the industry may face a similar problem to those of machinists: namely, lack of cheap labour, absenteeism and recruitment problems.

PAY AND UNIONIZATION

The unequal distribution of jobs is reflected in the relative pay of men and women in the industry. Women's weekly earnings are only just over 70 per cent of men's earnings (DE, 1991a). For most workers, wages are negotiated on a national basis through the Wages Councils. The minimum rate for 1991 is £97.01 for a 39-hour week (LRD, 1991). Average wages for the industry in 1991 were £167 for all workers, representing just 59 per cent of average wages, £185 for men and £133 for women. These represent pay averages of around 84 per cent of women's, and 73 per cent of men's average manual pay (DE, 1991b). Given that machinists average £140 a week, and that this is just 55 per cent of average male manual earnings, it would seem that it is not just sex discrimination and attitudes which keep men out of the industry. Women, it seems, are forced to accept wages which men would not consider. This is not because they are only a secondary earner within the family. One firm stated, 'a majority of whom we employ are women...a large proportion of them are the main earner, because of the unemployment in the steel and coal industry.' This relatively low pay means that firms will continue to find it difficult to keep both men and women in the industry. One firm manager said: 'We [the clothing industry] must be one of the lowest payers generally speaking, particularly for school leavers.' The industry's reliance on low-paid workers creates a number of difficulties. Despite 38 per cent of plants in the survey recognizing a trade union, mainly the NUTGW (now part of the GMB), activity has traditionally been low. Discontent tends to manifest itself in high turnover and high levels of absenteeism rather than in collective action. There is a considerable amount

TABLE 6.3
Number and type of trainee in Welsh plants

Type of trainees	Number of trainees			
	0	1–5	6–9	over 10
YTS	32	16	5	3
Apprenticeship	47	7	2	0
ET	50	6	0	0
Other	42	8	2	4
Total	19	19	9	9
Number of plants = 56				

of poaching among clothing firms, but many workers also leave to go to other industries, offering better or different wages or working conditions. This is perhaps not surprising, given the low wages and intense work pressure which most operators working under piece work have to contend with. However, a number of larger companies with plants in Wales were moving away from industry-wide bargaining between the employers' federation, the BCIA, and the unions, towards negotiating locally over pay. This, they claimed, was because the national agreements were not allowing them to pay operators enough to keep them in the industry in areas such as Wales.

The industry does not really face a recruitment problem, but a high rate of labour turnover, which manifests itself in the need for continuous recruitment and training of new workers. This problem of retention could be related to the generally poor training given to machinists, the lack of status and pay given to their work and, in many cases, the lack of career advancement available in the industry for women. Many firms expect to employ only trained machinists and it is often left to the larger firms to undertake the majority of training. On average, the firms surveyed were found to have about 4 trainees each, representing about 5 per cent of the total workforce. Of these, 41 per cent were on YTS, 10 per cent on apprenticeship schemes, 6 per cent on Employment Training and 43 per cent on other forms of training. The latter was usually some sort of in-house training. Table 6.3 shows that 19 firms had no trainees at all and only nine firms had more than 10 trainees.

Firms were asked whether there had been any change in the amount of training they undertook. Over the past three years, only eight plants had increased the number of trainees, and only four had increased the number of apprenticeships. Although 40 per cent of firms claimed to have increased the number of skilled workers they employed, 43 per cent of firms said that they had reduced their trainees, and 23 per cent of firms had reduced the number of apprenticeships. Many firms stressed the lack of skilled labour or the cost of training as being two of the major problems they faced in the future. These problems are likely to be considerably enhanced by the reduction and changes in government support for the industry. Money was available at £25 per day per trainee from the Manpower Services Commission. Responsibility for funding has now been moved to the new Technical Education Councils, run by local industrialists. The problem is that they are responsible for YTS and ET, and most of the funding goes into these areas. There is little left over for older workers, such as women returners, who are a common source of labour in the clothing industry. The clothing training board (CABITB) is being transferred into a private consultancy, and there have been reductions in local authority support as many training centres close. These changes are likely to leave a significant gap in training provision. Firms have complained at least since the Second World War about the lack of skilled labour. Despite large job losses in the early 1980s, this continues to be their main concern: how to get cheap, trained labour. If firms are not prepared to undertake training or pay reasonable wages with good working conditions, it is likely that they will continue to find problems in this area during periods of economic growth.

A number of Welsh plants were suggesting that they would have to start thinking about crèches and flexible working patterns, because of the difficulty in retaining and attracting women into the industry. There were also some managers who were suggesting that their companies ought to be paying higher wages as a means to resolve some of these problems. This impetus for change appears to be a result of the shortages of women in the local labour market, particularly in South Wales, due to the growth in the service sector and other manufacturing industry. It is uncertain whether the recent recession will affect the priority these types of working practices were beginning to be given.

CONCLUSION

The Welsh clothing industry offers large numbers of women full-time jobs in manufacturing, although at lower wages than in many other industries. They continue to be predominantly segregated into semi-skilled and unskilled work. Despite high levels of male unemployment in parts of Wales, occupations such as machinists remain virtually unopen to men. I have suggested that this is related to the interlinked 'sex' typing of clothing jobs and low pay for machinists. The pressure on firms to minimalize costs means that this is unlikely to change in the foreseeable future.

A process of feminization is occurring in the pre-assembly parts of the production process, as it is becoming acceptable for women to do some of the lower-grade jobs in many Welsh firms. It would seem that this is a gradual process involving the breakdown of craft skills. However, computerization has rapidly changed jobs and recreated new ones, and at the present time there is a period of struggle over job definitions and status. It seems likely that grading and marking will become feminized, associated with office work and accordingly paid less. The job of computer programmer is very rigidly defined as a male occupation. Whether male cutters will be able to defend their position is still being determined. Given the high cost of computerized cutting and the continued need for some manual cutting even where it does exist, this area may still remain male-dominated and higher paid.

ACKNOWLEDGEMENT

I would like to thank Mike Bresnen for comments and advice on this paper.

NOTES

1 This research was supported by a grant from the Welsh Office.
2 These results are part of a larger research project on the Welsh clothing industry, which included a detailed questionnaire and plant visits. Manufacturing plants in Wales were identified by a data base held by the WDA. All were contacted and, of the 120 who were believed to be still operating, 57 responded, answering questions about products, markets, technology, production process and employment levels. A further nine plants were involved in further interviews with managers and workers. Discussions were also held with the regional NUTGW and the WDA's Garment Initiative.

REFERENCES

Bettio, F. (1988) 'Sex-typing of Occupations, the Cycle and Restructuring in Italy', in J. Rubery (ed.), *Women and Recession* , London, Routledge.
Bradley, H. (1989) *Men's Work, Women's Work*, Cambridge, Polity Press.
Bythell, D. (1978) *The Sweated Trades: Outwork in Nineteenth Century Britain*, London, Routledge.
Cockburn, C. (1985) *Machinery of Dominance: Women, Men and Technical Know-how*, London, Pluto Press.
Cockburn, C. (1986) 'Women and Technology: Opportunity is not enough', in K. Purcell et al. (eds), *The Changing Experience of Employment*, London, Macmillan.
Crewe, L. J. (1988) *Picking up the Threads? An Investigation into the Changing Dynamics of the Clothing Industry*, Working Paper 513, School of Geography, University of Leeds.
DE (1991a) *Employment Gazette*, May, Department of Employment.

DE (1991b) *New Earnings Survey* Department of Employment.

Dobbs, S. P. (1926) *The Clothing Workers of Great Britain*, London, Routledge.

Hoffman, K. and Rush, H. (1988) *Microelectronics and Clothing: The Impact of Technical Change on a Global Industry*, Geneva, Praeger.

LRD (1991) *Labour Research Bargaining Report* no. 109, September, London, Labour Research Department.

Lloyd, C. (1990) *The Welsh Clothing Industry: A Report to the Welsh Office*, Cardiff, Welsh Office.

Mitter, S. (1986) 'Industrial Restructuring and Manufacturing Homework: Immigrant Women in the UK Clothing Industry', *Capital and Class*, 27.

Morris, J. (1986) 'The Characteristics of Sweating: The Late 19th Century London and Leeds Tailoring Trade', in A. V. John, *Unequal Opportunities: Women's Employment in England 1800–1918*, Oxford, Basil Blackwell.

Phillips, A. and Taylor, B. (1986) 'Sex and Skill', in Feminist Review (ed.) *Waged Work*, London, Virago.

Phizacklea, A. (1990), *Unpacking the Fashion Industry: Gender, Racism and Class in Production*, London, Routledge.

Rubery, J. (ed.) (1988) *Women and Recession*, London, Routledge.

Rubery, J. and Tarling, R. (1988) 'Women's Employment in Declining Britain', in J. Rubery (ed.), *Women and Recession*, London, Routledge.

Schmiechen, J. A. (1984) *Sweated Industries and Sweated Labour: The London Clothing Trades 1860–1914*, London, Croom Helm.

Short, J. (1987) *The Garment Industry in Wales: A Report to the WDA*, Wales Cooperative Development and Training Agency.

Totterdill, P., Farrands, C., Gawith, M. and Gillingwater, D. (1989) *Industrial Policy and the Regeneration of British Manufacturing Industry: The Case of Clothing*, LEPR, 1.

Winterton, R. and Winterton, J. (1990) 'Enterprise Culture and the Restructuring of the UK Clothing Industry', paper to the 'Employment Relations in the Enterprise Culture' Conference, Cardiff Business School.

Wray, M. (1957) *The Women's Outerwear Industry*, London, Duckworth.

7. WOMEN AND THE ORGANIZATION OF THE LABOUR FORCE IN THE ABERYSTWYTH HOTEL TRADE

Anna Walker

INTRODUCTION

I took part-time work because of Patrick. I work from 9 to 3 and then I take him from school. I'll never take a full-time job while he's at school. Not until he's 16. The trouble begins when you're not at home – children can get into trouble. (Mary, aged 41, a cleaner and single mother)

I'm doing teachers' training in Liverpool. My parents live here. I usually come here in the summer and work. I've been doing that for a few years. I work mornings in the hotel and afternoons in the chippy. Then I'm going on holiday and then back to college. (Eileen, aged 24, a chambermaid)

I worked for 12 years at the University [as a catering assistant and chambermaid], but I had to retire at 65. I didn't want to give up working...I only paid half stamp so I didn't get my pension...The office told me I only had to pay half stamp. My husband works part-time behind the bar at the 'Crossroads' but it's not enough to keep us. He earns less than £30 a week. (Liz, aged 65, a chambermaid)

During the summer of 1985 I interviewed 30 women and 13 men working in 12 Aberystwyth hotels. The words quoted above came from some of the women employed in the hotels and give an indication of the diversity of their labour market experiences. In this article I want to suggest that this diversity is the main feature of the Aberystwyth hotel labour market: women were very differently placed in that labour market, and therefore did not constitute one homogeneous group of employees. Similar patterns emerged amongst the male employees. Thus I discovered that in the specific context of the Aberystwyth hotels gender divisions were cross-cut by other social factors, especially age and recognized skills.

In addition, there were few definite and discrete social groups of women which would fit neatly into the explanatory frameworks of dual/segmented labour market theories which are commonly used by sociologists and radical economists when examining the female labour market. As such, the study raised questions concerning the usefulness of such general theories when discussing women employed in hotels – and possibly, by implication, female employees in the private service sector in general.

In brief, dualistic theories attempt to divide the labour market into two discrete segments, with women constituting a disadvantaged secondary or peripheral sector and men constituting an advantaged primary or core sector. In one of the most influential accounts of this model, Barron and Norris describe the dual labour market as follows:

A dual labour market is one in which:
(1)   there is a more or less pronounced division into higher paying and lower paying sectors;
(2)   mobility across the boundary of those sectors is restricted;
(3)   higher paying jobs are tied into promotional or career ladders, while lower paid jobs offer few opportunities for vertical movement;
(4)   higher paying jobs are relatively stable, while lower paid jobs are unstable. (Barron and Norris, 1976, pp.48–9)

Barron and Norris claimed that the secondary labour market in Britain is predominantly female because women are very likely to have most of the five main characteristics which constitute secondary sector employees. These are: dispensability – they are easily made unemployed by employers; clearly visible social difference for which they are likely to be discriminated against by employers; little interest in acquiring training; low economism – in other words, little interest in economic rewards; and lack of solidarity with other workers – for instance, little interest in joining a trade union. These characteristics also describe the minority of men who are employed in the secondary sector.

Two major problems with Barron and Norris's theory have been identified by feminist sociologists. Firstly, they have been criticized for treating all women as one homogeneous group, seen to be located within a limited number of occupations in the manufacturing industry. This ignores the diversity of women's labour market involvement. As Beechey (1986) points out: 'Dual labour market theory has little to say about horizontal occupational segregation – that is, about the segregation of women into jobs like clerical work and selling, and men into jobs like security and protective services.'

Beechey argues that this problem arises because Barron and Norris base their analysis on an account of employers' strategies in particular kinds of manufacturing industries, and it is in this area that the theory applies best. She cites the car industry as a good example, where men are employed in skilled, technical work and women in unskilled work on the production line. This type of work is not, however, characteristic of all women's employment – some women do skilled work. As Beechey argues,

> Many kinds of women's jobs do not fit easily into the category of secondary sector work...Much secretarial work throughout all sectors of the economy requires considerable training and secretarial workers are an integral part of the workforce...although it may not actually be defined as skilled, it is not marginal or insecure.

A second problem with the theory is that it is overly descriptive: it examines surface forms of employment relations and not underlying causal factors. In particular it fails to recognize *patriarchal* power relations which constitute one of the main underlying social processes affecting the structure of the labour market. Walby (1983) takes up this issue and suggests that it is through patriarchy that male employees exclude women from the better-paid, primary sector jobs, resulting in the vertical and horizontal sexual division in the labour market. This system exists alongside and cross-cuts the other main power relationship in the labour market between capitalist employers and their employees. Thus, Walby criticizes Barron and Norris for

> their lack of appreciation of, and analysis of, patriarchal structures in the labour market...They treat sexual differentiation as determined largely outside the labour market by the sexual division of labour in the household. It is then incorrectly...treated as a given which is unmodified by the workings of the labour market. (Walby, 1983, p. 155)

Subsequently there have been various attempts to produce a more sophisticated theory to explain the 'balkanisation' of the labour market (Atkinson, 1984). These theories tend to be grouped together under the title 'segmented labour market theories' and they attempt to provide a theoretical framework which is able to take into account the complexities of the labour market. In practice they tend to make similar points to Barron and Norris while rejecting a simple dualistic division of the labour market for three divisions or more.

A major problem with this approach is that it is often difficult to define where one labour market begins and another ends. Richard Brown (1985) makes this observation on the basis of a 10-year study of the male labour market in Newcastle-upon-Tyne. He concludes that 'in general our respondents' experiences in the labour market...formed a continuum, rather than displaying sharp breaks between different "types" of worker or labour market sectors' (Brown, 1985, p. 470). Graham Day also points to this problem, suggesting that:

> The scope for disagreement as to how many layers within the working-class should be accorded significance reflects the problem already mentioned of making break lines within a continuum of market situations. While some regard the divisions as marking qualitative discontinuities, others are prepared to see them as matters of degree. (Day et al., 1981, p. 6)

In the course of examining the hotel labour force, these problems came to the surface.

ABERYSTWYTH: THE LOCAL LABOUR MARKET

In order to make observations about the position of women in the hotel labour market it is necessary to examine the wider context of the Aberystwyth labour market to form a general picture of the availability of alternative sources of employment for these women and to discover to what extent unemployment is a significant factor.

Aberystwyth is situated on the Mid Wales west coast in a predominantly agricultural area. It has a population of 11,000–12,000, which fluctuates according to the time of year, particularly with the comings and goings of the large student population attached to the university (which now incorporates the former Library College), the Welsh Agricultural College and the College of Further Education.

These students and the workforce employed in the educational institutions and attached concerns constitute an important part of the town's character and population. The presence of the various educational institutions has transformed a medium-sized market town into a students' town (at certain times of year) with cafés, bars, shops and other services being well utilized. The economic spin-off from the presence of the university in particular is vital in sustaining a thriving personal services industry.

The other major income earner in the town is tourism: over the summer and bank holidays the town swells in numbers with influxes of holiday-makers – mainly from the English Midlands. The various hotels, guest-houses, bed and breakfast establishments and camping and caravan sites absorb this influx, and there is, of course, a large economic boost to the town's consumer service industries.

The other main employers in the town are also located in the service sector. The National Library of Wales employs approximately 200 people. The Mid Wales British Rail line terminates in the town, and this provides some employment (predominantly for men), as does the local bus and burgeoning taxi service. As Aberystwyth is the only big town serving a relatively large hinterland, it has become a busy shopping centre. It also contains various public services such as a magistrates' court, hospital, fire station, gas and electricity depots and so on. In addition, there is a sizeable government sector employing mostly white-collar workers, for instance tax and social security offices. Aberystwyth's manufacturing sector is represented by a small number of 'light' industries located on an industrial estate on the edge of the town.

Ceredigion is the lowest-level geographical area for which relevant statistics are provided in the 1981 General Census for Wales and England. There are, however, some problems with this – for instance, as Ceredigion is a predominantly agricultural region, the statistics will be weighted towards agricultural employment when compared to the town of Aberystwyth. However, taking this into account, these figures do provide the best indication of employment in the town in the years immediately following 1981. In addition, it should be noted that the government statistics lack detail and tend to lump together disparate groups of employees. This is particularly so where women's employment and unemployment are concerned (Rees, 1988). Unemployment statistics for married women are especially problematic in that they are only a partial account of the numbers of women out of employment in Wales and/or Britain. State legislation actively discourages married women from registering as unemployed. For instance, in 1985 when this study was done, as in other years, a married woman could not claim unemployment benefit if her husband was already receiving such benefits.

This legal policy is backed up by popular and state ideology which asserts that married women should not be economically active in times of high unemployment, thereby taking scarce jobs from men. During the mid-1980s this ideology was being particularly promoted by the Thatcher government at a time of very high unemployment. In examining unemployment statistics for women, then, it should be kept in mind that they underestimate the actual numbers involved.

In November 1984 I was informed by a local government officer that Aberystwyth had one of the lowest unemployment rates in Wales at 11.1 per

TABLE 7.1
Unemployment in Aberystwyth travel-to-work area, September 1984. LS1

	Women	Men	Total
September 1984			
No. out of work	472	99	1271
Unemployment rate	9.4	12.4	11.1
September 1983			
No. out of work	389	749	1138
Unemployment rate	7.8	11.6	9.9

Source: Local Government Statistics, Planning Dept., Ceredigion.

cent. Only two Welsh towns had lower rates: Brecon (10.7 per cent) and Carmarthen (9.3 per cent). However, although the Aberystwyth statistics looked good, unemployment figures had begun to rise rapidly. Thus in June 1983, 1051 people in the local travel-to-work area were unemployed. By June 1984 this number had risen to 1160. If we examine the position of women in Aberystwyth in 1984 (table 7.1) we can see that in contrast to the rest of Wales women were in a better position than men, although they might have been beginning to catch up with male unemployment rates.

It would seem from these statistics that women as an aggregate were in a relatively strong labour market position. This impression changes, however, if we look in more detail at what kinds of employment women were located in. Considering the occupation distribution of women and men in Ceredigion in table 7.2, which includes the top four employing industries for both women and men, it can be seen that in Ceredigion the majority of women worked in education, retail distribution, hotels and catering, and the medical services. Thus, the top four employing occupations for single women in Ceredigion (1981) were in the private and public service sector. They were: clerks (1060); secretaries and receptionists (720); shop assistants (630); domestic staff and school helpers (380). All of these occupational groups were almost exclusively 'feminine' with the exception of clerks and farmers/horticulturalists. Farming and horticulture is a relatively large occupational group for married women but not single women. This reflects the organization of farm work amongst owning families whereby women often work alongside their husbands, their labour being vital to the survival of the farm as a business.

Of the four highest employing occupations for men, farming and horti-culture constituted the single largest occupational group. The next largest occupational group was building and construction workers (610). Following this were bus, coach and lorry drivers (480), clerks (450), and woodworkers

TABLE 7.2

Economically active population in employment in Ceredigion: industry classes by sex and marital status (10 per cent sample)*

	Women	Married women	Men
Industry Classes			
Total in employment	782	513	1333
Education	142	95	119
Retail distribution	125	80	62
Hotel and catering	84	58	66
Medical and other health services inc. Vet services	72	50	25
Agriculture and horticulture	66	49	271
Construction	7	4	77
Public administration, national defence and social service.	49	32	96

* Included are the top four employing industry classes for each sex.
Source: 1981 census, Govt. Stat. Office, HMSO.

and pattern makers (410). Again, apart from clerks, these would all seem to have been typically male, mostly skilled, manual jobs although one would need to know more about the *types* of clerical and construction jobs – for instance, whether they are skilled or unskilled, low paid or well paid – in order to categorize these occupations clearly.

Thus the Ceredigion labour market is often horizontally segregated between women and men in terms of occupations, with women tending to work in service occupations where male employees are in a minority. These statistics tell us little, however, about vertical sexual segregation – in other words, divisions of pay, skill and general conditions of work within occupational groups. An indication of such divisions can be gained from table 7.3.

These statistics illustrate that there existed in Aberystwyth a fairly strict vertical segregation in the labour market between women and men, with women being grouped in the low-skilled, service occupations – occupations commonly associated with low pay and poor working conditions (Hakim, 1979) – and men being grouped in the better-paid skilled, manual work sector and self-employed business groups. In addition, the occupations that women worked in tended to be sex-specific, 'feminized' service industries which have been consistently and historically commonly defined as unskilled or less skilled – and therefore low-paid. The exceptions to this might be in employment in education and clerical work.

TABLE 7.3
Ceredigion economically active population: socio-economic group by sex (and married women) (10 per cent sample)

Socio-economic group	Women	Married women	Men
All economically active	815	520	1441
Junior non-manual workers	256	154	111
Intermediate non-manual workers	123	82	114
Ancillary workers and artists	120	80	108
Personal Service Workers	108	69	21
Skilled manual workers	17	11	212
Farmers - own account	38	31	185
(other than professional)	33	26	133
Employers and manufacturers in industry, commerce, etc.			
Smallest	59	44	130

Source: 1981 Census, Government Stat. Office, HMSO.

The poor labour market position of women is highlighted if hours of employment are examined. In Ceredigion the majority of women worked full-time (3840) but with a large minority working part-time (2600). Among men, 8810 worked full-time and only 210 part-time. Married women were more concentrated in part-time employment than either single women or men, with the majority (2140) working part-time and 1930 working full-time.

If we take part-time employment to indicate poor pay and employment conditions (*Department of Employment Gazette*, 1987, p. 544) – especially in the service occupations – then these statistics back up the general picture of women experiencing a weak labour-market position as compared to men. Many married women would seem to have been ghettoized, in addition, into part-time employment within these industries and occupations.

THE ABERYSTWYTH HOTEL TRADE

During 1985 I carried out interviews with 12 hoteliers in Aberystwyth. There were 20 hotels in the town in total. The hotels where I carried out the interviews ranged in size from the smallest, having a maximum bedspace capacity (m.b.c.) of 23, to the largest with an m.b.c. of 80, and all fell into the category of traditional coastal resort hotels: they were relatively small, and owned and managed by a live-in family.

The determining link between demand for a product or service and the way in which that product or service is produced at the workplace is as fundamental in the Aberystwyth hotel trade as it is in all industries. It was therefore vital to examine the nature of the demand for the services offered by the hotels in order to discover how the hotel owners organized the production of services by themselves and their employees. This in turn affected the nature of the hotel workforce and the labour market. The main feature of the Aberystwyth hotel trade is that it fluctuates. Demand for the various hotel services oscillates within the day, from day to day, and at different times of year.

Firstly, within each day there are specific times when services will be in greater demand, for instance before and during meals, preparing and serving food; cleaning up after meals; serving drinks at night in the bar; cleaning rooms and changing bed linen in the late mornings when most guests are out. The one type of labour which would seem to require fairly continuous work is reception work.

Secondly, many hoteliers specified a busier time within each week, often on Saturdays, when tourists tended to arrive in greater numbers, or at the beginning of the week when trades people would arrive. Thus one hotelier commented: 'we get busier times...the busiest time is Monday and Tuesday throughout the year. It reflects the commercial trade.'

Lastly, the hotel trade was seasonal in that it was reliant on tourists in the summer for most of its overnight staying guests. There was therefore an influx of guests in the summer months and a slackening off of numbers in the winter. All the hoteliers divided up each year into the busy seasons in the summer and the quiet season in the winter, especially from Christmas to February.

There were differences, however, in the hoteliers' accounts of the degree of these fluctuations in demand for overnight accommodation. For instance, one hotelier stated: 'The hotel's never full. We're least busy in January and February or some nights we get no one and usually it's under 10', while another stated: 'We're full all year round...In the time we've been here (3 years) there have been no more than 10 days when we've been empty.'

In claiming to be busy all year round, the latter hotelier was referring to patterns of demand for hotel services in Aberystwyth which helped to offset the seasonality of the trade. This was the low-level but year-round trade in non-tourist overnight guests; and the demand for the use of other facilities provided by the hotel apart from bedspaces. The former was facilitated by Aberystwyth's position as a commercial centre with a steady flow of travelling business people constituting a main source of trade on a year-round basis. University-related trade was also mentioned in this context. The latter was provided by the use of general hotel facilities by residential and non-residential guests alike. The use of such facilities – especially the bars and restaurants – was an extremely important factor in keeping the hotel profitable.

Despite these offsetting tendencies, however, the hotel trade remained basically seasonal, especially where overnight guests were concerned. This was confirmed by the fact that all the hoteliers hired extra summer-season employees in order to cope with the increase in trade. One hotelier summed up the situation well: 'Trade's not particularly seasonal and we're just extra busy in the summer. Only the accommodation's not in full use just after Christmas. The restaurant's very busy and the bar's steady.'

These patterns of demand for trade are important as they help to determine the nature of the organization of the hotel workforces and labour market patterns. Thus, as demand oscillated in short-term and long-term cycles, hoteliers tended to utilize a flexible labour force in order to meet waves in demand. This flexibility manifests itself in the use of part-time employees, split-shift employees, temporary seasonal staff and casual workers. In addition, flexibility was the criterion most cited by hoteliers as the quality they were looking for in employees. Often this meant that women in particular were employed as 'general' menial employees required to shift from task to task within the hotel on a daily and hourly basis. Such *ad hoc* labour organization was a typical feature in the hotels.

WOMEN IN THE HOTEL LABOUR MARKET

The 43 interviews represent just under one third of the total number of employees which the proprietors said they employed as a maximum (134). The ratio of women to men in my sample roughly equated to the overall ratio of women to men that the hoteliers said they employed. Likewise, my sample was on the whole representative of the hoteliers' figures in terms of other criteria – for instance, age, temporary/permanent status, job category and so on. Thus, although the overall number in my sample was not high, it provided a good indication of the main patterns in the Aberystwyth hotel labour market.

In 1985 the hotel labour force consisted predominantly of female, single, young, permanent employees who mostly worked on a full-time basis with a significant minority working part-time. Most of these women worked in low-paid, menial jobs which were type-cast as unskilled and 'women's work'. A minority of mainly young men were also employed in the hotels. They were equally divided between those defined as skilled and those defined as unskilled with the concomitant disparities of pay between the two groups. The vast majority of the male employees worked on a full-time basis and were single.

Within these broad patterns, however, it was possible to identify three main categories of hotel employees: the small 'core' group of relatively privileged, mostly male employees who were employed on a long-term, more well-paid basis and whose labour skills were pivotal to the running of the hotel. Also identifiable was a minority of very poorly paid, unskilled employees – for the most part teenagers who were either at school or students in higher education. Between these latter two groups there lay a 'grey area' of employees (mostly female) who were not part of the central 'core' group but were neither subject to the low pay and unfavourable conditions of employment of the very young employees.

These three groups of employees were not strictly delineated from each other, apart from the 'core' group. It would be more accurate to describe their differences in labour market position as lying along a continuum. I will examine each group of employees, paying especial regard to the position of women beginning with the role of the owning families who also worked in the hotels on a day-to-day basis, often alongside their employees.

The Owning Family

The owning families did not constitute a part of the hotel labour market as their labour was not for sale alongside other workers. In this sense they fall beyond the scope of this article. However, the labour they performed in the hotels was vital to the running of the hotels and as such they formed an inner core group of labourers within the core group of employees – their labour was central, long-term, mostly defined as skilled and with promotional prospects for the younger members of the family. Many of the hoteliers told me that they were training up their children to take over the hotel when they retired. Furthermore, the hoteliers had a profoundly different relationship to the means of production – the hotel itself – and the provision of services from that of their employees. Thus their financial rewards for working in the hotel were manifested in the form of profits for the owner (either the husband or the husband and wife) and mostly relatively high wages and numerous 'perks' for the wider family. Lastly, the family was separated from the other employees in that they had economic and social power over their employees through their position as employers.

These divisions between the owning family and their employees were often blurred and complicated by the fact that various family members worked alongside their employees in a variety of jobs and promoted an ideology of 'pulling together' and the workforce constituting 'one happy family' in order to gain the maximum co-operation from their employees. Thus the very real employer–employee power relationship tended to be obscured by the actuality of employers 'mucking in' with employees and the assertion that this rendered the hotel workplace one where employers and employees were somehow 'on the same side'. Several of the female employees interviewed used the term 'one happy family' to describe their workplace relations. However, other employees had a conflicting view of their relationships with their employers.

It is worth quoting here at some length a discussion I had with Jane. Jane was employed as a hotel bar worker. She worked alongside Aled, who ran the bar. Aled's mother, Mrs Jenkins, co-owned and managed the hotel.

Jane: You see, because it started out as a family business, everyone who comes into it is like 'join the family' and there's no 'this is your job, this is my job'. If something needs doing you do it, and that's the same with everybody...Really, if Aled worked when he was supposed to...he's supposed to be behind the bar all night. You know, it'd be no problem. It's when Aled says: 'I'm going to the flat to watch "Brookside" ' or 'I'm going down the road to see John'. Or sometimes he'll go out.

Me: But that puts you in an awkward position. If he was just another worker you might go to her [his mother] after a while and say he's not pulling his weight...

Jane: But he's my boss.

Me: But that's the thing. He's your boss but he's also your fellow worker, isn't he?

Jane: Yes, but I don't know how much Mrs Jenkins really expects him to do. I don't know whether he's just supposed to be there in a supervisory capacity in which case it doesn't matter if he goes out as long as one of the others is around...When it comes down to it, it's his money, his job, his profit...and it's his fault. So if he's not there and there's something I can't cope with then that's just tough.

Jane's words highlight the ambiguous position of family members within the workforce. They also illustrate how the notion of the employees 'joining' the owning family to 'help out' with the running of the business creates added flexibility amongst the workforce.

The position of daughters and sons of the hotel owners was particularly ambivalent: they were neither totally in charge of their own labour, nor were they totally in charge of the labour of paid employees. Their position was often one of working as a paid employee for their parents but also as a manager or trainee business owner. Jane summed up their position well:

I can't stop him [going out when he should be working]...I can't do it because he's my boss and he's always there. The only reason he can do it is because *his* boss, which is Mrs Jenkins, *isn't* always there. If she catches him going he gets a thick ear and gets sent back behind the bar.

Families would seem, therefore, to have been the vital form of hotel ownership in Aberystwyth with family labour constituting an important part of managerial and other labour. Given the nature of the hotel trade and the type of work organization it throws up, the reasons for this family involvement become clear: in a trade where demand is uneven, with surges in demand for services followed by periods of little or no demand, and labour is needed in different parts of the hotels at different (often unsociable) times, perhaps the family is the only social unit which is at once adequately flexible and resilient to meet such fluctuating demands. The family provides a ready supply of labour which is continuously available and which can be heavily exploited through the power-relations within the family, backed up by the state, whereby parents are able to exploit children, and husbands are able, to a lesser extent, to exploit their wives. Alternatively, a child or wife might voluntarily labour in a hotel as a joint or future owner. Lastly, there is the possibility that a combination of those two sets of relationships exists – for instance, a child's labour might be exploited but she/he might ultimately own the hotel business.

The Employees

The majority of hotel employees were women, and it was mostly women who looked for employment in the hotels.

The fact that it was women who actively sought work in the hotels, as opposed to men, is underlined by the numbers who had directly asked hoteliers for a job: 11 went to the hotelier and asked for work (no men did this) and a further eight used informal contacts, for instance asking friends who already had a hotel job. A much higher ratio of men used formal means for getting a job (answering advertisements in the press or using the local Job Centre) and said they were looking for work, but not necessarily hotel work.

It is immediately obvious, therefore, that the image of women being pulled into hotel work somehow against their will by the demands of employers is a misleading one: they participated in the construction and maintenance of hotel jobs as 'feminine' jobs. This could be for various reasons – for instance, the part-time hours and informal work structure often found in hotels could suit women, allowing them to fit in their unpaid domestic labour around their

TABLE 7.4
Age/gender of interviewees

Years old	Women no.	Men no.
Under 20	11	5
20–29	10	5
30–39	1	3
40–49	6	0
50–59	1	0
60 +	1	0
Total	30	13

paid hotel labour. Alternatively, they might be aware that much hotel work is seen by employers as 'women's work' and 'unskilled' and they might be making a realistic choice by opting for such work if they did not have other formal work qualifications.

Another feature of the workforce, whether female or male, was that it was mostly young: 16 employees were under 20 and a further 15 were aged between 20 and 29. This youthful nature of the labour market was particularly pronounced amongst the male employees. Twenty-one female employees were under 30, with 11 being under 20 (see table 7.4). Although the hotel trade attracts mainly young adults, it also attracts a significant minority of middle-aged women. These women tended to be married or divorced, with adult children. They had re-entered the labour market once their child-rearing commitments had lessened.

Whereas the total number of employees interviewed was 43, they were involved with 63 job categories (see table 7.5). This is because 13 of the 43 interviewees had two or more jobs. Quite clearly, the majority of jobs were sex-typed: waitressing, chambermaiding, bar work and reception work were the most predominantly 'female' jobs, while chefs were predominantly male. There was therefore horizontal segregation along the lines of sex in the labour force. Such divisions cannot be totally reduced to differences in levels of skill – men were employed as waiters and porters but not as chambermaids despite the equally 'unskilled' nature of the labour involved.

Twelve of the thirteen employees with more than one job were women, mostly permanently employed. In addition, six women carried out three or more jobs within the hotel. No men fell into this category.

This highlights the informal, *ad hoc* nature of the work relations within the Aberystwyth hotels: just over 30 per cent of the employees had no formal job

TABLE 7.5
Jobs performed by hotel employees by sex

Job Category	Women	Men
Waitress	12	–
Waiter	–	4
Chambermaid	13	–
Reception	7	–
Chef/cook	1	2
Assistant chef	–	2
Head Chef	–	2
Pastry Chef	1	–
Managerial	2	1
Barstaff	7	–
Laundry	1	–
Cleaner	2	–
Kitchen porter	1	3
Dishwasher	2	–
Total	49	14

definition. Even when an interviewee described herself, for instance, as a waitress, it would often become evident during the course of the interview that she would in fact perform other subsidiary tasks such as cleaning and bar work. One bar worker described how she performed waiting work as follows:

'Well Anne gets all of the food up from the kitchen. But it's really difficult because there's so much overlap between jobs... I'll go down to the kitchen and bring up bar-food, it's not my job but if there's nobody about and they're sitting there waiting for their food and the bell rings then I'll go down and get it.

These findings would tend to support the arguments of feminist theorists, that gender plays a crucial part in determining flexibility in the use of labour. On the basis of their study of employment in the Coventry labour market, Beechey and Perkins contend that

even if men's and women's jobs are governed by broadly similar requirements (in other words by similar needs for flexibility) it is generally only the women's jobs which are organised on a part-time basis. Manual work in hospitals illustrates this point well. Within the hospital sector there was total segregation between portering, which was done exclusively by men, and domestic manual work which was done by women...It is hard to escape the conclusion that gender is a significant element of the difference between the two occupations and moreover that it enters into the construction of women's jobs (and especially manual jobs) as part-time. (Beechey and Perkins, 1987, p. 101)

Similarly in the Aberystwyth hotels, although it should be noted that more than half the women experienced clear job definitions, women in the less skilled jobs were likely to be constructed into flexible work patterns, whereas men were not, even though all such menial work required the same levels of flexibility to cover peaks and troughs through any one day.

In the case of hotel employees, the gendered nature of flexibility did not manifest itself in the organization of hours of work – most employees worked full-time. Rather, lack of job demarcations and the moving of employees from one job to another within one working day, week, etc. was the way in which hotel owners achieved a flexible workforce.

None of the employees defined as 'skilled', whether female or male, experienced a similar lack of job demarcation. Male employees were more likely to be defined as skilled overall. For instance, of the eight chefs/cooks, six were male employees. These jobs were considered to be skilled, involving several years of training in an apprenticeship and often in college. Further, they were seen to be pivotal to the running of the hotels and were strictly demarcated and given the sole attention of one employee. Such work was seen by employers to be hard to replace on an *ad hoc* basis as it involved specialized staff consistently planning, co-ordinating and producing meals of a certain standard. Without that service, the hotel would not have been a hotel.

Chefs were not the only group of employees who were defined as skilled by employers – to a lesser extent reception and clerical work, which was mostly carried out by women, was defined as skilled. These definitions of skill often centred on strict job demarcations: thus two receptionists did reception work only, and they received significantly greater rates of pay than the women who performed additional, less skilled work alongside reception work. Likewise managerial workers, of whom none did solely managerial work, were not paid high rates of pay.

In contrast to these employees, waitresses, waiters, chambermaids, bar workers, cleaners, dish washers, kitchen porters, and laundry workers have been historically constructed into the category of unskilled workers. With the exception of kitchen porters and waiters, these jobs were done by women. There was no chance of promotion within women's unskilled jobs: a waitress remained a waitress, and there was no career ladder a chambermaid could climb and no possibility of her acquiring 'skills'. In contrast, assistant chefs might carry out a good deal of menial work but they were seen to be apprentices and by watching the chefs and learning skills from them, they had a chance of promotion.

The importance of skill to the structuring of sexual divisions in the labour market emerges repeatedly in feminist writings in the area, but it should be noted that feminist theorists themselves often have an oversimplified notion of skill. For instance, it is frequently argued that women end up in poorly paid, part-time personal service sector employment because in such feminized occupations they are able to use the skills they have learned in the home in their role as wives and mothers. Here the notion of skill is partially based in material reality and partially in ideological constructions – for instance, the ideology of femininity and motherhood. It is thus presumed that all women learn to cook, clean and make beds in the home, and that this equips them with the necessary skills to work in paid employment as, for instance, chambermaids, cooks, waitresses and nurses.

Beechey and Perkins make such an assumption: they discuss women employed as part-time cooks and cleaners in hospitals and school canteens and state that

> this work is quintessentially women's work, which requires the skills which women have learned in the home as wives and mothers. Since older married women are seen to be ideal employees for these jobs, they have been organised at least in part, to dovetail with women's domestic commitments. (Beechey and Perkins, 1987, pp. 100–1)

This argument is too generalized and hides the complexities of unpaid reproductive labour in the family household. It must not be presumed that all daughters learn the same skills from their mothers (or other older female relatives), and neither are all women wives or mothers.

Some social theorists provide a more sophisticated analysis, narrowing their focus to mothers working part-time and suggesting it is this social group which constitutes the secondary labour force which is predominantly made up of 'female' jobs. However, even in this case it cannot be supposed that all mothers learn the same sets of skills in the home. Family forms differ as to the divisions of labour within them (Pahl, 1984). In the instance of hotel employment, to have prepared food for a family of five does not equip a woman with the skills and speed necessary to produce food in the volumes needed in large hotels or catering establishments. Lastly, how do we explain, within the above framework, the existence of waiters alongside waitresses? What presumptions are made, on the part of employers, about their skills for the job?

Some pertinent criticisms of the equation between domestic skills and service skills are made by Janet Bujra in her discussion of Tanzanian domestic servants. Her study is intended to 'question both the view that domestic skills are naturally or necessarily feminine, whether by genetic inheritance or socialisation, and that gender segregation in the workplace can be explained as simply a common sense reflection of this' (Bujra, 1987, p. 1).

Bujra is arguing against what she describes as an 'oversocialised' conception of women, whereby schools and families provide a 'smoothly functional role' in moulding girls for domesticity. Instead, she suggests that we should separate the process of gender socialization from the acquisition of skills. Bujra backs up her arguments by showing that in Tanzania it is men who are thought to be better servants because they do not have to unlearn domestic skills as women do. However, the men have to overcome an aversion to performing what they see as 'women's work'. Bujra therefore illustrates in her paper the contingent nature of the equation between women's domestic skills and their paid labour.

In sum, therefore, it is necessary to note that a hierarchy of skills exists in the labour force and that most, but not all, skill definitions tend to coincide with gender divisions. However, the issue of skill is itself a contestable notion: such definitions are open to question, and if the tasks performed by employees are closely scrutinized, skill definitions are highly spurious. One woman employed to work behind a bar gave a graphic example of how 'women's work' often involved responsibility, ability to deal with customers and a good deal of skill while not receiving any credit for these qualities from employers. She described one night's work as follows:

> There's nobody in reception. So when you're in the bar, the phone's redirected to the bar so all the incoming calls have to be taken at the bar. And if there's just you there – like this has happened to me a few times – and the phone rings and you're in the middle of serving and you can see two more people coming in the door and somebody's standing at reception. And the 'phone goes and somebody says: 'Hello, we're calling about the possibility of a double room for three days in August' and you're panicking.
> The booking book and all that's in reception and you stand there behind the bar and say 'sorry 'bout all this', and you say: 'Hold the line please I'll just put you through to reception'. Then you re-dial reception, hang it up, run into reception, pick up and go: 'Hello reception'. And you're scrabbling

around reception with the books saying: 'Oh, yes Sir, I'll be with you in a minute' and '32? Here's your keys, Sir'. And you're doing everything at once...And they don't actually teach you to do anything...nobody's taught me anything really since I've been here.

In this instance the crucial factor would seem to be formal training: this woman had no formal training for her skills, which she had picked up as she worked in the hotel. She therefore only received the pay of an 'unskilled' bar worker.

In summary, although women could be employed in 'skilled' jobs and men in 'unskilled' jobs, it can be seen that amongst the Aberystwyth hotel employees a proportionately greater number of male employees were employed in central, 'skilled' jobs (or apprenticeships to such jobs) than female employees. Thus six of the 14 jobs carried out by men fell into this category (assistant chef, chef and head chef). In contrast, this was true of only nine of the 49 jobs carried out by women. The two receptionists who did solely reception work have been included in this group, along with the cook and pastry chef, although their jobs did not involve a promotional ladder equivalent to that of the chefs. None of the managerial employees did management work alone – such work was only a small part of their daily employment.

Closely related to the issue of skill is pay: hotel owners were willing to pay higher wages for those employees whose labour was defined as more skilled and more pivotal to the efficient running of the hotel. These 'core' employees often received a higher wage at the expense of the less skilled and more replaceable general body of employees. In other words, hotel owners were willing to invest money in the former group by saving money (through paying low wages) through the latter group. A certain dualism could be said to have been operating here, but it was a dynamic relationship: the high wages of the 'core', mostly male, group were dependent upon the low wages of the main group of employees, who were mostly women. The two groups were thus related to each other and were not two separate, independent yet coexisting groups of employees: the strong labour market position of the mostly male former group was dependent upon the weak labour market position of the latter group.

It should be noted that when referring to 'high wages' within the Aberystwyth hotel trade in 1985, this term is a relative one. In fact the highest wage I discovered was merely average in terms of British national wage scales. Amongst Aberystwyth hotel employees the average *hourly* rate of pay for full-time employees was £1.49 (table 7.6). This fell just below the recommended

TABLE 7.6

Hourly rates of pay for hotel employees by sex, job category and age

Women		Men	
Hourly pay	**Age**	**Hourly pay**	**Age**
		£2.50 Head chef	C
£2.00 Receptionist	B	£2.00 Head chef	C
		£2.00 Chef	C
£1.87 General	B		
£1.86 Pastry chef	A		
		£1.82 Kitchen porter	B
£1.67 Chambermaid	F		
£1.60 Receptionist	A		
£1.58 General	A		
£1.58 Cook	B		
£1.50 Waitress	B	£1.50 Waiter	A
£1.50 Waitress	B		
£1.50 Chambermaid	B		
£1.50 General	D		
£1.50 Chambermaid	D		
£1.48 Chambermaid	D		
£1.45 Chambermaid	B	£1.45 Kitchen porter	B
£1.33 Dishwasher	D		
£1.31 Chambermaid	D	£1.31 Assistant chef	A
£1.31 Waitress	E		
		£1.26 Assistant chef	B
		£1.25 Waiter	A
£1.23 Chambermaid	A		
£1.12 Waitress	A		
£1.11 Waitress	A		
£1.05 Waitress	A	£1.00 Waiter	A
£1.00 Waitress	A	£1.00 Kitchen porter	C
Total number: 22		Total number: 11	

Age:	A	= under 20	B	= 20–29
	C	= 30–39	D	= 40–49
	E	= 50–59	F	= 60 +

minimum Wage Council rate for service workers aged 18 and over. Female employees experienced lower rates of pay than male employees on the whole: the average hourly rate of pay for a woman was £1.39, whereas for men it was £1.55. This reflects the greater proportion of men who worked in skilled jobs.

If we take the directly comparable job categories of chefing/cooking and waitressing/waitering, we see that male chefs were paid significantly more than female chefs/cooks with the former group earning an average of £2.19 per hour and the latter group earning an average of £1.72 per hour. In this case, therefore, gender was used as a criterion to pay different wage rates as opposed to notions of skill. Waitresses and waiters, however, who worked in 'unskilled' jobs, received almost equal rates of pay with the former group earning £1.23 per hour and the latter £1.25 per hour. Age was a more significant factor than gender at the lower end of the labour market amongst 'unskilled', low-paid employees.

If table 7.6 is examined it becomes evident there existed a polarization in the hotel labour force between a small group of employees who were relatively well paid and defined as 'skilled' and a small, very low-paid group of employees who were defined as 'unskilled'. These patterns arose within the female *and* male workforces. Thus, although it can be said that a greater proportion of women than men were less skilled and less well paid, there existed a division in terms of skill and pay levels *within* each gender group.

Therefore it would be inaccurate to describe the hotel labour market as operating along strictly dualistic lines with women constituting a disadvantaged, 'peripheral' group and men constituting an advantaged 'core' group. Such patterns are better described as a tendency within the labour market as opposed to a strict division.

The complexity of the picture is added to when it is noted that although the most skilled received the highest pay, and the lowest paid were the least skilled, these two groups were in fact joined by a continuum of income and skill levels. Thus to introduce the notion of a sharp cut-off point somewhere along this continuum in fact falsifies the picture.

Age and skill were two factors which at times equalled gender in importance in positioning an employee in a strong or weak labour market position in hotel work. Thus, amongst the female employees the six lower-paid, unskilled employees were all under 20 years old with two being under 15 and a further two being aged between 16 and 17. Where youth and low skill-levels converge, pay tends to be very low. This pattern did not emerge amongst the male employees, although it should be remembered that, given the small numbers interviewed, it is less easy to provide a clear picture.

Lastly, the issue of seasonal work and part-time work was relevant to the make-up of pay levels in that none of the skilled and higher-paid employees – female or male – worked either on a seasonal or part-time basis. Additionally, the women employed in the summer season were divided amongst themselves along the lines of age with the women under 20 being paid less.

The criteria of age, seasonal status and hours worked in the day and/or night serve to reaffirm what I have already argued – that general patterns can be drawn at the top end of the workforce in terms of hourly pay (especially amongst women) but that there remains the 'grey area' of mostly female employees who were unskilled but achieved rates of pay ranging from fairly low to fairly high. These employees constituted the main body of hotel labourers and their pay levels did not seem to be linked to age, temporary status or part-time status in any clear-cut way. They provided the largest social group seeking employment in the hotels and were neither privileged in terms of skill nor disadvantaged in terms of age or skill.

Three employees – a chambermaid, a general worker and a kitchen porter – were notable in that their levels of pay seemed disproportionately high when compared to their co-workers doing similar jobs. Their position in terms of pay was in fact due to relatively strong labour market positions in that they were better trained, had more experience and were friends of their employers.

In the preceding discussion I have omitted one group of female employees who were a vital, though highly 'peripheralized', sector of the labour market: namely, casual employees. These employees constituted the other main group of married women employed in the hotels. Owing to the extreme *ad hoc* organization of their labour, however, I managed to talk to only a handful of such women. They were all married with young children; paid very low rates of pay; and were for the most part brought in to cover sudden increases in demand for hotel facilities: thus they worked as waitresses for private functions or bar workers during discos. I do not intend to provide any detailed analysis of their labour market position – however, their presence does need to be acknowledged as an important part of the female hotel workforce.

CONCLUSION

The great majority of employees working in Aberystwyth hotels in 1985 were women. For the most part they experienced poor working conditions with casualized, insecure forms of work practice and the concomitant features of few legal rights and high turnover rates. In addition, the work they carried out in the hotels tended to be defined as unskilled and low paid.

Given the prevailing poor conditions, the decision of these women to seek employment in the hotels might have taken the form of 'realistic choice' in a local labour market where women were already crowded into the low-paid, service sector of the economy: for the most part they had few alternative sources of employment. The vast majority of women in fact stated that they would prefer to work for higher wages or that they just had to 'make do'. In short, the majority of the women were working in the hotels owing to economic necessity – it would be difficult to discover any other motive given the repetitive and menial nature of the jobs they carried out.

Within the hotel trade it is possible to describe women as disadvantaged as compared to male employees at an aggregate level. They were divided, as against the male labour market, in two general respects: a far greater proportion of women were constructed into less skilled, menial jobs than men and, as a result of that, women found themselves in jobs where their average hourly income was lower than that of men. From this it would seem that the hotel labour market was simply divided into two sectors along gender lines.

However, I would suggest that such notions of dualistic divisions in the labour market are invalid and do not provide much in the way of analytical insight: labour market structures are more complex than such models would allow.

The hotel labour market constituted a complex and diverse set of social structures and relations which are irreducible to simplistic dualistic divisions. However, to describe the labour market as segmented, thereby identifying more than two discrete labour market structures of closure, would take us no nearer to understanding or accurately describing the hotel labour market. Segmented labour market theories describe a labour market which is fairly static and clearly delineated with discrete social groups operating in discrete labour markets. The labour market situation I discovered in the Aberystwyth hotels was more dynamic and less clear-cut than these theories would allow. Thus, following on from the arguments put forward by Brown, Day and others, it was difficult to identify definite cut-off points where one sector ended and another began – it would be more accurate to describe the differences between employees as lying along a continuum. Even if it were possible accurately to pin down labour market segments, this would tell us nothing about the dynamic or historical construction of those segments: in other words, it would not provide an analysis of *why* certain groups of employees got certain types of jobs.

There remain two points to be raised. I have restricted myself in this article to examining women employed in hotels at the level of the labour market, and shown that at this level dualistic/segmented labour market theories are inadequate both as descriptive categories and analytical models. However, in order to understand fully the position of women, it would be necessary to examine the relationship between their economic and work role in the family household and their role in paid production. To carry this out would require looking in detail at the family-household position of the women working in hotels – in other words what they bring to the labour market in terms of recognized skills, training and education, and so on; the demands of domestic labour and the constraints this places on the time available to them to seek paid labour; and their economic position in the family-household.

Additionally, dual/segmented labour market theories are unable to explain *why* the hotel labour force was sex-typed as 'female': more specifically, why the hotel industry consisted of jobs which were mostly seen by employers and female and male employees as 'women's work'. Existing alongside these 'feminine' jobs were 'male' jobs such as chefing and portering. I encountered three women who had taken on such typically male jobs in the pastry chef, the cook and the woman who worked as a kitchen porter amongst other jobs. These women were the exception to the rule. There was no cross-over of men into female-stereotyped jobs. I would argue that these gender divisions were amongst the strongest in the hotel labour market, despite the few cross-over examples. Thus, the fact of being female placed a woman in a hotel labour market which was horizontally divided along gender lines. In order to address these fundamental issues it would be necessary to look at the historical construction of the hotel industry and the occupations within it, and particularly the three-way struggle between employers, female and male employees over access to certain jobs and definitions of skill.

REFERENCES

Atkinson, J. (1984) *Manning for Uncertainty: Some Emerging U.K. Work Patterns*, Institute for Manpower Studies, University of Sussex.

Barron, R.D. and Norris, G.M. (1976) 'Sexual Divisions and the Dual Labour Market', in Sheila Allen and Diana Leonard (eds), *Dependence and Exploitation in Work and Marriage*, London, Longmans.

Beechey, V. (1986) 'Women's Employment in Contemporary Britain', in V. Beechey and E. Whitelegg (eds), *Women in Britain Today*, Milton Keynes, Open University.

Beechey, V. and Perkins,T. (1987) *A Matter of Hours: Women, Part-time Work and the Labour Market*. Cambridge, Polity Press.

Brown, R.K. (1985) 'Attitudes to Work, Occupational Identity and Industrial Change' in B. Roberts, R. Finnegan, and D. Gallie (eds), *New Approaches to Economic Life...*,ESRC, Manchester University Press.

Bujra, J. (1987) 'Men at Work in the Tanzanian Home: How did they ever Learn?' paper given to 'Women, Colonialism and Commonwealth Societies' Seminar, University of London, Institute of Commonwealth Studies.

Day, G. (1981) 'Introduction' to G. Day et al. (eds) *Diversity and Decomposition in the Labour Market*, Aldershot, Gower.

Hakim, C. (1979) *Occupational Segregation: A Comparative Study of the Degree and Pattern of the Differentiation Between Men and Women's Work...*, London, Department of Employment Research Paper.

Pahl, R.E. (1984) *Divisions of Labour*, Oxford, Basil Blackwell.

Rees, T.L. (1988) 'Changing Patterns of Women's Work in Wales: Some Myths Explored', *Contemporary Wales*, 2.

Walby, S. (1983) *Gender and Unemployment: Patriarchal and Capitalist Relations...*, PhD thesis, University of Essex.

8. COLLIERY CLOSURES AND PRODUCTIVITY GAINS IN THE SOUTH WALES COALFIELD 1983/84–1989/90

L. Mainwaring and V.J. Wass

INTRODUCTION

Deep-mine coal production is now all but extinct in South Wales, and it may seen odd that so much attention is still being paid to what is only a very minor part of the Welsh economy. Nevertheless, the dispute of 1984–5 and its aftermath had a profound social and economic impact on the valley communities of South Wales, the consequences of which will be felt for decades to come. The euthanasia of the industry and the motivation behind it therefore deserve close scrutiny. In a previous paper in *Contemporary Wales* (Wass and Mainwaring, 1989) we discussed these social and economic effects in some depth.[1] The purpose of this note is to update some results from that paper concerning the impact of the post-strike colliery closure programme on the overall productivity performance for the South Wales Area. The availability of two years' additional data, relating to colliery operating results, together with the virtual demise of the industry, allows us to put the post-strike strategy of British Coal (BC) into clearer perspective.

BC's justification for the closure programme was based almost entirely on the grounds of profitability. South Wales as a whole was unprofitable, on average losing £32.8 million per annum between 1979/80 and 1983/4, and it was anticipated that the closure of the least efficient capacity would raise average productivity and lead the industry towards solvency.[2] In fact, average coalfield output per manshift (OMS) had risen from a pre-strike level of 1.57 to 2.30 tonnes by March 1988, some 80 per cent (see table 8.1). Using colliery operating results, employment, production and productivity, for 1983/84 and the three years from March 1985, we estimated the direct contribution of colliery closures to the improvement in average coalfield productivity. We also predicted that, because: (1) returning miners would attempt to make up for earnings lost during the strike; (2) the productivity gains from closure would diminish as the least efficient collieries were taken out; and, (3) management would be anxious to meet production targets, productivity gains on this scale

TABLE 8.1
Trends in coal production in South Wales 1983/4–1990/1

Year	Output[a] (million tonnes)	Employment[b] (thousands)	Output per man shift[c] (tonnes)	Collieries[d]
1983/4	6.6 (7.3)	20.2 (10.5)	1.57 (64.6)	28
1984/5*	0.3 (1.1)	19.3 (11.0)	0.39 (18.8)	28
1985/6	6.6 (7.5)	13.4 (8.7)	1.87 (68.8)	17
1986/7	6.5 (7.4)	10.2 (8.1)	2.47 (75.1)	14
1987/8	5.0 (6.1)	7.5 (7.2)	2.30 (63.5)	11
1988/9	5.0 (4.8)	5.5 (5.2)	2.88 (70.0)	9
1989/90	3.5 (4.6)	3.7 (4.4)	3.04 (70.4)	6
1990/1**	3.2 (4.4)	1.9 (3.3)	5.00 (106.4)	4

Source: NCB *Report and Accounts*, various editions.

[a] Output is from NCB deep mines, excludes open cast and private licensed mines, but includes capital and tip coal. Figures in parentheses show South Wales output as a percentage of UK output.

[b] Employment is measured at the end of the financial year and includes manpower at closed collieries. Figures in parentheses show South Wales employment as a percentage of UK employment.

[c] Output per manshift is an overall figure for all employees and includes production from closed collieries. Figures in parentheses show South Wales OMS as a percentage of UK OMS.

[d] Number of collieries is measured at the end of the financial year.

* Figures affected by strike.

** See remarks in note 4.

would prove unsustainable over the longer term. With information relating to operating results at the individual colliery level for 1988/9 and 1989/90, we are able to analyse later efficiency gains in coal production and to test our prediction that the magnitude of productivity growth in the immediate post-strike years was a short-term phenomenon.

OUTPUT, EMPLOYMENT AND PRODUCTIVITY: 1983/4–1990/1

In the year following the end of the 1984–5 coal strike, the South Wales coalfield suffered a rapid series of closures, 11 collieries in all. This contraction has continued, and by April 1991 only four collieries remained.[3] The data reported in table 8.1 show that between 1983/84 and 1990/91 employment in coal in South Wales has declined by 90.6 per cent, and 18,300 jobs have been lost. Output has declined from 6.6 million tonnes to 3.2 million tonnes over this period. Contraction in South Wales has exceeded the GB average. The purpose of the programme of rationalization was to raise average coalfield productivity, and indeed OMS had risen from 1.5 tonnes in 1983/84 to 3.04 tonnes in 1989/90.[4] However, the productivity gains were concentrated in the first four years.

Following our previous analysis, three aspects of productivity improvement are distinguished, and an attempt is made through 'shift share' analysis to quantify the contribution of each to annual productivity gains in the post-strike period to 1990.[5]

Average coalfield productivity may be affected in three ways: through the closure of some pits, through the contraction or expansion of activity in surviving pits with differing productivities, and through actual on-site increases in efficiency. It might be supposed that BC would close the most inefficient pits, reallocate manpower from less to more efficient pits, and attempt to induce pit-by-pit improvements to productivity. Even assuming that this was the intention, it does not follow that the strategy would be successful nor, therefore, that each of these components will necessarily be positive over any period.

The problem for analysis is to disentangle the contribution of the three components to overall productivity change. In order, first, to isolate the effect of *closures* on average productivity over any period a hypothetical figure is estimated for what average productivity would have been if only those pits surviving to the end of the period had been operating at their productivity levels at the beginning of the period. Secondly, as we have seen, the *reallocation of manpower* from low-productivity surviving pits to high-productivity pits raises average productivity even if the level in the individual pits remains constant. This effect is estimated by deriving a hypothetical figure calculated by applying start-of-period productivities to end-of-period man-power levels. Thirdly, the effects of *within-pit improvements* are determined by applying the new productivity levels of surviving pits to their initial manpower levels. The three sums derived from these calculations account fully for the overall average productivity increase.

This exercise has been carried out for the period between the financial years 1983/4 and 1989/90 and for two sub-periods, 1983/4–1986/7, which can be described as the immediate strike aftermath, and 1986/7–1989/90. The results are reported in table 8.2. For the period as a whole average productivity rose by a remarkable 52.7 per cent. This gain did not, however, occur at an even pace over the period, but was concentrated entirely in the first sub-period. In the second sub-period productivity actually fell, albeit marginally.[6] (This is not true of the individual components of productivity change in this sub-period, some of which therefore contributed negatively and some positively.) During the whole period, 22 of the original 27 collieries were closed, so it is hardly surprising to find, taking the entire six-year span, that closures were the prime cause of productivity gain: 80.5 per cent, to be precise.[7] However,

TABLE 8.2
Sources of productivity change 1983/4–1989/90

	1983/4–86/7		1986/7–89/90		1983/4–89/90[a]	
	A	B	A	B	A	B
Percentage increase in						
productivity over period due to:	A	B	A	B	A	B
Closures	19.76	(37.8)	−2.41	(−2773.8)	42.39	(80.5)
Manpower reallocation	0.97	(1.8)	0.86	(986.2)	−6.01	(−11.4)
Within-pit improvements	32.05	(60.7)	1.47	(1687.8)	16.27	(30.9)
Total[b]	52.79		−0.09		52.65	
No. of closures	13		9		22	

A   Percentage growth in productivity due to each source
B   Percentage contribution of each source to total sub-period productivity growth.
[a]   The estimates in column 3 (1983/4–1989/90) do not represent the cumulated total of estimates in the two
      sub-periods (columns 1 and 2). The reason for this is explained in note 8.
[b]   These figures for productivity change are derived from the coalfield average output weighted OMS
      estimates which are not the same as the coalfield average (unweighted) OMS figures reported in table 1.

examination of the sub-periods gives rather more insight into the contribution of closures.[8]

What is notable is that closures account for less than 40 per cent of the gain in the first sub-period and actually had a negative contribution in the second (for which the large percentage share is not particularly meaningful, given the magnitude of the total change). Most of the gains in sub-period 1 came from within-pit improvements, but these, too, collapsed in absolute terms in the following sub-period. Generally speaking, manpower reallocations were the weakest of the three sources, possibly because the desire to move on the part of miners was small, given the general decline in the industry (Thomas, 1991).

The main question is what underlay the within-pit improvements. If they were the result of physical investments then, given the gestation lags, such investments must have been in the pipeline at about the time of the strike. Yet this suggests either that BC was banking on a remarkably quick pay-off period (for by April 1991, 23 out of the 27 post-strike pits had closed), or that there was something wildly inconsistent in BC's planning, for it makes no sense to commit large investments to short-life projects.

It could, of course, be that BC simply had no clear medium/long-term plan for the industry, but other explanations are possible and more plausible. One is that immediately after the strike BC pursued an opportunistic policy of intensifying work practices by exercising greater discipline over a broken and humiliated workforce. In addition, they appear to have followed a strategy of concentrating on 'easy pickings' by rapidly abandoning many less productive seams. If these explanations are valid, they mean that BC was concerned to get as much out of the coalfield as quickly as possible and then leave it to its inevitable fate. The work intensity of the immediate post-strike period could not be sustained for long, and any attempt to do so would necessarily lead to increasing demoralization. That morale did fall is supported by anecdotal evidence. The strategy of easy pickings, unsupported by adequate capital investment, could only lead to a cumulative pattern of decline, each pit being quickly worked for what it would readily yield, then closed.

These explanations, though tentative, are clearly consistent with the collapse of within-pit productivity gains between the two sub-periods. They would also help explain why closures had such a small (in fact, negative) impact on total productivity gains in the second sub-period. For at the beginning of that sub-period some of the pits which were subsequently closed would have had high but unsustainable productivity levels. Thus, so far as one can tell over such a short time-span, this process of induced cumulative decline and closure appears to be consistent with the facts. If such a strategy is still being pursued then it is only a matter of time (a short time) before the few remaining pits disappear.

CONCLUSION

In October 1991, the media reported results of a study commissioned by the Energy Secretary and undertaken by the government's merchant banker, N.M. Rothschild. The study recommended the closure by 1994 of all but 14 of the (then) 61 pits operated by BC throughout the UK and the loss of 33,000 jobs. It was said (see, for example, *The Guardian*, 8 October 1991) that BC was 'closely involved' in the selection process. Moreover, of those pits chosen for survival, half had 'relatively short-term reserves and may not be producing in ten years' time'. Under the proposals, the South Wales coalfield would be completely eliminated. Provisions included in the new Coal Industry Act, introduced to Parliament on 1 November 1991, raise the grant available to BC for restructuring and redundancy compensation by £1.5 billion to £3 billion for the period 1993 to 1996, and would appear to confirm the government's intention to act upon the Rothschild recommendations. Whether, in fact, they are successful or whether the recommendations are watered down under political pressure, it seems that BC has been willing to co-operate with the government to bring about its own demise. Indeed, even on its own pre-Rothschild plans, more than 20 pits were to go by early 1993 (*The Guardian*, 7 October 1991).

These recently announced plans help us to understand more clearly the changes which have been analysed in this note. Our results are consistent with what appears to have been a 'smash and grab' approach by BC in South Wales. With the 1984/5 strike resolving decisively in favour of the Coal Board and the government, the conditions were perfect for a conclusive assault on a powerful Area union and for the writing-off of assets which were insufficiently attractive to private buyers wanting quick and relatively riskless returns. It would not, perhaps, be fanciful to speculate that the dismemberment of the South Wales coal industry was something of a 'trial run' for the bigger task on which BC and the government are about to embark. Their experience has shown how rapidly a process of contraction can be prosecuted, with minimal effective opposition from a workforce once noted for its strength and determination.

NOTES

1   See also Wass (1988) and Thomas (1991).
2   There is a close relationship between financial performance (profitability) and labour productivity (output per man shift). Labour productivity is a major determinant of operating costs and therefore of profitability in the short-run.
3   With the closure of Penallta on 31 October 1991, only three collieries now remain, Betws, Taff Merthyr and Tower, employing less than one 1,000 miners.
4   The reported OMS figure for 1990/1 of 5.50 tonnes (implying an annual increase of 64 per cent) is completely out of line with historical trends. It is impossible to explain it solely in terms of the small numbers of pits surviving but it may have something to do with the extensive use of subcontract labour (which does not appear in the denominator of the OMS estimate) after 1989/90. Whatever the explanation, readers are advised to treat this figure with extreme caution.
5   Data at the colliery level are available only up until 1989/90
6   The reported figures are output-weighted averages. Employment-weighted averages differ in detail but convey essentially the same story. The main difference is that overall productivity grew by 50 per cent in the first sub-period and by 9 per cent in the second.
7   Lewis Merthyr colliery closed just after the strike, but work had ceased before the strike and therefore colliery operating results for only 27 collieries were used in the shift-share analysis.
8   It should be noted that, by the nature of the exercise, calculations for the sub-periods involve different bases and base-weights. Thus it does not follow that the effects for the whole period can be obtained by cumulating the effects for the two sub-periods. A simple stylized example may clarify the point. Suppose there are three pits, A, B and C employing the same numbers in period O and for as long as they survive thereafter. Pit A closes in period 1, pit B in period 2. The numbers in table 8.3 represent output per man.

TABLE 8.3

Period	A	B	C
0	10	20	30
1	–	25	30
2	–	–	30

Consider the nature of the productivity gains (by construction there are no manpower reallocation effects). Between O and 1 there are effects due to closure of low-productivity pit A and improvement within pit B. Between 1 and 2 there is only a closure gain. Equally, between 0 and 2 the entire gain is due to closure. Thus, although the within-pit gain is positive for the first sub-period and zero for the second, its overall contribution is zero, the initial gain being nullified by the closure of pit B. Likewise, sub-period gains from closure fall short of 100 per cent – the proportion of overall gain arising from closure.

REFERENCES

Thomas, M. (1991) 'Colliery Closure and the Miner's Experience of Redundancy', *Contemporary Wales*, 4, pp. 43–66.

Wass, V. (1988) 'Redundancy and Re-employment: Effects and Prospects following Colliery Closure', Coalfield Communities Campaign, Working Papers, vol. 5, pp. 3–21.

Wass, V. and Mainwaring L. (1989) 'Economic and Social Consequences of Rationalisation in the South Wales Coal Industry', *Contemporary Wales*, 3, pp. 161–85.

9. MANAGING CARE: SPECIAL NEEDS HOUSING IN WALES

Ian Shaw, Rodney Bull and Howard Williamson

The housing association world is in ferment. Within that ferment the provision of special needs or supported housing for those people in need of additional care and support, together with a more intensive style of housing management, faces a series of sea changes. Local authority Social Services Departments are midway through the preparation of Social Care Plans which will lead to major changes in the relationship between state and voluntary sector provision, and to significant shifts in the position of the service consumer, each of which are heavy with implication for special needs housing. National Health Service reforms could readily lead to a substantial redrawing of the boundaries between the health and social services. Promised local government reorganization adds a further layer to the change and uncertainty affecting special needs provision of all kinds.

Closer to home, the capital and revenue funding systems for housing associations have radically changed in Wales over the past two years. Allied to a marked gravitation towards quality assurance monitoring and strategic planning initiatives, these changes all take place in the context of a newly distinct policy and funding framework for special and general needs housing provision in Wales, which is still in its infancy.

The 1980s witnessed a continued reaction against traditional large-scale hostel provision, with shared eating, sleeping and living facilities. Following the 1988 Housing Act, Tai Cymru (Housing for Wales) was established in April 1989, taking over the previous role of the London-based Housing Corporation. In parallel, the Welsh Federation of Housing Associations (WFHA) was formed, thus giving distinct identity to Welsh developments in the housing association field that have already been traced in *Contemporary Wales* (Smith and Williams, 1991). Support for special needs developments is also provided through the Special Needs Housing Advisory Service in Wales (SNHAS).

Special needs housing is, as we have noted, housing for people who need additional care and support as well as a home. In order to count as 'special needs housing', schemes in Wales should have a minimum ratio of one staff member to every fifteen residents. In practice the range varies from schemes with no staff on the premises to heavily supported schemes with about four members of staff for each resident. Comparisons with England are difficult, though it is likely that staffing ratios are fairly similar (cf Garside et al., 1990, pp. 94–8; Randolph, 1990, p. 48). Such housing encompasses hostels, group homes and shared housing, but may also include people living in ordinary flats or houses.

Schemes are provided for a range of housing need groups including young single homeless people, offenders, people with learning difficulties, those with problems involving alcohol or drugs, adult single homeless, women at risk of domestic violence, people with a disability, and those with mental health problems. Projects are, by and large directly managed by the owning housing association, or indirectly managed by a voluntary or statutory agency, although other forms of partnership and management also exist.

This wide range of provision is thus part of a complex of interlocking policy, funding and service networks, where *resources* and negotiated, but officially binding, *advice and guidance* are fed down from Tai Cymru to housing associations and, through them, to voluntary, statutory and independent managing agencies.

Moves to raise the quality of provision has led to a number of concerns. Capital costs for developing such schemes are often higher than for ordinary housing, and revenue costs to cover staffing are considerable. In April 1990 Tai Cymru introduced, a year ahead of the Housing Corporation, a new revenue funding system, Special Needs Management Allowance (SNMA), based on a given sum per bedspace, paid up-front, and tiered to allocate a proportionately higher allowance to smaller schemes. This replaced the previous complex and cumbersome Hostel Deficit Grant funding arrangements.

There are several ways in which the Welsh system may prove significantly preferable to the corresponding English one, despite the fact that the early development of the idea owes much to housing associations in England working through the National Federation of Housing Associations. The SNMA levels are more generous than those in England. Also, the negotiations about transitional funding arrangements for longer-established schemes, while the subject of active debate, have not been marked by the rancour which led in England to repeated breaks in the tripartite negotiations between the Department of the Environment, the Housing Corporation and the National

Federation of Housing Associations. The tiering system could also lead to a further emphasis on smaller, more intensively supported schemes in Wales as compared to England.

Yet major issues remain. The new revenue funding system does not cover all revenue costs for providing care and support staffing, and a recent WFHA/ SNHAS report describes the current basis for gaining additional 'topping-up' monies for care and support and management as 'a shambles' (WFHA/ SNHAS, 1991). The Welsh Office and Tai Cymru have both commissioned recent studies of the impact of the new revenue funding on the management of schemes and on residents living in them, and continuing Treasury commitment to funding existing SNMA levels is an underlying preoccupation.

Funding is not, however, the only concern. The welcome rise in housing standards has led to concern whether there has been a resultant fall in the number of bedspaces for the homeless, though recent research for Tai Cymru illustrates how difficult it is to gain a precise figure for bedspace provision (Shaw and Williamson, 1991). A related concern is the increasing anxiety regarding the lack of 'move-on' accommodation for people who have lived in special needs projects (e.g. Garside et al., 1990).

The existence of a distinct Wales policy and service dimension should not be overstated. In various respects the key Welsh actors are mirror-images of their English counterparts, issuing policy and good practice guidance that is a Welsh repackaging of basic development work done elsewhere. The infant Tai Cymru is understandably anxious to flex its muscles, claim the high ground and create its own identity.

Yet the Welsh orbit of debate and practice *is* significant. Smith and Williams (1991) point out how the implications of scale have shaped discussion about Welsh housing policy in general, making it less adversarial and marked more by dialogue. A similar point can be made about special needs housing, and we have already contrasted the relations between Tai Cymru, the Welsh Office and the Welsh Federation of Housing Associations with those between the Department of the Environment, Housing Corporation and National Federation of Housing Associations.

More substantively, the direction of special needs housing in Wales must be understood within the threefold context of the shift towards strategic policy planning, the development of a social care planning approach in the personal social services, and the permeation of ideas about quality assurance in service provision.

The introduction of the *All Wales Strategy for Mental Handicap* (Welsh Office, 1983), with its emphasis on strategic service planning, led in the special needs housing field to a situation of *relatively* well resourced housing schemes for people with learning difficulties. The more recent introduction of strategic planning for mental health services has created the potential for corresponding developments in the mental illness field. Both of these strategies have led to the establishment of planning at a county level.

During 1991 Tai Cymru introduced a shift to district level strategic planning for a diverse spread of single homeless people (Tai Cymru 1991). Hostel provision for offenders has also come under a series of county level local forums, which, since 1988, have been required to produce area accommodation strategies, though the reality of strategic planning is highly variable in this and other fields.

The mental handicap strategy has influenced local authorities in their work on developing social care plans in the context of the new contract cultures within Social Services Departments and the Health Authorities, following the implementation of the NHS and Community Care Act 1990. With the planned implementation of social care plans in 1993, local authorities will be making decisions about purchase of service which will have far-reaching implications for the future development of housing schemes. For example, high-cost, high-care projects may well lose out unless they can convince purseholders of their value and negotiate a partnership with service purchasers.

The emphasis on a planned rather than an incremental approach, and the present stress on consumer involvement in both the 1989 Children Act and social care planning, form a bridge to the growth of performance monitoring and quality assurance in supported housing provision. Inspection and the application of performance expectations – described by a rather jaundiced English Director of Social Services at a recent conference in Wales as the 'checklists and truncheons approach' – are increasingly used as the tools for developing special needs housing in Wales.

Yet quality of service remains an intangible, deceptively meaningful aspiration, and it can readily slide across the border into invasion of privacy. An American consumer has recently sounded the warning that standards

> strain the richness from peoples' lives...They do not get at the heart of the quality issue because they dance around the agony of truly disgraceful masquerades for community programs and suppress the spirit of good ones with lethal threat and excruciating detail. (Bradley and Bersani, 1990)

The policy and service contexts outlined here, raise a series of substantive questions. What kind of service is currently offered within supported housing schemes in Wales? How are principles established and implemented in these schemes? How adequately are the very different housing needs of different groups met within the existing framework of provision? Do performance expectation and quality assurance mechanisms operate within schemes, and if so to what effect? What are the outcomes of special needs housing? And where does such provision actually fit into the wider picture of housing provision and need in Wales?

Evidence relevant to these issues has been obtained through a recent national bilingual evaluation of all supported housing in Wales funded through Tai Cymru (Shaw and Williamson, 1991). The research was carried out in 1991, through a survey of all schemes together with eight qualitative case studies of a range of projects.

Survey information was obtained on 144 schemes in operation on 1 January 1991 (77 per cent response rate), 589 staff employed in those schemes, and 602 people who had left those schemes during 1990. The case studies included 57 interviews with residents, staff, managers and members of local networks. Other supported housing is provided directly through local authorities and voluntary agencies. However, schemes included in this research provide housing of a semi-permanent nature or as preparation for moving into independent living in the community, for people with learning difficulties or mental health problems, offenders, those with addiction problems, young single homeless people leaving local authority care, adult single homeless, women at risk of violence, people with disabilities and several other groups.

SERVICE PATTERNS

Taking the results from this survey and making reasonable estimates for schemes not participating in the research, the number of bedspaces provided in all schemes operated through Tai Cymru at the beginning of 1990 was about 1,450. Some schemes, for example those providing for women at risk of violence, have a very high turnover of people moving through their project in any one year. Others, for example those providing for people with learning difficulties, have a much lower turnover rate.

Following a similar line of reasoning to allow for the minority of projects for which no evidence is available, it seems likely that about 2,000 people moved through Tai Cymru's special needs schemes in 1990, though, with the steady addition of new schemes into management, that figure will need constant updating.

Four hundred and ninety (57 per cent) of the current adult residents in these schemes were men and 276 (43 per cent) women. These figures may be misleading if we conclude that there are more men than women using supported housing schemes. In reality the reverse is the case. Women stay in schemes for shorter periods of time than men. Of the 602 leavers for whom we have information, 327 (58 per cent) were women, and women have a turnover rate more than twice as rapid as that for men, suggesting that not only is the experience of being homeless different for women, but also that their experience of supported housing is different.

The experience of being homeless is different for women than for men, and these figures strongly suggest that women's experience of supported housing is also different.

It is possible that similar conclusions need to be drawn regarding the experience of people from ethnic minorities, in that the rate at which people from ethnic minority backgrounds move through Welsh schemes is twice that for white residents.

It may come as little surprise that, relative to England, there are fewer black and Asian residents in Welsh special needs schemes. They account for only just over 3 per cent of residents (recent figures for English schemes give figures of 16 per cent [Garside et al., 1990, p. 107] and 14 per cent [Randolph, 1990, p. 59]). Almost nine out of ten schemes in the study were accommodating only white residents.

Who works in special needs housing? Staff numbering 589 provided confidential details about themselves. Three-quarters are women, and one in seven is Welsh-speaking. Too little attention has been given to the potential significance of shared language, culture and tradition between Welsh-speaking residents and staff. One woman with learning difficulties had been labelled as having virtually no speech for several years until moving into a project with Welsh-speaking staff, where her capacity to relate to people who shared her own language was immediately apparent.

This anecdote incidentally illustrates that information about the numbers of Welsh-speaking residents is not routinely recorded by many housing associations or care agencies.

When asked about their ethnic and cultural origin, an overwhelming 98 per cent (570) of staff describe themselves as white. Just eight said they were black, and one person said s/he was Asian. Given the evidence about the ethnic origins of both residents and leavers, this figure leaves some cause for concern. A recent comparable figure for staff in English schemes suggests that 83 per cent may be white (Randolph, 1990, p. 52).

We have observed already that staffing patterns cover a very wide range. More heavily staffed schemes are not necessarily better-staffed schemes - need

TABLE 9.1
Care and support services given in the previous twenty four hours

	Given in last 24 hours	
	No.	%
Practical/personal care	106	76
Counselling	114	81
Education, skills training	90	64
Budget skills	75	54
Information, advice	67	48
Establishing social/family networks	73	52
Rehabilitation and move-on	49	35
Links to statutory services	72	51
Links to voluntary services	35	25
Total	140	

levels vary and high staffing can induce dependency. However, responses from staff do point towards the conclusion that staffing levels are influenced by a range of factors other than need. In addition, staff training levels are variable and slight. Almost two-fifths mentioned no qualifications at all, and less than one in ten had some kind of social welfare-related qualification.

People move into supported housing schemes with a mix of acute and chronic needs arising from being homeless. What kind of care and support service is given to residents in the projects? A snapshot of care and support given in the twenty-four hours prior to the research shows that each scheme provided on average about five different kinds of care and support in the preceding day. This is a fairly impressive output of provision.

Personal counselling and practical assistance with personal care were given by over three-quarters of the schemes. Two kinds of service were less commonly given. These were advice and assistance about move-on and rehabilitation, and establishing links with voluntary agencies.

We conclude at more than one point that one of the key issues differentiating schemes is the degree of their engagement with rehabilitation as a central or peripheral aim of their project. And, given current preoccupations in Wales with social care planning, the sharply limited extent to which services are engaging residents with the local network of voluntary agencies points up the potential gap between rhetoric and reality in delivering effective social care service packages.

In their efforts to mount care and support programmes, scheme staff were preoccupied with twin clusters of dilemmas in creating satisfying role performances. First, the whole question of 'professionalism' was central to their self-image. This affected their stance regarding the need for group work or counselling skills within their work. Most staff were at best ambiguous, refusing to accept the role of 'social worker'. 'Professional' training was often dismissed as 'too vague and useless', and lacking relevance to the 'real' demands of the job. Their attitude to professionalism also created a chronic sense of tension in their relationships with the wider network of agencies. Staff often felt subject to an inappropriate professional agenda created by outside bodies, while those same outside professionals were likely to criticize staff.

> The staff have tended not to handle the problems properly. This has caused tension – the staff tend to feel that *our* way of dealing with [one type of] clients is so different...and can't see why things have to be so different. We have tried to explain but they did not understand what we're trying to do. (Professional worker within wider network)

This mistrust of professionalism interacted with their daily attempts to cope with the burden of care. Reference was frequently made to the crucial contribution of additional voluntary support which functioned as 'invisible strands of help' sustaining effective care and support for residents. Staff talked of working considerable additional hours or at least 'bending' their working week to accommodate the needs of residents, resulting in a fragile web of support and care, with paid staff and volunteers in an unspoken, uneasy loose liaison of service maintained by frequent strokes from the project leader and personal loyalty to her. With the injection of this extra commitment and time, most schemes 'got by', but were unable to cope easily with unpredictable events. As one staff member put it, 'Things are just about OK (though we could do with more) when everything's ticking along smoothly. But it's no good at all when all hell breaks loose.'

This precarious equilibrium produced damaging results. In the first place, care and support programmes, however structured or informal they were, were subject to a variety of pressures which limited their effectiveness. Programmes shaped by outside 'professionals' or even by scheme managers were subject to *reshaping* by staff according to perceptions of their validity. Even programmes which had the full support of staff were often subverted by competing demands on scheme employees, who are caught in an 'altruistic poverty trap'.

Second, resource limitations produced in many schemes a day-to-day preoccupation with counteracting or mitigating financial shortfalls. Some schemes struck deals (such as in effect 'selling' nomination rights to other providers) in order to ensure greater financial stability. But such deals entailed a trade-off involving some loss of control and independence. Others adopted different strategies, such as stalling move-on to keep bedspaces full, or filtering referrals to accept only non-problematic residents in order to function with minimal staff. Each strategy had its costs, but was considered to be essential to survival.

Special needs housing constitutes a significant resource for people with housing problems in Wales. Varied needs are met by staff offering diversified and often impressive packages of care and support. Operating with highly varying staffing levels, paid workers pilot a course through dilemmas over their role and resources which entails a precarious equilibrium leading to the negotiation of strategies of expediency. Schemes walk a constant tightrope of caring and being careful.

But how do projects, housing associations and managing agencies understand their *aims*? What principles underlie their practice, and how do they attempt to act on these principles?

IMPLEMENTING VALUES?

Widespread policy guidance exists within the housing association movement on the principles which should govern special needs housing provision. Values are attached to integrating residents into the community, allowing resident involvement and choice, ensuring quality of life, operating an equal opportunity policy, privacy, confidentiality, and so on.

However, this advice is marked by three limitations. First, there is very limited consensus or explicit discussion on the extent to which these principles are believed to have similar *operational* implications for different housing need groups. To take just one example, integration into the community will mean something very different for a permanent housing project providing for people with learning difficulties in contrast with a refuge for women at risk of violence. The more that operational values diverge, the more room exists for debate over what counts as a principled action in any given situation. Second, and arising from this point, virtually nothing has been known about the impact of this guidance on the beliefs and practices of staff, residents and others in the immediate networks of individual people living in projects.

The third problem is that unresolved tensions do exist in guidance on good practice in special needs housing. For instance, it was pointed out to us more than once that conformity to fire regulations, through the provision of fire doors for example, made a completely 'home-like' atmosphere impossible.

Also principles of care and support were sometimes felt to conflict with principles of resident choice.

The exercise of discretion thus becomes a key feature of behaviour by staff, residents and managers. It seems reasonable to assume that associations, projects and managing partners engage in a variety of day-to-day strategies to accommodate the demands of prescriptive and discretionary guidance from Housing for Wales, the Welsh Federation of Housing Associations and others who hold the purse-strings. Inevitably these practices will include aspects which may be seen as forms of 'rule-breaking'. We do not mean to suggest that rule-breaking of this kind necessarily involves poor practice. Formal and informal rules are interpreted within the resources and capacities of those expected to observe them.

Rule-breaking will be damaging in some cases, while in other cases rule-*keeping* may be seen as having a negative effect on standards of good practice. In a world of limited resources, rule-breaking in one area may be precipitated by rule-keeping in another area.

To assess staff views about discretion in implementing guidance about principles of care, staff in this study were presented with a list of operational statements of the five general values of integration, choice, quality of life, equal opportunity and privacy. For example, one operational translation of privacy was, 'Clear agreement should exist on circumstances in which staff may have access to residents' rooms', and commitment to involvement and choice might invite assent to the statement that 'residents should have a say in who moves into their house.' Staff were asked to say how strongly they *agreed* with this list of statements, and how well they had *implemented* them.

With a few significant exceptions, staff said they were in overall agreement with these statements. They were also confident that they had been at least reasonably effective in implementing all five principles of care. Indeed, one initially curious feature of this study was the sanguine outlook of staff on the ease with which such principles can be implemented. Thus, almost four out of five schemes did not think that it was *difficult* to enact an equal opportunities policy, and only one in 20 schemes thought they had been remiss in implementing such a policy. Part of the explanation may be that 'equal opportunity' is interpreted more in terms of consistent and fair treatment of individual residents rather than broad strategies concerning specified categories of people.

But this is not the whole explanation. One hundred and five (73 per cent) schemes did not have a written equal opportunity statement, yet of these only five thought they were doing fairly badly or very badly in implementing equal opportunities in their scheme. An analogous point can be made about grievance procedures for residents. Seventy-five projects did not have a written statement on grievance procedures to give to residents coming into their scheme. Yet of these schemes only two expressed any doubt when asked whether clear grievance procedures should exist for residents. Such apparent inconsistencies may of course be nothing less than contradictory practice – we see no reason to assume that the world of special needs housing is exempt from charges of inconsistency or complacency. Yet we also found recurring evidence from the case studies suggesting a widespread mistrust of written documents and central guidance.

MEETING DIFFERENT NEEDS

The range of views about implementing *values* of good practice is related to the still more divergent *housing needs* of people provided for through supported housing programmes.

Thus, schemes providing for people with learning difficulties appear to entertain far *fewer* doubts about the various ways of acting on operational principles than did most other schemes. Women's aid schemes, providing for women at risk of domestic violence, expressed considerably *greater* doubt about the appropriateness of such guidance. Schemes providing for young single homeless people expressed *more* doubts about principles of integration and resident involvement, but far *less* doubt about implementing ideas of privacy.

Again, it is not our view that schemes with doubts are deviants which need to be brought into line. It may be that policy makers need to give more appropriate guidance on how to operationalize principles. One possible way to make sense of these findings may be that guidance on housing management within Tai Cymru may have been shaped extensively by developments within the field of learning difficulties, and that this in itself explains the relative comfort felt by these schemes in applying such principles.

Thinking about social care planning in local authorities and the Welsh Office is influenced to a considerable degree by the model of the *All Wales Strategy for Mental Handicap*. An emerging conclusion from the kind of data presented here is that there needs to be an appropriate pluralism of interpretation and application of such models and frameworks within a healthy special needs housing movement.

This conclusion is reinforced by strong evidence that the actual content of care and support programmes varies significantly from one housing need group to another, and once again highlights the extent to which women's aid,

TABLE 9.2
Selected patterns of care and support for women's aid, learning difficulty and young single homeless schemes

Care and support	Needs groups	Given in last 24 hours		Total schemes
		No.	%	No.
Practical assistance	Women's aid	2	18	11
	All schemes	106	76	140
Rehabilitation	Learning difficulty	6	9	69
	Womens aid	11	100	11
	Young single homeless	7	70	10
	All schemes	49	35	140
Information and advice	Learning difficulty	15	22	69
	Young single homeless	9	90	10
	All schemes	62	44	140

learning difficulty and young single homeless schemes depart from the pattern for schemes as a whole.

Our emphasis upon women's aid, learning difficulty and young single homeless schemes is not arbitrary. Together they represent the three most important kinds of provision in Wales. Learning difficulty schemes account for almost a half of all schemes in this study, and women's aid and young single homeless schemes together contribute well over 50 per cent of all people moving out of schemes and on to the housing market in Wales.

Table 9.2 shows that women's aid schemes are less likely to offer practical assistance with personal care and more likely to offer advice and assistance with move-on and rehabilitation. Young single homeless schemes provide more assistance with move-on and rehabilitation, and also more advice on welfare benefits and related matters. Learning difficulty schemes are less likely to provide care and support in relation to rehabilitation, and also less likely to give advice and information on welfare benefits.

These differences in the patterns of intervention appear to mirror clear differences in views about the aims of schemes, and the extent to which housing is seen as permanent or temporary. The picture is far from straightforward however. Some schemes, especially those providing for young single homeless, argue that residents have few care and support needs beyond the presenting one of homelessness (or at least no greater needs than their peers who are not homeless). Also, 43 (62 per cent) of the learning difficulty schemes *do* provide help with rehabilitation *at some time*. Ambiguities of this kind provoke recurrent tensions regarding the aims of any given project, and a chronic lack of agreement as to what counts as 'success'. Thus in one project examples of residents moving out into the community were quoted by a staff member as instances of where the project had succeeded, whereas a committee member described success as 'to see someone settled, and that they don't want to move'.

This diversity of views and practices about the care and support needs of residents resulted in very little clarity or consensus between projects over what exactly constituted 'care and support'. There appeared to be a broad menu of options, from which staff selected according to their judgements of residents' needs and residents' receptivity to different forms of intervention. Whatever the particular choice made, it was imbued with inevitable tensions. Perhaps the fundamental issue mentioned most frequently by respondents was that planned programmes of care and support risk conflicting with principles of resident choice. All such dilemmas were the product of an overriding endeavour to strike a balance between 'crowding' and 'neglecting' residents. Staff often spoke of attempting to promote independence whilst not compounding isolation.

This may result in the situation encountered in a case study where staff said that residents have the right to go out of the building without staff permission, whereas residents in the same scheme clearly regarded it as a 'rule' of the project that permission is always necessary. Staff generally expected residents to say where they were going. This is the critical point: what staff saw as responsible care, residents perceived as regulation.

Evidence of this kind points to the danger of assuming that general policies and practices can be applied in a similar way across all housing need groups. Attempts to do so are likely to lead to a straitjacket that will either constrict projects, or fracture and thus militate against a real consensus of policy in the world of special needs housing. Discordant models of what constitutes 'success' will also lead to problems in estimating the outcomes of these programmes.

EFFECTIVE OUTCOMES?

A major weakness of recent studies of special needs housing has been the almost total neglect of any attempt to appraise its effectiveness (e.g. Garside et al., 1990; Randolph, 1990). Until it *is* addressed, attempts to extol any virtues of supported housing projects will remain like the sound of one hand clapping.

Not that any easy strategy suggests itself. While there has been a growth of concern about quality assurance, targets and monitoring, the underlying questions of what is meant by 'effectiveness' and whether it can be measured have hitherto scarcely been addressed in the special needs housing field. We have implied already that key stakeholders will hold a variety of constructs of 'success'. These are unlikely to be entirely compatible from one person to another, or even within the account given by one particular person. This is partly because explanations of success or failure are situated accounts given to audiences, and serving functions of demonstrating to that audience the value of work done.

Research of this kind has still to be started. For the present it is possible to recognize that the values and disvalues of special needs housing lie partly in the 'product' of provision, and partly in the 'process'. Some kind of product measure is needed – are people better off in some identifiable way on leaving schemes than they were when they first moved in?

Some kind of 'process' measure is also needed – is the housing being offered to the appropriate target group, and is it of good quality? Thus, moving residents on to independent living in the community is not an official policy for schemes providing for people with learning difficulties, nor for some schemes providing for those with mental health problems. Such schemes need to be measured in terms of 'input' (for example, how do levels of housing and care and support compare with what was received prior to admission?) and 'process' (the quality of life experience of the residents). The picture is not as simple as this suggests, however, in that a significant number of people *do* leave 'permanent' housing schemes, and whatever the official policy, there is an abiding ambiguity and frequent contradiction about grassroots move-on policy and practice in individual schemes.

People responsible for the day-to-day management of schemes expressed considerable confidence about the quality of service provided by them. For example, when asked whether standards of design, care and support and housing management had declined or improved during the previous year, a significant proportion asserted that an improvement had taken place, and comparatively few detected a decline. Thus, two-thirds of schemes thought that standards of care and support had improved over the previous twelve months.

A similar kind of confidence was evident when staff were asked to judge their effectiveness in meeting the needs of their residents. Over 90 per cent of schemes judged themselves more or less effective in meeting the personal needs of their residents. More than three-quarters conveyed a similar confidence

TABLE 9.3
Changes in needs of residents during time in housing scheme

	Greater than	Same as	Less than	Not known	Total
		when admitted to the scheme			
Number	118	202	173	108	601
Percentage	24	41	35	–	100

regarding their impact on residents' needs in society, and four-fifths when assessing the quality of their work in meeting people's accommodation needs.

However, a less up-beat picture emerged when staff were asked to judge the impact of their scheme on the needs of individual residents who had moved through the projects during the previous twelve months.

In more than a third of cases the needs of individuals were judged to be less at the point of leaving than they were at entry. Given the intractable nature of the problems that bring many people into the supported housing sector, this achievement is not to be underestimated. However, there remain over a fifth of the scheme users whose needs were judged to be actually *worse* at the point of leaving than they were when they entered the project, and two-fifths where their needs are assessed to be much the same as at the point of entry. Given that people come to special needs projects with fairly acute and chronic needs, this figure illustrates the major task facing people working in the supported housing field.

Is it possible to draw any conclusions about the factors which were likely to contribute to identifiable impacts on needs levels? To some degree, yes. The research points towards an explanation that suggests that certain schemes do better than others. In other words, analysis yielded no evidence to support the view that age, gender, ethnic background or disability were related to outcome. Rather than such *individual* differences, 'success' was associated with three key *structural* factors. More 'successful' schemes tended to be those where levels of care and support were judged to have improved, where residents were not housed in traditional hostels with shared sleeping, cooking and bathroom facilities, and where standards of design and fabric were estimated to have advanced. Each of these factors is open to policy targets, although there was no evidence that the smaller projects, preferred by Housing for Wales, with higher than average levels of staffing, and the top levels of revenue funding under the new Special Needs Management Allowance, were any more effective in impacting on need levels than slightly larger schemes.

A considerable amount of work remains to be carried out on setting sensitive, flexible, coherent measures of effectiveness in this field. Work done elsewhere in the field of residential and hospital care has shown that criteria of 'success' and 'failure' are different between medical staff, social work staff, residents and their carers (Smith and Cantley, 1984). This pluralist picture of evaluation is likely to apply to special needs housing. Residents, funders, managing agencies, professionals in the housing and needs networks, voluntary committee members and project staff are all likely to operate varying criteria. However, rather than justify a relativist let-out, where 'anything goes', this points up the need for a quality assurance model that reflects a genuine consumer involvement.

THE WIDER NETWORK

Judgements about the value of services provided through special needs housing must be set in the context of wider housing and service networks occupied by the schemes. Our research suggests that schemes exist in two different kinds of networks, namely a 'housing' network and a 'welfare' network. These networks were both vertical (concerning both funding and policy structures affecting the operation of schemes) and horizontal (concerning referral, care and support and move-on affecting the client group).

To those involved in particular schemes, the housing network was perceived as largely 'above' and 'outside' the world of the individual scheme. While accepted as crucial for resourcing the project, staff had very little knowledge of Tai Cymru. Where views were expressed, they tended to be critical of its emphasis on ideals, models and strategies, which were perceived to be too mechanistic and failing to acknowledge the complexity of 'special needs' – the different needs of the various client groups and the different human interests at play. Housing associations were often seen as almost equally distant.

The day-to-day awareness of scheme staff is centred on what we have called the needs-related or welfare network. Thus, if a scheme provides for people with learning difficulties, then the network horizon is shaped and limited by agencies, organizations and systems operating within the same boundaries. There is little apparent sense of belonging to a housing movement.

If this reflects the networks in which voluntary and paid programme providers move, what is the role of special needs housing in terms of the housing and care networks occupied by people using the schemes? It is schemes with higher turnover rates that make the greatest demands on the housing market. Thus, while schemes providing for people with learning difficulties or mental health problems (the two areas funded under national

TABLE 9.4
Scheme inputs and outputs

	Where from		Where to	
	No.	%	No.	%
DSS hostel	23	3.9	9	1.7
Voluntary hostel	41	6.9	24	4.5
Probation hostel	8	1.4	5	1.0
Other scheme/association	14	2.4	83	15.6
Hospital	57	9.6	9	1.7
Custodial	17	2.9	10	1.9
Local authority housing	96	16.2	113	21.2
Private rented	50	8.1	88	16.5
Bed and breakfast	16	2.7	13	2.4
Family or friends	94	15.9	102	19.1
Night shelter	2	0.3	1	0.2
Street homeless	59	9.9	12	2.3
Local authority care	53	8.9	6	1.1
Other (e.g. owner-occupied)	63	10.6	58	10.9
Totals	593		533	

Welsh Office strategies) account for 64 per cent of all *schemes* in the study, people whose main housing problem arose from these needs accounted for only 21 per cent of those *leaving* schemes.

The reverse is true for young single homeless and women's aid schemes. While they account for only 15 per cent of *schemes*, they inject a massive 55 per cent of *scheme leavers* on to the housing market.

What kind of housing did these people *come from* at the point they entered housing association projects? And what kind of housing do they *move to* immediately on leaving the project? The figures in table 9.4 show the net effect of the schemes in mediating individuals' housing opportunities.

As a crude measure of the benefits of special needs projects on housing prospects, we can make a value judgement about the kinds of housing that would be regarded as generally 'negative', and compare the extent to which people find themselves in that kind of housing once they leave, in comparison with their housing before they arrived.

'Negative' housing may be roughly seen as that kind of housing which people may enter because they have a 'problem' of some kind. In this category we can include DSS hostels, voluntary hostels, probation hostels, hospitals, custody, commercial bed and breakfast, night shelters, street homeless and local authority care.

These categories of housing account for 46.5 per cent of the *input* into the schemes, but only 16.8 per cent of the *output*. While this is a rough-and-ready estimate, it certainly appears to indicate that – at the point of leaving – users of special needs housing were markedly less likely to find themselves in unsatisfactory housing than at the point they entered the projects.

Looking at the other side of the coin, scheme leavers were much more likely to find themselves in other housing association schemes, local authority housing and the private rented sector, and these scheme leavers were all rated as having fewer housing, personal and social needs than leavers as a whole. While we have no means of knowing how enduring these housing gains prove to be for users of the projects, there does seem to be real positive evidence about the impact of the housing association movement on the immediate housing fortunes of those who use its resources.

These conclusions should not hide the central preoccupation of special needs staff and managers with the problems of finding adequate move-on resources for people leaving the schemes. Move-on was accepted as a good ideal for many schemes, but realistic opportunities were heavily constrained by resource limitations. A more textured account of reality would also suggest that within this broad consensus lay a range of competing attitudes towards move-on policy. For example, it was in the interests of schemes on occasion to impede move-on possibilities because of other pressures to keep bedspaces full. There was also general agreement that levels of care and support for those who had moved on were often inadequate. Sustaining differential levels of support in the community was naturally closely related to the location of move-on accommodation. Thus, being close to 'old' networks was deemed patently undesirable for people with drink or drug problems, or for many women leaving refuges. Yet move-on provision away from these networks posed new problems of non-existent support frameworks.

FUTURE POLICY AND PRACTICE

Our canvas has been broad. We are not about to embark on simplistic solutions for the future of special needs housing. The policy and service contexts for our research make this impossible. Yet there are recurring themes that ought to shape future debate.

For example, we have repeatedly pointed up the differences between the varied housing need groups. There has been an unhelpful tendency to assume that the application of policy can be made in an undifferentiated manner to all housing need groups. While it is *not* our view that supported housing can or should be parcelled out into discrete areas of need, there *are* distinct policy needs facing each area of housing need. There appears to be a lack of any clear specialist advisory function built into consultation and decision-making. There is a persuasive case for a role operating at the interface of housing policy and provision and consumer aspirations and needs.

This tendency to act as if an undifferentiated policy can be applied across the board is particularly evident in the debate about the aims and principles underlying special needs provision, and active consultation is needed with grassroots staff in schemes. The voices of staff and people living in projects are not being clearly heard. For example, appropriate indicators of *outcome* are one issue where both the research and previous experience of quality assurance show that varied viewpoints are almost certain to exist.

The general principles of integration into the community, resident choice and involvement, privacy, quality of life and equal opportunities are clearly beyond dispute. Yet we are convinced that there needs to be flexibility in the ways in which these principles are *operationalized* in each kind of scheme. It is at this point that a distinctively Welsh dimension calls for emphasis, in drawing together considerations of language, integration, community and normalization policies.

If integration and community are seen in terms of support networks, then language is crucial. Language structures a community built out of interaction and identity. In parts of Wales there are at least two communities structured by language. One consists of local, Welsh-speaking people, involved in Welsh-language institutions and kinship networks, and whose support structures are partly conditioned by language. The other consists of recent in-migrants, and is spatially much more dispersed, focusing on institutions which are much less localized. While there is a degree of overlap in the sense that some individuals may have a foot in both camps, they are essentially separate communities.

From the standpoint of special needs housing, there is a problem of which of these communities integration is or should be applied to. If the measure of integration is interaction, then it will probably depend on management, length of residence in the area, extent of kinship and institutional involvement, gender and language.

Flexibility in implementing principles is not a recipe for evasion or laziness, but for a clear obligation on the part of the housing association movement to explore ways in which quality and outcomes can be sensitively appraised and reviewed.

In trying to reach beyond the rhetoric of special needs housing we have repeatedly stressed the problematic nature of policy-making in this field. The ambiguity of staff attitudes to 'standards' is a case in point. The debate cannot be reduced to a question of progressive policy-makers meeting the resistance of traditional and self-protecting project staff. Neither can we turn the argument on its head and present a picture of hidebound bureaucrats imposing a rigid system on liberal, well-meaning service providers. Rather, we think the issue can be seen more discriminatingly as a question of the operation of policy *models* (cf. Shaw, Williamson and Parry-Langdon, 1992). We detect a reality of distinct and competing models, each of which is vying for 'space' in the debate.

In one sense none of these models describes the real world. For example, supported housing is not and cannot be a 'normal home'; neither, for the majority of residents, can it be a 'preparation for independent living' – hence the debate about care and support needed in move-on provision. These models are aspirations. They are none the less important, for it is from within the tensions and contradictions they uncover that clearly thought-out practice can emerge, giving a properly balanced consideration of the 'housing' and 'welfare' needs of different consumer groups.

Such 'good practice' demands proper funding. The case for appropriate models of provision, quality assurance, strategic planning and care in the community is unequivocal, but it cannot be used to cloak the central debate about resource issues in relation to supported housing in the wider arena of social policy development in Wales.

ACKNOWLEDGEMENT

We should like to acknowledge the invaluable contributions of Sarah Fielder, Nina Parry-Langdon and Glyn Williams to the work reported in this paper.

REFERENCES

Bradley, V. and Bersani, H. (1990), *Quality Assurance for Individuals with Development Disabilities: It's Everybody's Business*, London, Paul H. Brooks.

Garside, P.L., Grimshaw, R.W. and Ward, F.J. (1990) *No Place Like Home: The Hostels Experience*, London, HMSO.

Randolph, B. (1990) *Housing People with Special Needs,* London, National Federation of Housing Associations.

Shaw, I. and Williamson, H. (1991) *Management and Welfare: An Evaluation of Special Needs Housing in Wales,* Cardiff, School of Social and Administrative Studies, University of Wales College of Cardiff.

Shaw, I., Williamson, H. and Parry-Langdon, N. (1992) 'Developing Models for Day Services', in *Social Policy and Administration,* 26, pp. 73–86.

Smith, G. and Cantley, C. (1984) 'Pluralistic Evaluation', in J. Lishman (ed.), *Evaluation,* Aberdeen, University of Aberdeen.

Smith, R. and Williams, P. (1991) 'Taking Stock: The Changing Dimensions of Housing Policy in Wales', *Contemporary Wales*, 4, pp. 167–87.

Tai Cymru (1991) *Report of the Working Party on Single Homelessness*, Cardiff, Tai Cymru.

Welsh Federation of Housing Associations and Special Needs Housing Advisory Service in Wales (1991) *The Revenue Funding of Special Needs Housing in Wales*, Cardiff, WFHA/SNHAS.

Welsh Office (1983) *All Wales Strategy for the Development of Services for Mentally Handicapped People*, Cardiff, Welsh Office.

10. EVALUATING A HEALTH CAMPAIGN: THE HEARTBEAT WALES NO-SMOKING INITIATIVE[1]

Ceri J. Phillips and Malcolm J. Prowle

INTRODUCTION

The issue of how health services should be provided and the extent of resources utilized is clearly one of the most contentious political issues of the day. However, aside from the short-term political controversy, there is a more fundamental issue which is taxing the minds of all governments in the developed world, namely that of longer-term health policies. This is brought about as a consequence of what we have termed the health service dilemma.

At the time the NHS was formed, there was a belief that the demand for health services was finite, and that all we had to do was provide sufficient financial resources and all the health demands of the population would be satisfied. With the benefit of hindsight that view seems unbelievably naive, and it is conventional wisdom now to say that the demands for health services are infinite, or at least approaching infinity. There are probably three main contributory factors at work here:

(1)   The increasing health needs and demands of an ageing population.
(2)   The continual advances in medical science.
(3)   The increasing aspirations of the population.

Clearly, the resources available for health services (public or private) are finite, and thus we come to the dilemma of health service provision. How do we reconcile infinite demand with finite resources without ending up in a position where 100 per cent of GDP is devoted to the provision of health services, and still fails to meet demand? There are a number of broad policy options, and these are briefly outlined below:

(1)   *Increase efficiency*   This option covers a whole variety of themes ranging from reducing the costs of catering or domestic services (through

competitive tendering) to reducing the unit costs of treating patients through, for example, a move from in-patient surgery to day-case surgery. The overall aim is the same, to get the NHS to deliver more care for the same amount of money. Broadly speaking, the recent reforms to the NHS are concerned with promoting greater efficiency in service delivery.

(2) *Limit service range* The NHS is charged with providing a comprehensive range of health services to its population, reaffirmed by the role of district health authorities as 'providers' of health care under the NHS reforms. However, a number of health authorities are beginning to question the interpretation of this duty and, in the light of resource pressures, are contemplating restricting the range of services they are prepared to provide.

(3) *Additional funding* The option favoured by most NHS staff and, according to opinion polls, a large proportion of the general public would be to increase the level of funds going into the existing NHS. This could be done in a number of ways, such as levying charges, increasing taxation proceeds or shifting resources from other parts of the public sector.

(4) *Alternative financing structure* A fourth alternative would be completely to restructure the method of organizing and funding health services in this country. This could involve the deployment of some form of health insurance system similar to that in many other European countries and the USA.

(5) *Reduce demand for health services* A key policy plank of most governments would be to try and reduce the demand for health services by preventing people from getting ill in the first place. It is not always appreciated that a large proportion of human sickness is preventable by changes in people's lifestyles (e.g. no smoking, improved diet), and thus health promotion and preventive health care is becoming increasingly important as a means of reducing sickness levels and the pressure on NHS resources. However, the key problem with such approaches is that quite often they require long-term investment, and the benefits of such investment are not always easy to identify.

HEALTH IN WALES AND HEARTBEAT WALES NO-SMOKING INITIATIVE

The NHS in Wales is not exempt from the dilemma referred to above, of reconciling finite resources with infinite demands. Indeed, there may be grounds for suspecting that the problem is exacerbated in Wales by the underlying poor health status of the population. For example, the incidence of cancers in Wales is amongst the highest of any region in England and Wales (HPAW, 1990a), while for cardiovascular disease, Wales has one of the highest rates of premature death in the world (HPAW, 1990b). Not surprisingly, in these circumstances, Wales has been the home of a major initiative to reduce the incidence of such preventable disease through health promotion activity.

The Heartbeat Wales (HBW) programme was initiated in April 1985 as the national (UK) demonstration project for reducing the prevalence of coronary heart disease. The programme employed a multi-faceted approach to coronary heart disease prevention by focusing on the major risk factors such as smoking, physical inactivity, poor nutrition etc, and also a multi-sectoral approach to health promotion involving, amongst others, local authorities, commerce and industry and the voluntary sector.

This article is concerned with the economic evaluation of one particular part of the HBW programme, namely that devoted to reducing the prevalence of smoking in Wales. The No Smoking intervention consisted of a number of activities which sought to educate people and change behaviour thereby reducing the incidence of smoking in the Principality.

Education for Young People

HBW aimed to prevent young people from starting to smoke in the first place, and also to support existing smokers in stopping. The emphasis was placed on ensuring that existing smoking education projects available for use in schools were fully disseminated and utilized. This school-based work was also supplemented by an unique project for younger children, aged 10–12 years. The Pulse Club was launched in 1986 as a mechanism for reaching young people outside the school environment. By 1988, 1,500 young people were members of the club, regularly receiving the newsletter and other materials. Evaluation of the project has indicated its positive effect, both on the children and their parents in terms of smoking behaviour (Newman and Nutbeam, 1990), and there is evidence to show that between 1986 and 1988 both experimental smoking and regular smoking reduced among both boys and girls (Nutbeam, 1989).

Education and Support for Existing Smokers

The 1985 Health Heart Survey indicated that more than two-thirds of current smokers in Wales wished to stop smoking (WHPD, 1986). The HBW programme sought to enhance existing opportunities for personal education through a number of mechanisms, including primary health care, adult education (through the 'Look After Yourself' programme) and occupational health services.

Mass Media

The HBW Programme used mass communication techniques directly, e.g. exhibitions and special events, and also collaborated with the mass media in joint initiatives, e.g. in the making of television programmes. In relation to smoking, most of the exhibitions established on a regular basis by HBW contained information and included follow-up literature on smoking. During the first three years of the programme, an estimated third of a million people visited HBW exhibitions, and 70,000 smoking cessation guidebooks were distributed.

In addition to exhibitions and collaborative work with television, HBW has regularly contributed to the print and broadcast media on smoking-related issues. This output has also been monitored, and during the 1985–8 period approximately 100 newspaper column inches and an average five radio items and one television news item were generated each year on the subject of smoking.

Environmental Support

HBW made a deliberate effort to create a supportive environment for both non-smokers and ex-smokers by promoting widespread restrictions on smoking in public places. Collaborative efforts with the health authorities resulted in the introduction and enhancement of smoking restrictions in most Welsh hospitals during the 1985–8 period. Collaboration with local authorities resulted in smoking restrictions on transport services in three districts, and in leisure amenities, such as sports centres.

Furthermore, a special programme to promote healthier catering, the Heartbeat Award Scheme, also included provision for non-smokers, in that to obtain an award a minimum of one-third of all seating must be designated non-smoking. Out of 37 district authorities in Wales, a large proportion now operate this scheme, and to date over 150 restaurants, cafeterias, canteens and public houses have achieved the award in Wales.

Finally, collaboration with organizations has led to important changes in many work environments as, within the period, 27 per cent of organizations employing more than 300 people either initiated or developed restrictions on smoking in the workplace.

TABLE 10.1

Percentage of current smokers by age and sex in Wales, 1985 and 1988

Age	Sex	Percentage Current Smokers	
		1985	**1988**
18–24	male	34.9	30.9
	female	32.4	30.9
25–34	male	41.6	38.0
	female	35.3	34.4
35–44	male	45.7	40.7
	female	37.0	30.5
45–54	male	43.0	40.5
	female	32.6	29.6
55–64	male	39.4	35.3
	female	29.0	27.3
18–64	male	41.2	37.1
	female	33.4	30.7

THE HBW NO-SMOKING INTERVENTION: RESULTS SO FAR

Smoking prevalence in Wales was measured by population surveys in 1985 and 1988 involving 22,000 and 8,000 subjects respectively. Table 10.1 shows that there was an overall decline of 4.1 per cent among men and 2.7 per cent among women. Thus the target of reducing prevalence by 1% per year was exceeded among males and almost achieved amongst women. Smoking declined among men and women of all ages, with the most marked decline among 35–44-year-olds (− 5 per cent men, − 7 per cent women).

Table 10.2 shows that the decline in the incidence of smoking is found among all social groups in Wales. However, there is one major exception in that there is a small rise in prevalence among those from households where the head of the household was unemployed at the time of the survey.

ECONOMIC EVALUATION OF HBW NO-SMOKING PROGRAMME

One of the major aims of the National Health Service set out in the White Paper, 'Working for Patients' (1989), is 'make the best use of the resources available to it. The quest for value for money must be an essential element in its work.'

As questions of priority setting and resource allocation become more apparent within the health service, similar attention should be paid to the

TABLE 10.2
Percentage of current smokers in Wales by social class, 1985 and 1988

	Percentage current smokers	
Social group	1985	1988
I	22.5	18.5
II	30.0	23.6
IIIN	32.5	27.8
IIIM	39.0	35.5
IV	42.5	37.4
V	49.5	45.0
Economically inactive	44.5	42.8
Total	37.0	33.4
All unemployed	49.5	52.4
Long-term unemployed	53.5	54.5

economic evaluation of preventive measures within health care, because
'budget holders have a responsibility to ensure that the money is being spent
with maximum benefit and efficiency' (Jones and Baker, 1986). Although
Cohen and Henderson (1988) have demonstrated the way in which economic
principles can assist in undertaking analysis and evaluation within the area of
health promotion, to date very limited attention has been given to the
economic evaluation of programmes designed to alter behaviour patterns,
partly because of the less direct relationship between behaviour and disease,
partly because of the time-lags between behaviour change and subsequent
disease reduction, and also because of inadequate data relating to the
effectiveness of such programmes (Cribb and Haycox, 1989; Drummond,
1986; Engleman and Forbes, 1986).

In undertaking an economic evaluation, the fundamental principle of
economic efficiency in the allocation of resources implies that choices should be
made so as to derive the maximum total benefit from the resources available.
However, whilst it is the case that economic appraisal is more relevant for
longer-term decision-making about the relative success of health promotion
programmes, the short-term financial dimension cannot be ignored. In reality,
short-term political pressures frequently dictate that financial considerations
take precedence over economic ones. Thus proponents of health promotion
need to take cognizance of both the financial and economic impact of their
activities if they are to make headway in the real political world.

This study is essentially a cost-benefit analysis of the HBW No-Smoking
intervention. Although improvements in morbidity and mortality will

undoubtedly lead to increases in health status through reduced pain and suffering, longer life etc., no attempt has been made to quantify or evaluate these factors in this study. Instead there has been a consideration of the non-health status impact of improvements in morbidity and mortality such as increased economic output and reduced public spending, with the changes in health status being simply noted. The evaluation of the programme is undertaken from two perspectives, namely a 'public sector appraisal', where the resource costs and benefits attributable to the public sector in Wales as a consequence of the no-smoking intervention will be considered, and secondly an 'economic appraisal', where attention will be focused on the full resource costs and benefits across all sectors of Welsh society attributable to the no-smoking intervention.

There are three basic stages to the investigation. Firstly, the identification, measurement and assessment of the costs incurred in the intervention programme. The second stage deals with the identification, measurement and assessment of the benefits of the intervention, recognizing the difficulties involved in attributing the outcomes to the particular input of HBW. The third stage combines the costs and benefits, and (after allowing for the difference in timing between the costs being incurred and the benefits being derived) arrives at a series of measures of the net present value of the HBW no-smoking intervention, based on the 'impact' of HBW on the reduction in smoking prevalence. However, it is accepted that some of the data are rather soft, and hence a sensitivity analysis is also undertaken to examine the impact on the net value of variations in the inputs and outcomes. Furthermore, whilst there are likely to be implications for the UK Exchequer resulting from the intervention, no attempt has been made to incorporate them into the evaluation, because this is a self-contained study of the impact of a particular public health policy within Wales.

The Costs of the Intervention

The no-smoking intervention of the HBW programme has resulted in costs being incurred by a range of organizations within the Principality. The most obvious case is, of course, the costs incurred by HBW itself, and such costs are relatively easy to identify from the information systems of the Health Promotion Authority for Wales. However, other participants can be identified who have contributed directly or indirectly to the HBW project. Consideration must therefore be given to any costs incurred by such organizations as a consequence of their contributions to HBW activities in general and the no-smoking intervention in particular.

TABLE 10.3
Health service costs (£000s) of no-smoking programme

	1985/86		1986/87		1987/88		1988/89	
---	cash	real	cash	real	cash	real	cash	real
Health Promotion Authority	72	82	65	72	93	98	126	126
District health education depts.	–	–	17	19	24	25	41	41
Health service	72	82	82	91	117	123	167	167

The following organizations have been identified as having been participants in the no-smoking interventions: district health authority health education departments; Welsh Office; other district health authority functions (e.g. community nursing); general practitioners; district councils (e.g. environmental health officers); voluntary sector; commerce, industry and other employers; individuals. The costs incurred by each of these groups of participants will be considered in turn.

Health Promotion Authority for Wales   For the years 1985/6 and 1986/7, the HBW programme was a discrete entity which came under the auspices of the University of Wales College of Medicine. For those years audited accounts were prepared separately for the HBW organization showing the total expenditure of the programme. For this two-year period, using available information, estimates have been drawn up of the amount of resources that were committed to the no-smoking intervention, incorporating both direct costs (staff and consumables) and a proportion of the organization's overheads.

On 1 April 1987, the Health Promotion for Wales was created as a statutory health authority and as such took over responsibility for the HBW programme, the Welsh AIDS campaign and other health education activities. For 1987/8, the Authority prepared accounts in the standard health authority format. Again, using available information, estimates have been prepared of the direct and indirect costs of the no-smoking intervention.

The results of this exercise are shown in table 10.3, in cash and real terms, by making adjustments in line with the retail price index to bring all costs to 1988 price levels. The costs shown in table 10.3, however, exclude the costs of health authority local programmes which are discussed in the next section.

Health education departments[2] Since its inception in 1985, HBW has provided financial assistance to each of the nine district health education departments (DHED) in Wales to support a variety of locally managed programmes of health promotion. It has been estimated that over the period 1985/6 to 1988/9, the proportion of resources which were committed to anti-smoking activities was approximately 20 per cent. Summarized in table 10.3 are the total costs of the no-smoking intervention associated with HBW local programmes both in cash and real terms.

Welsh Office Clearly the main source of finance for the HBW programme has been the financial allocation it receives from the Welsh Office, and these costs have been dealt with above as costs of the Health Promotion Authority. However, in addition there are the resource costs incurred by the Welsh Office in administering the programme. In practice, no information is publicly available about what such costs amount to, and so no provision can be made for this item.

Other district health authority functions A large number of health care professionals employed by district health authorities are undoubtedly involved, in various ways, in attempting to deter smoking. Examples of this could be medical staff, community nurses, physiotherapists etc. As noted earlier, there is a clear opportunity cost to the health authority and to the public sector at large in these staff undertaking this activity. However it is not possible to measure these resource costs.

General practitioners As with district health authority staff, general practitioners in Wales spend part of their time, to a lesser or greater degree, in health promotion activities, including that of encouraging smoking cessation; with the introduction of the new GP contract, which encourages the provision of specific health promotion sessions, better information may become available in the future. However, at present no figure for the resource costs of GP no-smoking activities can be prepared, but the existence of such a cost, as with other 'missing costs' is allowed for in the sensitivity analysis.

District councils The main activity in which district councils in Wales have been involved is the Heartbeat Award scheme. This scheme, which was initiated by HBW, involves the district council making an award to those catering establishments which meet certain 'health' criteria, including the provision of no-smoking areas.

The scheme is administered by Environmental Health Departments, which link the scrutiny for potential applicants of the award with their normal day-to-day food hygiene responsibilities. Consequently, it does not seem that there are any significant incremental resource costs associated with this work, and nothing has been included in the costs of the no-smoking intervention.

Voluntary sector   The term 'voluntary sector' is an all-embracing one which includes a wide range of disparate organizations. During its life, HBW has worked with and through a variety of voluntary organizations, e.g. Citizens Advice Bureaux, Shelter, Women's Institutes, Lions, Round Table, and pressure groups, such as ASH. However, it is not likely that any of these organizations have incurred additional costs as a result of the HBW programme and therefore, no costs from this sector are included in the analysis.

Commerce and Industry   The main resource commitment to health promotion by commerce and industry (and other employing organizations) in Wales has been via the acquisition of Well Welsh services. The Well Welsh service involves the employing organization paying the Health Promotion Authority for Wales for the provision of health screening and counselling services. The aim of this service is to screen the workforce and to offer advice about promoting better health, including that of no smoking. It is estimated that 20 per cent of the costs of the screening service can be attributed to no-smoking aspects. In addition to the costs of the screening itself, the employing organization will incur additional resource costs resulting from activities associated with the screening (e.g. administrative costs, loss of production). It is estimated that these costs will amount to 150 per cent of the cost of the screening itself. The various costs are summarized in table 10.4, where the total costs of the no-smoking intervention are displayed.

There are some additional costs to commerce and industry in Wales associated with the 'Make Health Your Business' Award' but these are felt to be not significant and can be ignored for the purposes of this exercise.

Individuals   In considering the costs that might be incurred by individual members of society, it is suggested that such individuals can be classified into two types: (1) those individuals who are themselves in the process of quitting the smoking habit, who may incur some loss of utility as a result of the loss of enjoyment of smoking tobacco, but who, on the other hand, will have additional resources available for expenditure in other areas; (2) those

TABLE **10.4**

Total costs (£000s) of no smoking programme

	1985/86		1986/87		1987/88		1988/89	
	cash	real	cash	real	cash	real	cash	real
Health service	72	82	82	91	117	123	167	167
Industry and commerce	–	–	–	–	33	35	38	38
Total	72	82	82	91	150	158	205	205

individuals who are somehow involved in providing any form of support to other individuals who are quitting the smoking habit.

With the second class of person, there may be some loss of time as a consequence of the need to provide forms of emotional support to others attempting to give up smoking. However it is extremely difficult to identify, let alone quantify and evaluate, such costs, and so their possible existence is merely noted.

The Benefits of the Intervention

Reference has already been made to the difficulties of attributing outcomes to input, but the range and extent of the activities of the HBW programme has acted as a prompt and trigger to those who either are contemplating stopping smoking or have started on the process. Given that the target of the HBW programme to reduce smoking prevalence in Wales by 1 per cent per year for the first five years of the intervention was achieved for the first three years, the result will be a series of outcomes eventually leading to a stream of benefits being produced, as can be seen in figure 10.1.

Attention is focused on two of the three final outcomes, namely reduced morbidity and displaced mortality,[3] and the benefits derived from these outcomes categorized into:

(1) Benefits to the health service in Wales.
(2) Benefits to Welsh commerce and industry.
(3) Benefits to the individual.
(4) Benefits to Welsh society.

Reduced Morbidity

The first area to be examined is the effect of reduced smoking prevalence on morbidity rates. Much clinical and epidemiological evidence exists about the

FIGURE 10.1
Structure of benefits from HBW programme

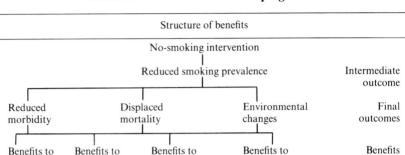

TABLE 10.5
Estimated costs to the NHS in Wales of disease attributable to smoking

	£million	
Disease	**Male**	**Female**
Lung cancer	3.55	0.77
Coronary heart disease	1.92	1.35
Chronic bronchitis/emphysema	3.71	1.38

impact of tobacco smoking on levels of morbidity. A whole range of clinical conditions can be quoted where smoking is believed to be a major contributory factor. For the purpose of this study, the analysis has been restricted to the impact of smoking on three categories of disease, namely coronary heart disease, lung cancer and bronchial disease.

Benefits to the health service in Wales   There are no precise data relating to the costs to the NHS of smoking-related illnesses and disabilities, so table 10.5 is adapted from Cohen's figures (1984) and indicates the total costs of treating lung cancer, coronary heart disease and chronic bronchitis/emphysema as a result of smoking in Wales.

Given the reduction in smoking prevalence within the Principality, the savings and benefits to the NHS can be calculated by multiplying the percentage reduction in smoking prevalence by the costs of treating diseases attributable to smoking. Table 10.6 indicates the extent of savings to the NHS as a result of the decline in smoking within Wales.

TABLE 10.6
Annual savings to NHS in Wales as a result of decline in smoking

Disease	Cost of treatment (£m)		Annual saving (£000)	
	Male	Female	Male[1]	Female[2]
Lung cancer	3.55	0.77	44.375	5.775
CHD	1.92	1.35	24.000	10.125
Chronic bronchitis	3.71	1.38	46.375	10.350

1 Based on annual reduction in smoking prevalence amongst males in Wales of 1.25 per cent.
2 Based on annual reduction in smoking prevalence amongst females in Wales of 0.75 per cent.

TABLE 10.7
Number of working days lost in Wales as a result of smoking-related illnesses

Disease	Number of days[1]		Attribution rate (%)	Days lost[2]	
	Male	Female		Male	Female
Lung cancer	21,650	1,850	75.9	16,433	1,423
CHD	2,950,150	265,000	20.0	590,030	53,000
Chronic bronchitis/ emphysema	716,900	73,350	68.4	490,360	50,172

1 Number of days of certified incapacity.
2 Working days lost as a result of smoking.

Benefits to commerce and industry   The number of working days lost through sickness absence in Wales by disease group is shown in table 10.7. In order to estimate the extent to which such certified incapacity can be attributed to smoking, 'attribution factors' are utilized. The 'attribution factors' are based on figures quoted in an ASH report (1989) and a study in the USA by Almer and Dull (1987), which was applied to English and Welsh data by Godfrey et al. (1989). It has to be remembered that such factors are based on what is termed 'avoidable life years lost', and therefore are mortality- rather than morbidity-related. Table 10.7 also indicates the factors of attribution, which are the most conservative quoted in the above studies, to be applied to the costs of treating the three disease groups in Wales.

Using the attribution factors for smoking as a causal factor in each of the disease groups it is possible to determine the number of working days lost as a result of smoking, as shown in table 10.7.

The benefit to industry and the economy from a reduction in smoking prevalence and thereby sickness absence caused by smoking-related illnesses

TABLE 10.8
Reduction in working days lost as a result of a decline in smoking

Disease	Reduction in working days lost	
	Male	Female
Lung cancer	205	11
CHD	7,375	398
Chronic bronchitis/emphysema	6,130	376

TABLE 10.9
Reduction in lost output (1988 prices)

Disease	Reduction in working days lost	Gross cost of employment (£)	Value of output not lost (£)
Lung cancer	216	56.20	12,139
CHD	7773	56.20	436,842
Chronic bronchitis	6506	56.20	365,637

and disabilities is obtained by multiplying the percentage reduction in smoking prevalence by the number of working days lost owing to smoking-related problems. The results can be seen in table 10.8.

In order to estimate the value of the output that would be lost to the economy as a result of working days lost, it is the convention to multiply the number of working days lost by the gross cost of employment (including wages, employers' national insurance contributions, etc.). Thus the benefit to the economy in terms of the value of output that would no longer be lost as a result of fewer smoking-related illnesses and disabilities can be seen in table 10.9.

However, the above analysis has assumed that the economy is operating at full employment levels. This obviously is not the case, and consideration has to be given to the effect of unemployment levels on the value of increased output as a result of fewer lost working days. However, since the data are based on working days lost through sickness absence, thus only considering those who form part of the employed workforce, it is legitimate to assume that output levels from the employed workforce are not at full potential owing to the existence of sickness-related absenteeism. Support for this view comes from the fact that value of output lost through industrial stoppages is widely used in political discussions.

TABLE 10.10
Annual benefits of reduced morbidity (£000)

Benefits to the NHS	
Savings in treatment of lung cancer	50.2
Savings in treatment of CHD	34.1
Savings in treatment of chronic bronchitis/emphysema	56.7
Benefits to commerce and industry	
Potential increase in output resulting from reduction in sickness absence	814.6
Benefits to the individual	
Potential increase in utility and reduction in sickness absence resulting in increased time for leisure and work	
Benefits to society	
All of the above plus any synergy created	

Benefits to the individual   The benefits to the individual from reduced morbidity as a result of a reduction in smoking prevalence are merely identified as being the physiological and psychological benefits less the negative psychological effects of giving up smoking, given the complexities associated with the measurement of these factors.

Benefits to Society   The consequences of reduced morbidity as a result of a reduction in smoking prevalence for society are obviously a combination of the benefits which accrue to individuals, industry, the economy and the NHS. A healthier population places less demands on the resources of the NHS and contributes more to GDP, thereby stimulating economic growth and improving living standards (assuming price levels are constant). Furthermore, third parties would not be adversely affected by the consequences of smoking-related illnesses and disabilities, nor would they be subjected to the illnesses brought about as the result of passive smoking (acknowledging that the epidemiological evidence for the effects of passive smoking is not clear cut).

Table 10.10 summarizes the benefits derived from reduced morbidity. In addition, it should be remembered that synergy exists when adding the benefits of the individual components to arrive at a measure of the benefits to society.

Displaced Mortality

The reality is that health promotion, in common with the bulk of medical science, is not in the business of providing immortality. The best that can be done is to postpone mortality until a later date. Various data are available on done is to postpone mortality until a later date. Various data are available on the amount of premature mortality that exists in Wales through the incidence of the three diseases to illustrate the magnitude of the task. Consequently, there is considerable scope for believing that a reduction in the incidence of smoking can displace mortality and result in a considerable reduction in the magnitude of premature death. However, identifying the benefits of such displacement is somewhat more problematic.

Benefits to the health service   The question here is whether the displacement of mortality to future years is doing anything other than pushing the cost burden on the health service further into the future with no real reduction in its magnitude. For example, St Leger (1989) suggested that reducing the level of ischaemic heart disease would increase overall hospital costs. However, it can be argued that the opposite is the case. Whereas reductions in the level of smoking prevalence could easily lead to more people living longer with the consequent increased burden on health and other social services, this need not necessarily be the case and, as suggested by Jagger et al. (1991), the elderly of today may well be fitter than previous cohorts of elderly, whilst Elliott (1972) offered the view that there may be real benefits to be accrued by the health service from displacing mortality to future years.

The existing position shows a population suffering an increasing level of morbidity and disability from the age of 45 onwards, as a consequence of preventable disease, with ultimate death around the age of 70. Obviously this implies a considerable burden on the health service over a 20-year period. The alternative position shows a picture of the population being relatively free of illness and able to maintain an independent existence for most of their lives, as a consequence of freedom from preventable illness caused by smoking. The age of death would be closer to what is thought to be the biological maximum, with a relatively short period of time between the onset of severe disability and ultimate death. Under this hypothesis the burden on the health service would in fact be less than that under the existing position, a very important consideration in the light of demographic changes.

Benefits to commerce and industry   The displacement of mortality would seem, at first examination, to have considerable benefits to employers and the economy as a whole. The death in service of employees robs the organization of skills and experience that may be of great benefit in terms of skills and productivity. However, leaving aside the humanitarian aspects, there are two important caveats that need to be made on this point. Firstly, much of the

TABLE 10.11
Years of working life lost as a result of smoking (1987)

Disease	Male	Female
Lung cancer	1.97	0.91
CHD	2.42	0.58
Chronic bronchitis/emphysema	0.64	0.22

TABLE 10.12
Value of output lost through premature mortality (1988 prices) (£m)

Disease	Male	Female
Lung cancer	16.17	7.47
CHD	19.86	4.76
Chronic bronchitis	5.25	1.81

displacement of mortality may take place beyond the normal retirement age. Thus, there will be no benefits accruing to the employing organization, although there may be an implication for the company pension fund. Secondly, dependent on the state of the labour market, the skills and experience lost by the death of an employee may be easily replaced or even improved by the recruitment of a younger person, although it is very difficult to generalize across industry and occupational groups. However, the existence of the demographic gap in the 1990s and the opportunities for job creation afforded by the Single European Market would seem to reduce the force of this argument quite considerably.

Nevertheless, premature death results in potential working life years and their associated output being lost. Utilizing the attribution factors, indicated earlier, it is then possible to determine the years of working life lost as result of smoking, as shown in table 10.11.

Multiplying the resultant number of working life years lost through smoking by the average output per head, £8,208 (1988 prices) per annum (albeit a crude indicator across occupational groups and skill areas) gives an indication of the potential output lost due to premature mortality. The results can be seen in table 10.12.

The benefits to the economy of the reduction in smoking prevalence can be calculated by multiplying the percentage decline in smoking by the potential output lost through premature deaths in Wales. The results are seen in table 10.13.

TABLE 10.13
Value of output saved by reduction in smoking (1988 prices) (£000)

Disease	Male	Female
Lung cancer	202.10	56.00
CHD	248.25	35.70
Chronic bronchitis	65.63	13.58

However, another consequence of displacing mortality is to increase the supply of labour, and an increase in the number of people of post-retirement age. Dependent upon the state of the labour market, the increase in the supply of labour could reduce income levels leading to reduced demand for output and increases in unemployment. However, demographic changes would seem to indicate that this is unlikely to be so, since there will be a reduction in the proportion of the population of working age.

Benefits to the individual   It would seem to be self-evident that there are benefits to individuals from postponing their own death. However, arguments are advanced that consideration needs to be given to the quality of life enjoyed by individuals during that period. It will suffice to say that the hypothesis discussed earlier suggests that reductions in smoking can lead to a longer life coupled with an enhanced quality of life. This is the case irrespective of age. Much of the premature mortality associated with smoking occurs in the post-retirement age group and therefore has not been considered in the discussion on potential output lost.

Since society does care for the elderly and other non-working groups such as the mentally handicapped, it is the case that the value of their lives is greater than zero, and therefore all individuals, irrespective of economic activity, need to be considered in identifying the benefits of displaced mortality to the individual.

Benefits to society   The premature death of an individual can bring increased pressures and anxieties on those left behind, over and above the grief and sense of loss. For example, where the family breadwinner is cut down in the prime of life, at peak earning power, the financial burden on the remaining family can be quite intense. The avoidance of such early death, together with the enhanced quality of life, is thus of benefit not just to the individual but to his or her family, and furthermore if this benefit is distributed on an equitable basis

FIGURE 10.2
Timescale of benefits from HBW programme

Timescale of benefits	
Time period	**Event**
0	No-smoking intervention occurs
1	Occurrence of intermediate outcomes (with some direct benefits)
2	Occurrence of final outcomes in terms of reduced morbidity
2–3	Benefits from reduced morbidity
3	Occurrence of final outcomes in terms of displaced mortality
3–4 (age 70)	Benefits from displaced mortality

there is an increase in social welfare, i.e. efficiency plus equity. Society also reaps rewards from the benefits which accrue to the health service and to the economy as a whole – again a potential increase in social welfare if lower socio-economic groups enjoy a relatively larger share of the benefits.

THE NET IMPACT OF HBW

In order to arrive at an indicator of the net value of the HBW no-smoking intervention it is necessary to consider three particular issues, namely which benefits are to be included in the appraisal, the timing of such benefits, and accounting for the occurrence of the costs and benefits.

As already mentioned, over the period 1985–8, there was a reduction in smoking prevalence in Wales of some 5 per cent. It is important, therefore, that only benefits that accrue as a result of that particular cohort of people either giving up or not commencing smoking are included. It cannot just be assumed that the reductions in smoking prevalence (and hence benefits) already achieved can be attributed to the no-smoking intervention. Furthermore, there is no guarantee that the benefits will be automatically recurring and that additional groups of persons will either give up or not commence smoking as a result of a health promotion activity that took place over a four-year period. In other words, the benefits that may be derived from future health promotion activity cannot be included unless the costs are included as well.

The second issue concerns the timing of benefits, in particular, projecting the final outcomes that will be derived from the intermediate outcomes and the benefits to be gained. Consequently, in considering the impact of the HBW programme, the model shown in figure 10.2 has been applied.

In using this model, it is recognized that certain of these events may take place simultaneously. However the two key points are to recognize that there

FIGURE 10.3
Timing profiles of benefits from HBW programme

	Timing profiles		
Disease type	Reduced smoking prevalence	Benefits from reduced morbidity	Benefits from displaced mortality
	year	year	year
Lung cancer	1	8 to 12	13 to 30
CHD	1	2 to 16	17 to 30
Chronic bronchitis	1	2 to 26	27 to 30

Mention has also been made that only three smoking-related diseases were to be considered, namely coronary heart disease, lung cancer and bronchial disease. Although much medical evidence is available on the ultimate impact of smoking with regard to morbidity, the timing of the onset of that morbidity is much less clear-cut. The basic problem is that the precise physiological effects of smoking are not fully understood. Therefore, it is not clear how soon after smoking cessation an individual benefits in the sense of reduced risk of particular diseases, and consequently it is not clear how quickly benefits to society at large will accrue. Consequently the time periods identified generically in the above model will vary, in practice, from disease to disease. This study has therefore made certain assumptions about the timing of benefits for the three disease groups considered, and applying these to the first year of reduced smoking prevalence included in this study (1985/6) gives the picture shown in figure 10.3.

The third and final issue concerns the method of accounting for the time dimension of the costs and benefits. It has already been stated that the costs of the intervention more or less occur during the duration of the intervention, whilst the benefits accrue over a long period of time. However, in order to compare like with like it is necessary to place today's value on benefits, whenever they occur, in order to compare them with the costs.

Using the data on costs and benefits discussed earlier, and applying the timing factors referred to above, standard discounting techniques[4] are used to compute net present values for both the public sector and economic appraisals. Applying all the assumptions referred to above gives the results shown in table 10.14.

Such results indicate that the benefits (public sector and economic) derived from reduced smoking prevalence in Wales are far in excess of the costs

TABLE 10.14
Net present values of HBW programme

Appraisal	Present value of costs	Present value of benefits
	£(000)	£(000)
Public sector	394	4,134
Economic	394	43,503

TABLE 10.15
Net present value of projects

Impact percentage	Public sector (£000)	Economic (£000)
100%	3,740	43,109
50%	1,673	21,358
25%	640	10,482
10%	19	3,956

associated with the Heartbeat Wales no-smoking intervention. However it is a far more difficult task to prove that the reductions in smoking prevalence (and hence the benefits) are directly caused, in whole or in part, by the HBW programme.

One possible approach might have been to compare the reductions in smoking prevalence in Wales with that in a comparable part of England which did not have a HBW-type programme, thereby inferring something about the effectiveness of the programme. Such an approach has been considered as part of the overall evaluation of the HBW programme. However, in practice it has proved virtually impossible to achieve the necessary *ceteris paribus* conditions to permit such an evaluation to take place. This is because of the problems of 'leakage' from Wales into the reference area. By this we mean that many of the innovative ideas in health promotion developed by HBW have been picked up and initiated in various parts of England, thus spoiling the chance of having a suitable reference area.

In these circumstances one is forced to rely on selective pieces of evidence which might enable us to infer something about the impact of the HBW programme. The following points should be noted:

(1) Reductions in smoking prevalence have been greater in Wales over the past four years than in England (see OPCS General Household Survey data for comparison).

(2)   The HBW programme is very well known by the general public throughout Wales and its objectives are understood.

However, given the uncertainty about the extent to which the benefits of reduced smoking prevalence can be attributed to the HBW intervention, an analysis has been performed of the net present value (NPV) of the project based on a range of 'impact percentages'. The resulting net present values are shown in table 10.15.

Thus it can be seen that even with an impact percentage of 10 per cent, the HBW intervention still gives a small net present value to the public sector in Wales and a larger net present value to the Welsh economy at large. Given the discussion in the previous section about the impact of the HBW project in Wales, it is suggested that it is not unreasonable to assume that an impact percentage of at least 10 per cent has been achieved.

SENSITIVITY ANALYSIS

Throughout this investigation no attempt has been made to disguise the fact that much of the information needed for a definitive cost-benefit appraisal of the no-smoking intervention is unavailable.

In addition it is recognized that much of the available information used in this study is rather 'soft' in character. No apology is made for this since all available data have been used to undertake our analysis. What has been done, therefore, is to conduct various forms of sensitivity analysis to identify the robustness of the net present value calculations.

From what has been stated earlier, it can be seen that the costs of the HBW no-smoking intervention are dwarfed by the value of the benefits that are generated by the reductions in smoking prevalence. Consequently the results of the cost-benefit analysis show very little sensitivity to variations in the levels of cost incurred. What has been done therefore is to concentrate on the benefits side of the equation and look at the impact of variations in the magnitude and timing of benefits on the net present values. For each impact percentage, the following variations have been made and the impact on net present values assessed:
(1)   Reduce overall benefit levels by 10 per cent.
(2)   Reduce overall benefit levels by 25 per cent.
(3)   Delay receipt of all benefits by an additional five years.
(4)   Reduce benefit levels by 10 per cent plus delay of five years (i.e. (1) and (3))
The results are shown in table 10.16.

TABLE 10.16
Results of sensitivity analysis

(1) 100% impact percentage	Net present values	
	Health service	Economic
	£(000)	£(000)
Main scenario	3740	43109
Variations		
(a) 10% benefit reduction	3327	38759
(b) 20% benefit reduction	2914	34409
(c) 5-year delay in receipt	2607	29759
(d) 10% reduction plus 5 year delay	2307	26744

(2) 50% impact percentage	Net present values	
	Health Service	Economic
	£(000)	£(000)
Main scenario	1673	21358
Variations		
(a) 10% benefit reduction	1466	19182
(b) 20% benefit reduction	1260	17008
(c) 5-year delay in receipt	1106	14683
(d) 10% reduction plus 5-year delay	956	13175

(3) 25% impact percentage	Net present values	
	Health service	Economic
	£(000)	£(000)
Main scenario	640	10482
Variations		
(a) 10% benefit reduction	537	9394
(b) 20% benefit reduction	434	8306
(c) 5-year delay in receipt	356	7144
(d) 10% reduction plus 5-year delay	281	6390

(4) 10% impact percentage	Net Present Values	
	Health Service	Economic
	£(000)	£(000)
Main scenario	19	3956
Variations		
(a) 10% benefit reduction	− 22	3521
(b) 20% benefit reduction	− 63	3086
(c) 5-year delay in receipt	− 94	2921
(d) 10% reduction plus 5-year delay	− 124	2620

From this sensitivity analysis, it can be seen that for all impact percentages and variations, the NPV of the economic appraisal always remains positive. The public sector appraisal gives positive NPVs for all variations and impact percentages with the exception of the 10 per cent impact percentage, where reductions in benefit levels and/or timing delays will result in negative NPVs being produced.

CONCLUSION

The aim of this study was to assess the costs and benefits associated with a health promotion campaign designed to reduce the incidence of smoking, using the HBW Programme for this purpose. From the outset the study recognized the difficulties of isolating the benefits which could be directly attributable to HBW and therefore attempted to compare the overall benefits from the reduction in smoking prevalence in Wales with the costs incurred in the HBW programme, whilst also estimating the extent to which reduced smoking levels in Wales and its associated benefits could be attributed to the HBW intervention.

Two perspectives to the evaluation have been taken. The first perspective limits itself to the overall impact of the no-smoking intervention on public expenditure within Wales. The second perspective takes a wider look at the impact of the intervention on the Welsh economy at large. Given this emphasis on the Welsh dimension, this study should be seen as a basis for making policy decisions within Wales.

It has been shown that on both evaluation bases the no-smoking intervention generates positive net present values even with HBW impact percentages as low as 10 per cent, and generates a financial payback within a reasonable number of years. Although the information is not available to prove that the HBW intervention is the causal factor in achieving reduced smoking prevalence in Wales, it is reasonable to assume that HBW has been, at least, a significant factor.

What can be stated with some confidence therefore is that programmes such as HBW, designed to reduce smoking prevalence, are extremely worthwhile economically, financially and for many other reasons. In terms of future policy directions in Wales it should be stated that even if Heartbeat Wales was responsible for only 10 per cent of the decline in smoking prevalence, there would still have been a surplus, and the programme has been a successful and 'profitable' investment of public funds. Although the level of benefits generated through reduced smoking prevalence may seem very large, only relatively small changes are needed to achieve this level of benefits. For example, it requires only a saving of approximately £2 per annum from each of the individuals who make up the reduction in smoking prevalence to achieve the level of benefits shown in the public sector. In the case of the economic appraisal a saving of approximately 21p per person per annum would be needed. In crude terms, such savings would be generated respectively through one less drug prescription and one less day lost from work per annum from each individual involved in the make-up of reduced smoking prevalence. In addition, as such programmes will not necessarily add to pressure on NHS funds at some later date, and the pension implications of more people living longer can more than be accommodated from the surplus generated by such programmes, the results of this study should ensure that programmes designed to reduce smoking prevalence feature high on the list of NHS spending priorities.

NOTES

1 This article is based on a report undertaken for the Health Promotion Authority for Wales by Don Nutbeam (formerly Head of Research at Health Promotion Authority for Wales), Malcolm Prowle (formerly Head of Resources at Health Promotion Authority for Wales) and Ceri Phillips, entitled 'The Heartbeat Wales No-Smoking Intervention', Heartbeat Wales Technical Report no. 22, Health Promotion Authority for Wales, Brunel House, Fitzalan Road, Cardiff, CF2 1EB.
2 In conducting an appraisal of the impact of the HBW interventions, it must be borne in mind that preventive activity in the no-smoking field has been carried out by DHED staff for many years prior to the formation of HBW. It is possible to speculate that some incremental activity in this area might have been catalysed by the activities of HBW with consequent additional resource costs to the DHAs concerned. If so then such additional costs should be attributed to the HBW intervention. However, in practice it is not possible to establish whether the activities of HBW did result in additional district health authority resources being committed to no-smoking activity, and hence no attempt has been made to assess any possible incremental costs.
3 The third outcome, environmental changes, is dealt with in less detail, but allowance is made for this in the sensitivity analysis.
4 In undertaking the discounting, the following three factors have been applied:
    (1) A discount rate of 6 per cent has been used, this being the official test discount rate recommended by HM Treasury as being the Social Opportunity Cost Rate. This rate is the marginal rate of return on private sector investment and thus represents the opportunity cost of public sector investment.
    (2) The benefits have been included up to the year 2016, this being 30 years from the commencement of the HBW programme. Although benefits will undoubtedly accrue beyond that date, they will not materially affect the overall present value of the project.
    (3) All costs have been expressed in terms of mid-1988 prices. All benefits are computed at 1988 price levels.

REFERENCES

Almer, R.W. and Dull, H.B. (eds) (1987) *Closing the Gap: The Burden of Unnecessary Illness*, Oxford University Press.

ASH (1989), Factsheet no. 1, *Smoking Statistics*.

Clarkson, J., Blower, E., Hunter, C. et al. (1990) *Overview of Workplace Action for Health in UK*, Dublin, European Foundation for the Improvement of Living and Working Conditions.

Cohen, D.R. (1984) *Economic Consequences of a Non-Smoking Generation*, University of Aberdeen, Health Economics Research Unit, Discussion Paper, 06/84.

Cohen, D.R. and Henderson, J.B. (1988) *Health, Prevention and Economics*, Oxford University Press.

Cribb, A. and Haycox, A. (1989) 'Economic Analysis in the Evaluation of Health Promotion', *Community Medicine*, 11 (4), 299–305.

Drummond, M.F. et al. (1986) *Studies in Economic Appraisal in Health Care*, vol. 2, Oxford University Press.

Elliott, C.G. (1972) 'Instant Medicine for the Elderly', *World Medicine* (5 January), p. 75.

Engleman, S.R. and Forbes, J.F. (1986) 'Economic Aspects of Health Education', *Social Science and Medicine*, 22 (4), 443–58.

Godfrey, C. et al. (1989) *Priorities for Health Promotion*, Centre for Health Economics, University of York, Discussion Paper no. 59.

Hayes, E. (1990) *Health Promotion Practice among GPs in Wales*, Cardiff, Health Promotion Authority for Wales.

Health Promotion Authority for Wales (1990a) *Health in Wales*, Cardiff, Health Promotion Authority for Wales.

Health Promotion Authority for Wales (1990b) *Health for All in Wales: Health Promotion Challenges for the 1990's*, Cardiff, Health Promotion Authority for Wales.

Jagger, C. et al. (1991) 'Getting Older – Feeling Younger: The Changing Health Profile of the Elderly', *International Journal of Epidemiology*, 20 (1), 234–8.

Jones, T.W. and Prowle, M.J. (1987) *Health Service Finance*, Certified Accountants Educational Trust.

Newman, R. and Nutbeam, D. (1990) *Evaluation of 'Pulse': Children's Health Club*, Cardiff, Health Promotion Authority for Wales.

Nutbeam, D. (1989) *Health for All Young People in Wales*, Cardiff, Health Promotion Authority for Wales.

Nutbeam, D. et al. (1987) 'The Health-Promoting School: Organisation and Policy Development in Welsh Secondary Schools', *Health Education Journal*, 46 (3), 109–15.

St Leger, A.S. (1989) 'Would a Healthier Population Consume Fewer Health Service Resources?' *International Journal of Epidemiology*, 18,(1), 227–31.

WHPD (1986) *Heartbeat Wales Awareness and Recall Survey Report*, Heartbeat Report no. 6, Cardiff, Health Promotion Authority for Wales.

11. WALES IN 1990:
AN ECONOMIC SURVEY

Dennis Thomas

THE BRITISH EXPERIENCE

The last few months of 1990 brought overwhelming evidence that the British economy was in recession. Formal recognition, however, had to await the publication of figures in early 1991 which confirmed 'two successive quarters of falling gross domestic product'. This recourse to semantics together with official criticisms of the Jeremiah voices of doom and gloom seemed to fly in the face of falling output, declining investment, low profitability, a record number of business failures and rapidly increasing unemployment.

The initial downturn in the economy could be traced back to late 1989 as the personal sector, largely in the housing market, began to respond to the high interest rate policy which had seen the base rate rise to 15 per cent. Southern regions of England were hit hardest and earliest, with the service, construction and property sectors, which had experienced strong expansion in the second half of the 1980s, suffering the most. Other sectors and regions experienced only a relative slowdown initially as buoyant export markets compensated for reduced domestic demand, but by the end of the year cutbacks, closures and job losses had become widespread. The general uniformity of recessionary effects contrasted with the recession of the early 1980s, in which the manufacturing sector and the industrial heartlands had borne the brunt.

During the autumn an appreciation that inflation was staying stubbornly high and that the authorities were reluctant to cut interest rates produced a growing business pessimism. The severe downturn in demand, together with the commitment to finance high borrowing undertaken in the late 1980s, combined to create large financial deficits. These problems were compounded by other pieces of 'bad news' which accumulated during the second half of the year, namely the developing crisis in the Gulf, the slowdown in world trade, and various difficulties facing the government, particularly with respect to the Community Charge and European issues. The general retrenchment in the corporate sector contributed to the highest level of company failures on record with the latest Dun and Bradstreet survey showing 24,442 company failures during 1990, some 35 per cent more than the 1989 figure and far in excess of the previous high of 1984.

During the second half of 1990 consumer spending fell by 1.5 per cent despite continued growth in real personal disposable income, with the personal savings ratio increasing to 11 per cent in response to increased debt servicing needs and a decline in personal sector wealth. Corporate spending also fell as industrial and commercial businesses cut back sharply on their borrowings. Investment peaked at record levels in early 1990 and began its downward trend in the second quarter of the year. In the final quarter, total fixed investment is estimated to have been 4 per cent lower than in the previous quarter and 6.5 per cent lower than in the same period a year earlier, while manufacturing investment was over 9 per cent down on the corresponding period in 1989. The flat housing market throughout the United Kingdom saw house prices falling on a year-to-year basis for the first time in two decades, and by the last quarter of 1990 house prices were generally down 3 per cent in nominal terms and over 10 per cent in real terms compared with a year earlier. As the year came to an end, the first set of consistent falls in house prices in 'northern' regions was accompanied by a bottoming out in the 'south'.

Although Gross Domestic Product (GDP) was provisionally estimated to have risen by some 0.5 per cent in the year as a whole the figures indicate a fall of 1.75 per cent between the first and second halves of 1990. The output of the service and construction sectors fell by around 1 per cent over the third and fourth quarters, with manufacturing output falling by more than 5 per cent. Unemployment had begun to rise in April 1990 after falling continuously for over three and a half years, and at the end of the year the seasonally adjusted figure for Great Britain stood at 1,745,400, compared with 1,516,600 in January 1990. The seasonally adjusted stock of vacancies remaining unfilled at Great Britain Job Centres in December 1990 was reported as 124,500, the lowest figure since 1983 and indicating further, substantial increases in unemployment. Employment peaked in the second quarter of 1990 and is estimated to have fallen by over 200,000 over the second half of the year.

The improvement in inflation and balance of payments figures which appeared during the final quarter of 1990 must be placed in the context of the considerable deceleration of demand. Having peaked at 10.9 per cent in October, compared with 7.7 in January, the headline rate of inflation measured as the twelve-monthly change in the Retail Prices Index declined to 9.3 per cent in December. Despite claims that the headline rate was overstating the problem owing to a number of factors, especially the Community Charge and mortgage increases which would soon fall out of the calculations, concerns remained regarding the underlying rate. The annual rate of inflation excluding housing costs stood at 7.5 per cent, well above the EC average. The underlying rate of increase in average earnings in the year to December was provisionally estimated at 9.75 per cent, while unit wage costs were estimated as having risen by 11.25 per cent in the year to the last quarter of 1990, the highest rate of growth since the first quarter of 1981.

The revised current account deficit on the balance of payments for 1990 was £12.8 billion, compared with £19.6 billion in 1989, with the fall basically explained by a 6.8 per cent rise in export volume, compared with a 1.4 per cent rise in imports excluding oil and erratics. Invisibles displayed a particularly buoyant performance in the second half of the year following a weak first half. These figures, however, should not detract from the fact that the year's current account deficit was still the third worst on record, and the fifth running with the much reduced fourth quarter current account deficit of £0.8 billion occurring in a period of deepening recession.

It was against this background that Great Britain joined the Exchange Rate Mechanism (ERM) of the European Monetary System (EMS) on 8 October at a central rate of 2.95 Deutschmarks to be varied within a 6 per cent band. Although the decision to enter the ERM had been long anticipated, its actual timing, together with the reduction in the base lending rate to 14 per cent, came as a surprise. Despite the official justification that inflation was at or near its peak, cynics saw the announcement as a politically expedient move in the complex game of European and domestic politics. There was also a widespread belief that the high central rate of exchange did not reflect the economy's underlying competitiveness, and that entry should have occurred earlier in the year when the exchange rate had been lower and the foreign exchange markets relatively calm.

While conventional opinion viewed ERM membership as producing a much-needed discipline in the economy and bringing greater stability to the exchange rate, most commentators were agreed that the high entry rate made for painful adjustment, with limited scope either for a rapid reduction in interest rates or a significant sterling devaluation to boost exports. With interest rates now having to be set with a view to their effects on international financial markets, further substantial cuts were regarded as improbable as long as sterling remained in the bottom half of its band. In the absence of a sterling devaluation, which was unlikely without a general realignment of currencies within the ERM, the need to sustain the high entry rate would inevitably seem to perpetuate the current account deficit on the balance of payments, and require a long and deep recession in order to bring wage and price rises into line with those experienced by other EC countries. While unit costs continued to rise faster than elsewhere the burden of maintaining the competitiveness of British industry would fall on job shedding. At the same time business would continue to struggle with high borrowing costs and little incentive to undertake new and replacement investment. Without a significant fall in the underlying rate of inflation together with appropriate interest rate cuts, government optimism regarding an upturn in the second half of 1991 seemed to be misplaced. The expected revival in the property market and in consumer expenditure might prove to be illusory, with the slowdown in European growth rates and problems with world trade preventing an export recovery. Whatever the actual scenario even the most optimistic forecasters saw unemployment rising well into 1992.

Entry into the ERM left the fundamental problems facing the domestic economy unresolved, and concerns about Britain's long-term future in post-1992 Europe remained. As the debate on European Monetary Union (EMU) continued, many commentators saw the full entry of the pound into the EMS at the chosen rate providing a glimpse into a future where the function of macro-economic policy-making is substantially transferred to the European level.

THE WELSH ECONOMY IN 1990

Along with other 'northern' regions of the United Kingdom, Wales experienced a delayed reaction to recessionary forces, but by the end of the year the recession had well and truly arrived. Dun and Bradstreet figures show that company failures almost doubled between the third and fourth quarters of the year, compared with a 60 per cent rise for England and Wales as a whole. Unemployment rose by some 10,000 during the last three months, while the number of unfilled vacancies reported at Welsh Job Centres contracted sharply, falling from 10,100 in November to 8,500 in December.

Successive business surveys displayed a rapidly diminishing confidence with respect to investment and employment prospects in the face of declining consumer demand, high borrowing costs, falling profits and a growing export pessimism. The CBI identified Welsh industry in its gloomiest mood since 1980, while the December survey for the Institute of Directors showed business confidence at its most pessimistic since the six-monthly surveys began in 1984. In January 1991 the Cardiff Chamber of Commerce and Industry claimed that the rate of deterioration was now worse in Wales than elsewhere. In contrast, the official view of the situation was optimistic and up-beat.

Current problems were described as serious but not debilitating with the 'new-look' economy, which had emerged during the second-half of the 1980s, well placed to ride out a relatively short-lived and shallow recession and to exploit the inevitable upturn when it came. This view was supported by a variety of independent forecasters, but doubts remained among some observers regarding both the length and depth of the recession and the validity of the new stereotype of a dynamic, diversified economy.

Inward investment, the financial and business service expansion in south-east Wales, and the success projected for the Cardiff Bay development featured prominently in the new images of Wales as portrayed, for example, by the Henley Centre for Forecasting report on Local Futures (July 1990). In contrast, survey evidence within Wales continued to highlight the increasing extremes of prosperity between areas. In north-east Wales a consultancy report on Social Deprivation in Clwyd (CENTRIS, October 1990) identified localities which exhibited some of the most acute features of deprivation in the country, despite the jobs and investment boom of the second half of the 1980s which had produced one of the lowest county unemployment rates in Wales. In South Wales, survey evidence collected as part of the Valley Skills Project showed the 'Valleys' continuing to lag behind other parts of Wales. As the effects of recessionary forces offset measures to stimulate the local economy the unemployment rate for the area covered by the Valleys Initiative rose above 10 per cent in December 1990 for the first time since September 1989. An account of regional variations within Wales, together with statistics detailing the aggregate picture of the Welsh economy, are contained in other sections of this survey.

In the course of the year preparations for the completion of the single European market in 1992 gathered pace amid concerns regarding Wales's preparedness and the implications for Welsh business. May brought the official launch of the Wales European Information Centre (EIC) funded by the EC and the Welsh Development Agency (WDA) with support from Clwyd CC and the University of Wales. The Wales EIC was part of a network established across the EC essentially designed to assist small- and medium-sized business enterprises (SMEs) prepare for a barrier-free Europe and to communicate with each other through the provision of information and advice. A related development was the hosting in Cardiff in June of Europartenariat 1990. Financed by the EC and the WDA, the event was the third in an annual series of five aimed at developing co-operative ventures between SMEs in different parts of Europe.

With European developments post-1992 in mind, the year also saw a growing emphasis on training and skill development. Various reports emphasized the need to ensure appropriate training in order to produce a better supply of skills in terms of volume, range and level to meet both current and changing needs of new industries and occupations. A particular emphasis was placed on skills which were easily transferable across a wide range of jobs as well as national boundaries. It was stressed that both new and traditional skills were required to attract firms to Wales and for Welsh firms to compete effectively in domestic and international markets, and also to enable Welsh workers to become more marketable. As well as occupational and business skills, language training was emphasized as an essential component in the new scheme of things.

By the end of 1990, the Training and Enterprise Council (TEC) framework introduced in 1989 was almost complete in Wales. Three out of the seven TECs covering Wales were operational – Mid Glamorgan, North East Wales and West Wales – with the other four – Gwent, Powys, North West Wales and South Glamorgan – all in their development stages. Whilst the debate concerning the philosophy and appropriateness of the TECs continued, difficulties were reported in the collection of information and preparation of strategy documents, while complaints were voiced regarding reduced incomes for training organizations because of reduction of government funding. Concerns were also expressed that employer participation in providing practical training had not materialized to the extent anticipated. Among the variety of initiatives introduced during the year was the New Training Solutions scheme announced by West Wales TEC. The scheme was aimed at assisting small- and medium-sized firms, which might not be able to fund appropriate initiatives themselves, to design home-grown training packages to solve their own skills shortages and develop existing employees.

Another major priority, if Wales is not to miss out on the potential opportunities offered by the European open market, involves the transport infrastructure, and 1990 saw increased calls from many quarters for im provements within Wales and linking Wales with the Channel Tunnel and Europe. March brought the long-awaited response by the Secretary of State for Wales to the report of the Select Committee on Welsh Affairs on the Channel Tunnel which had been published in June 1989. The report had called for extra government action on a number of issues in order to ensure that Wales did not lose out. Great emphasis was placed on boosting road and rail links between the tunnel and Wales, including a call for a cost-benefit analysis to justify the electrification of rail lines in North and South Wales. The official response, however, stressed that such transport issues were matters for commercial judgement rather than government policy, as befitted a scheme which was intended as a privately funded project. In June 1990 plans for a high-speed Channel Tunnel rail link were scrapped following the government announcement that they would not subsidize it, while electrification of the Paddington–Fishguard and Crewe–Holyhead lines was ruled out as commercially unviable according to British Rail's investment criteria. At the end of the year concerns for the future of rail in Wales were heightened by British Rail's reorganization of its provincial network under the Regional Railways banner. South Wales was to be combined with South West England with administrative offices in Swindon, while Mid and North Wales were similarly to be run from England.

Calls for road improvements within Wales focused attention on improved links between north and south, and a sustained campaign was launched for a new and more direct route to replace the current patchwork based on the A470. While improvements to the A55 Expressway across North Wales were embodied in the Welsh Office's development strategy for Gwynedd and Clwyd, a proposal for road improvements in Dyfed beyond Carmarthen was blocked as being too ambitious. In north Gwent, reclamation work at the former Marine Colliery site at Cwm formed part of improvements to the Valleys road link in preparation for the 1992 National Garden Festival to be held at Ebbw Vale, while in the south of the county proposals were mooted for a duplicate motorway. This new section would swing south of Newport as part of a package to service Cardiff Bay with direct access from the east. Calls were also made for extra motorway links to service a second Severn Bridge, plans for which were unveiled in June. Subject to legislation introduced in 1991, building on the bridge was anticipated to begin in 1992, with a projected completion date in late 1995 or early 1996. The whole issue proved extremely contentious, however, following the announcement that an Anglo-French consortium (Laing/GTM–Entrepose) had been chosen to finance, build and run the second crossing as well as taking over the existing bridge, whose tolls, it was simultaneously announced, were to be increased by 40 per cent. The successful bid was criticized by proponents of state funding, and concern was expressed regarding the possibility of unfair competition from French suppliers because of French design specification requirements and the project's financing by a French bank. Many critics also pointed out that the project reflected the changing face of European grants, which were moving away from such infrastructural projects.

The year 1990 also saw increasing concern regarding air services to and from Wales, particularly with respect to the lack of scheduled services from Cardiff-Wales airport which, it was argued, was an important consideration in locational decision-making in a European context, with an emphasis on effective communication and administrative co-ordination between Head Office and branch plants. A welcome development was the announcement in June of plans for Cardiff-Wales costing more than £45m. The main emphasis at the time was placed on building a reputation as a North American gateway, but November brought a potential boost to European air links, when Manx Airlines unveiled proposals for eight routes from Cardiff (including flights to Paris, Brussels and Düsseldorf).

While transport and communications may be regarded as the major factor influencing location outside the productive process itself, there were growing complaints during 1990 of the burdensome commercial rate bills arising from the combined effects of property revaluations and the Uniform Business Rate which had been introduced on 1 April. Particular concern was expressed regarding the disparity between the UBR for Wales and that for England, which was aggravated by the announcement of an 11 per cent increase for the 1991/2 financial year. In addition, surveys undertaken by National Utility Services during 1990 showed that Wales was a relatively high-cost region in terms of both water supply and electricity.

During the year a variety of government-backed development initiatives were introduced or extended. In North Wales activities were focused on the implementation of the 'Road of Opportunity' strategy unveiled in late 1989, while in South Wales the South East Wales Financial Services Initiative was extended to include the Swansea Bay Area. At the end of the year the Welsh Office announced that another £300m was to be pumped into the Valleys Initiative in a two-year extension, which was to see a switch in emphasis away from central and local government agencies and towards 'a partnership with the people'. This emphasis on community-based initiatives was also reflected in the WDA's new strategy plan for rural development as outlined in 'Rural Prosperity: Action Plans for Communities' (February 1990). The WDA established a Rural Affairs Division and emphasized the need to develop a range of business, environmental and social activities to be implemented in an integrated planning process sympathetic to the needs, opportunities, geography and culture of local areas. While continuing to carry out its core activities, the agency committed itself to devoting additional effort and resources to particular areas by the preparation and adoption of 'reasonable, realistic and cost effective' Action Plans for selected communities. Eleven communities in Clwyd, Dyfed and Gwynedd were targeted for 'Action Plan' regeneration schemes in the initial list – Corwen, Denbigh, North Pembrokeshire (including Fishguard, Newport, Nevern and Bro Preseli), Newcastle Emlyn, Llandovery, Llanrwst, Bethesda-Dyffryn Ogwen, Dyffryn Nantlle, Pwllheli, Porthmadog and Amlwch.

For its part the Development Board for Rural Wales (DBRW) built on the strategy plan announced in November 1989, emphasizing the need to focus on young people by improving the general quality of life in Mid and west Wales and providing opportunities for the young to live and work. November 1990 brought the announcement of an additional £1m funding for each of the next three years, to be spent on the DBRW's Special Rural Action Programme, which was to expand on the work of the Western Initiative aimed at creating more prosperity in the remoter areas of the Board's responsibilities. The westward slant to rural development during 1990 was also reflected in another report by the Institute of Welsh Affairs entitled 'West Wales' (March 1990), which focused attention on the problems and aspirations of Dyfed and West Glamorgan.

The housing problems of rural Wales were highlighted in a number of reports, including *Home Truths* produced by the Council for the Protection of Rural Wales (CPRW) and others. The report emphasized the need for more, and more affordable, homes in rural areas in the face of spiralling house prices which placed many local people at a disadvantage in competition with commuters and second-home owners, and stressed that environmental considerations would require a reorientation of planning policy and decisions. November brought another CPRW report entitled 'How Green Was My Valley', which urged the drawing-up of a green belt policy for Wales to combat the ever-increasing spread of development projects. Opponents of tighter restrictions, however, emphasized the deterrent effect for potential investors, which would hamper job-creation developments. Apart from proving particularly detrimental to high-technology industry looking for clean green field sites, it was argued, a green belt policy would hinder farm diversifications and generally choke economic development.

Despite the acceleration of rural initiatives during 1990, many critics maintained demands for a more rounded view of the social and economic needs of rural Wales, which was seen as essential for the implementation of a successful strategy. Among the claims was that for a Rural Development Commission, similar to that for England, responsible for housing, tourism, transport and a variety of other rural needs, and replacing many of the activities of the DBRW and the WDA. In a separate, but not unrelated, development, June 1990 brought the announcement of the formation of the Welsh Association of Local Enterprise Agencies, which brought together 21 organizations across Wales in an initiative to promote their work with a single voice, focusing on small firms.

June brought the announcement that rural Wales had been chosen by the EC as one of four regions in the United Kingdom for the adoption of a Community Support Framework. The financial allocation of some £88m was intended to help the area overcome the problems of peripherality and encourage economic development via tourism, training and diversification. May and November brought further awards of EC funds, totalling over £20m, to Dyfed, Gwynedd and Powys under the National Programme of Community Interest, established in 1988 as part of the Integrated Development Operation (IDO) programme to help fund infrastructure projects which contributed to industrial and tourism development. In Clwyd the Shotton, Rhyl and Wrexham Travel to Work Areas received a £23m package of EC funds from the IDO programme, while the year also saw the announcement of the first allocations by the Industrial South Wales IDO. Another EC development was the introduction of the RECHAR initiative launched in 1989, which provided for the channelling of funds as financial assistance to coal communities hit by pit closures. Eleven areas in South Wales were accepted as eligible in April. RECHAR projects were intended to cover infrastructure and environmental schemes, the promotion of new economic activities including tourism and training for new employment opportunities.

Despite these EC awards, there developed a growing fear that Wales was set to lose out in European aid through any reformation of regional policy and the criteria for aid receipt. The accession of Spain, Portugal and Greece to the EC had necessitated a reorientation of Structural Fund priorities and many anticipated that the recent improvement in Wales's position, particularly in comparison with the poorer Mediterranean regions, would involve a re-grading of certain areas currently receiving aid under Objective II status.

Provisional figures released by the WDA for the 1990/1 financial year show 344 new tenants occupying 1,755k. sq. ft. of Agency premises with a total jobs forecast of 4,376. Speculative floorspace amounting to 970k. sq. ft. was completed during the year, 239k. of which was purpose-built, while 55 industrial units were reserved (402.5k. sq. ft.) and applications received for another 262 (1,116k. sq. ft.). In all cases these figures were lower than the ones quoted in the WDA's annual report for 1989/90. At the end of 1990/1 total WDA stock was reported as amounting to 2,100 units covering 20,526k. sq.

ft., with 350 units (2,209k. sq. ft.) vacant. Employment in Agency premises stood at 42,500 compared with 47,385 a year earlier. In addition to its involvement in many of the developments noted elsewhere in this survey, the WDA's wide-ranging activities included an extensive marketing campaign to promote Welsh products to leading retailers, and various land reclamation projects such as the transformation of the site of the old Duport steelworks in south Llanelli. The WDA's new Welsh Property Venture sped up its programme of selling pieces of prime industrial land to the private sector amid concerns regarding the potential for increased factory rental charges.

The end-of-year press release by the DBRW reported that 93 units were allocated during 1990/1, amounting to nearly 300,000 sq. ft. of factory space and projected to create over 1,000 jobs during the next three years. Other figures indicated that some 135,000 sq. ft. of new factory space was created in the year, while 65,000 sq. ft. of new factory building, including extensions undertaken by established Mid Wales firms, was supported by grants and loans from the DBRW. Over £708,000 was paid out in Mid Wales Development Grants to job-creating projects that went ahead during the year, with approval given for grants amounting to £682,600 for ongoing projects to be completed over the next few years. Approval was also given for financial support for various projects which were to receive DRIVE grants worth over £219,000, while other projects received support from Redundant Building Conversion Grants (£116,000) and Subsidised Rural and Business Loan Schemes (£460,000). The DBRW also supported 32 job-creating Local Authority projects with grants of nearly £35,000 towards workshops, environmental improvement and tourism schemes. The DBRW reported that the effects of recession had produced activity levels which were lower than in previous years, but emphasized the encouraging end-of-year signs. The number of projects approved for grant aid over the year was some 20 per cent down on the previous year.

Regional aid statistics provided by the Welsh Office show that 194 offers of Regional Selective Assistance (RSA) amounting to £75,585,000 for projects costing £385,282,000 were accepted during 1990, while Regional Enterprise Grants offered for 258 investment and innovation schemes amounted to £2,345,000. Attached to the RSA figures were employment forecasts for 9,109 new and 4,022 safeguarded jobs. A substantial portion of this regional aid was associated with inward investment, with 142 projects from within and outside the United Kingdom reported for 1990 involving total capital investment of around £640m. A particularly noticeable feature of inward investment to

Wales was the growing presence of German firms, and at the end of the year 48 German subsidiaries were reported as being located in Wales, of which 38 were manufacturing operations. These accounted for some 15 per cent of the total number of overseas subsidiaries in Wales and one-sixth of all German manufacturing companies in the United Kingdom. Eight of the companies had their origins in Baden-Württemberg, a state with which Wales had developed a close relationship.

The regional agreement between Wales and Baden-Württemberg was signed in March 1990 and included a commitment to promote economic co-operation, technology transfer, research, education and training. Through the agreement Wales was also introduced to the European High Technology Confederation, which comprised Rhône-Alpes in France, Lombardy in Italy and Catalonia in Spain as well as Baden-Württemberg. The Confederation's broad aims involved control of the dissemination of high-technology industries and the provision of information and assistance to firms in the partner regions to seek locations or joint ventures in other parts of Europe. In July Wales received observer status in the so-called Four Motors programme, which had begun in 1987 with a predominant aim of building up a subnational R and D network including suppliers, customers, export-brokers, higher education establishments and consultants.

An assessment of the Baden-Württemberg system and that region's leading role in interregional co-operation is provided in a 1990 report produced by Philip Cooke and Kevin Morgan (*Industry, Training and Technology Transfer*). The authors point out that the received image of Baden-Württemberg as one of the most robust and innovative industrial regions in Europe, free of major problems, is somewhat misleading, and that the picture of a dynamically networked small-firm economy belies a reality in which large firms orchestrate the system. Nevertheless, it is argued, the Baden-Württemberg experience can provide a variety of lessons for Wales. These include the improvement of the level of information flowing through business networks, a strengthening of vocational training programmes, increasing levels of technology transfer, and the integration of public policy with education, business association networks and large firms, such as Bosch, which could play a crucial role as 'tutors' to small- and medium-sized enterprises. Despite such arguments, however, some reservations remain concerning the appropriateness of Baden-Württemberg as an economic model for Wales, with doubts concerning whether Wales's connections with the wider programme would ever be more than peripheral in all senses.

OUTPUT

The Index of Production and Construction for Wales aims to measure the movement in Welsh output in one quarterly series, and Table 11.A (Appendix) contains the full year results for 1990 as published in April 1991. Following increases of 2.6 per cent and 1.4 per cent respectively in the first two quarters, the 'all industry' index showed a decrease of 2 per cent in the third quarter of the year, followed by a fall of 3.7 per cent over the final quarter. The widespread nature of the contraction in production over the second half of 1990 is clearly shown in the sectoral breakdown. During the final quarter output in the Energy and Water Supply sector fell by 7.8 per cent, with the most significant component being a drop of 16.6 per cent in Gas and Oil Extraction and Mineral Oil Processing. Manufacturing output was down by 2.6 per cent, with that in Engineering and Allied industries down by 4.6 per cent. The most notable individual contractions occurred in Mechanical Engineering (8.6 per cent), Metal Manufacture (5.7), and Electrical and Instrument Engineering (5.4). Output in the Construction sector fell back by 3.5 per cent in the last quarter.

The year-on-year analysis shows that overall output in the final quarter of 1990 was 1.8 per cent less than the figure for the corresponding period in 1989. Output in Energy and Water Supply was down by 6.7 per cent, with production in Gas and Oil Extraction and Mineral Oil Processing down by more than a quarter. Although Manufacturing as a whole showed no change, some sectors showed significant falls in output – Metal Manufacture (14.5 per cent), Mechanical Engineering (9.4) and Other Minerals and Products (8.8). In contrast Transport Engineering was recorded as showing a 16 per cent increase over the year despite experiencing a 4 per cent fall in the final quarter.

Analysis by market sector records all three sectors, particularly Intermediate Goods and Investment Goods, falling back in the fourth quarter of 1990. While the output of Consumer Goods and Investment Goods stood at a higher level than a year earlier, output of Intermediate Goods showed a 7.2 per cent fall compared with the final quarter of 1989.

EMPLOYMENT

As in previous years, the results of the latest Labour Force Survey have been used to produce revised estimates of employees in employment, which enable a consistent annual series for comparison purposes. Table 11.B (Appendix) contains figures for the number of employees in employment in Wales, the United Kingdom and all regions for June 1990, together with revised figures for June 1989 and corresponding figures for June 1983. The number of total employees in Wales at June 1990, rounded at 993,000, showed an increase of 11,000 over the previous June figure. This 1.1 per cent increase was slightly above that experienced by the United Kingdom as a whole and exceeded that for six other regions – the North, Scotland, the East Midlands, Northern Ireland, the North West and the South East, with the latter region actually experiencing a decrease in employees in employment. Unlike the national trend, the greater percentage increase occurred in the male employee figure (1.7) rather than female employees (0.4). The number of self-employed in Wales (not tabulated) is estimated to have fallen by some 5,000 to 184,000 between June 1989 and June 1990 after successive yearly increases. Although considerable care must be taken when interpreting the accuracy of self-employment data the figures indicate a 50 per cent increase in the self-employed figure during the 1980s.

A provisional indication of the end-of-year employment situation in Wales is given in table 11.1, which provides a sectoral distribution of employees in employment in December 1990. A comparison with December 1989 shows that the total number of employees in employment is estimated to have fallen by some 4,000. Manufacturing employment declined by 6,000 with service sector employment, in contrast to the static picture nationally, increasing by a similar amount. Table 11.1 also provides a sectoral breakdown for 1980.

UNEMPLOYMENT

After 44 consecutive monthly falls, the seasonally adjusted unemployment figure for Wales began to rise in May 1990 and ended the year at 94,000. The seasonally adjusted unemployment rate for Wales at December 1990 stood at 7.2 per cent, compared with 6.6 per cent in December 1989 and a United Kingdom rate of 6.5 per cent. The Welsh rate was the same as that registered in Yorkshire and Humberside and exceeded by four other regions – Northern Ireland (13.4), the North (9.2), the North West (8.2) and Scotland (8.1). The male and female unemployment rates at the end of 1990 stood at 9.5 and 3.9 respectively, with the corresponding United Kingdom rates reported as 8.5 and 3.7.

The unemployment pattern across United Kingdom regions showed wide divergences during 1990 as a result of marked regional differences in the timing of the recession's onset. The figures reported in Table 11.C (Appendix) show all regions, apart from Scotland and Northern Ireland, experiencing unemployment increases between December 1989 and December 1990, with the seasonally adjusted figure for Wales showing a rise of 9.6 per cent compared

TABLE 11.1

Employees in employment, Wales, by sector, December 1980, 1989 and 1990

SIC 1980	1980	1989	1990
Agriculture, Forestry and Fishing	24,000	21,000	20,000
Energy and Water Supply	60,000	28,000	26,000
Total Primary Sector	**84,000**	**49,000**	**46,000**
Metal Manufacturing and Chemical Industries	78,000	53,000	51,000
Metal Goods, Engineering and Vehicles	104,000	103,000	102,000
Other Manufacturing	78,000	86,000	83,000
Total MFR Sector	**260,000**	**242,000**	**236,000**
Construction	**58,000**	**48,000**	**46,000**
Wholesale Distribution; Hotel and Catering	81,000	99,000	99,000
Retail Distribution	81,000	97,000	100,000
Transport/Communication	55,000	54,000	53,000
Banking, Insurance and Finance	50,000	68,000	67,000
Public Administration and Defence	109,000	106,000	108,000
Education, Health and Other Services	188,000	225,000	226,000
Total Service Sector	**564,000**	**647,000**	**653,000**
Total All Industries	**966,000**	**986,000**	**982,000**

The figures are quarterly estimates produced by the Department of Employment. They are based on monthly and quarterly sample surveys of individual establishments, and returns from major industries. These estimates are subject to periodic revision, particularly as a result of Labour Force Surveys. Totals do not add up due to rounding.

Source: Department of Employment.

with a United Kingdom increase of 12.6 per cent. The North, North West, Yorkshire and Humberside, and the West Midlands all had smaller percentage increases than experienced by Wales, while East Anglia and the two southern regions displayed increases in excess of 33 per cent. The increase in the male unemployment figure for Wales was 13.7 per cent, compared with 16 per cent for the United Kingdom, while female unemployment in Wales showed a continuing decline (2.8 per cent) along with six other regions, compared with a United Kingdom increase of 3.4 per cent.

Table 11.2 provides a breakdown of unemployment by duration at October 1990. Wales remained fourth lowest of the United Kingdom regions in terms of the proportion of long-term unemployed. Almost 23,000 persons were recorded as being unemployed for over one year in Wales, accounting for 26.6 per cent of the total unemployed, compared with 30.4 per cent for the United Kingdom. Of the total unemployed 6.6 per cent (5,650) had been unemployed for more than five years, compared to the United Kingdom figure of 8.6 per

TABLE 11.2
**Unemployment by duration and age, Wales, United Kingdom and Regions, 11
October, 1990**

| | **Percentage of Total Unemployed** | | |
	Unemployed for over one year	Unemployed for over five years	In 18–24 age group
South East	23.5	5.2	26.9
East Anglia	20.3	5.0	29.8
South West	21.4	5.1	28.0
West Midlands	31.7	9.9	30.8
East Midlands	27.3	7.5	30.1
Yorkshire & Humberside	31.1	8.5	31.7
North West	34.8	9.9	32.1
North	32.7	9.8	31.3
Scotland	35.5	10.0	30.1
Northern Ireland	52.2	21.1	27.2
WALES	26.6	6.6	32.0
UNITED KINGDOM	30.4	8.6	29.7

Information on the age and duration of the unemployed is available on a quarterly basis in January, April, July
and October.
Source: Department of Employment.

cent. All regions experienced a fall in the number of long-term unemployed
between October 1989 and October 1990, with Wales displaying the greatest
reduction in the 'over five years' category, 31 per cent compared with 22 per
cent for the United Kingdom. Only the West Midlands and the North showed
greater percentage decreases in the 'more than one year' category. The Welsh
figure fell by 20.6 per cent compared with a decrease of 17.2 per cent for the
United Kingdom.

The number of 18-to-24-year-olds unemployed in Wales rose by 5.6 per cent
between October 1989 and October 1990, compared with a 6.5 per cent
increase in the United Kingdom. This increase in the Welsh figure to 27,500
was accompanied by an increase in the proportion of total unemployed
accounted for by the 18-to-24-age-group to 32 per cent in October 1990
compared with 30 per cent a year previously. The final column of table 11.2
shows Wales possessing the second highest proportion of total unemployed in
this age category among the United Kingdom regions, marginally below that
of the North West and compared with the United Kingdom figure of 29.7 per
cent.

The annual average unemployment rates for each region over the period
1980 to 1990 are reported in table 11.3 and include the latest revisions as
explained in previous surveys.

TABLE 11.3

Annual average unemployment rates, Wales, United Kingdom and Regions, males and females combined, seasonally adjusted, 1980 to 1990

	1980	1981	1982	1983	1984	1985	1986	1987	1988	1989	1990*
South East	3.1	5.5	6.7	7.5	7.8	8.0	8.2	7.2	5.4	3.9	4.0
East Anglia	3.8	6.3	7.4	8.0	7.9	8.0	8.1	7.3	5.2	3.6	3.7
South West	4.5	6.8	7.8	8.7	9.0	9.3	9.5	8.1	6.2	4.5	4.4
West Midlands	5.5	10.0	11.9	12.9	12.7	12.7	12.6	11.4	8.9	6.6	6.0
East Midlands	4.5	7.4	8.4	9.5	9.8	9.9	9.9	9.0	7.1	5.4	5.1
Yorkshire & Humberside	5.3	8.9	10.4	11.4	11.7	12.0	12.4	11.3	9.3	7.4	6.7
North West	6.5	10.2	12.1	13.4	13.6	13.8	13.9	12.5	10.4	8.4	7.7
North	8.0	11.8	13.3	14.6	15.3	15.4	15.2	14.1	11.9	9.9	8.7
Scotland	7.0	9.9	11.3	12.3	12.6	12.9	13.3	13.0	11.3	9.3	8.1
Northern Ireland	9.4	12.7	14.4	15.5	15.9	16.1	17.6	17.2	15.6	14.6	13.4
WALES	6.9	10.5	12.1	12.9	13.2	13.8	13.9	12.0	9.8	7.3	6.6
UNITED KINGDOM	5.1	8.1	9.5	10.5	10.7	10.9	11.1	10.0	8.1	6.3	5.8

* Provisional estimate.
Source: Department of Employment.

EARNINGS

As reported in the New Earnings Survey 1990 the average gross weekly earnings of all full-time employees in Wales at April 1990 was £232.1. This figure was the lowest of any region in Great Britain and compared with a national figure of £263.1. A comparison of 1990 figures with those for April 1989 shows an increase of 7.5 per cent in Welsh average earnings, with Great Britain earnings increasing by almost 10 per cent. These changes left Welsh earnings, at 88 per cent of the Great Britain figure compared with 90 per cent in 1989. This relative deterioration is reflected in manual and non-manual categories for both males and females as shown in table 11.4.

The most significant change is recorded in the non-manual female category where average earnings, at £193, dipped below 90 per cent of the Great Britain figure (£215.5). The 7 per cent increase since April 1989, compared with a 10.5 increase for Great Britain, contributed to an increase of 7.3 per cent in the earnings of all full-time female employees, which at £180.3 now stood at 89.5 per cent of the Great Britain figure (£201.5), compared with 92.2 per cent in 1989. The earnings figure for all full-time males increased by 8.4 per cent, compared with 9.7 per cent for Great Britain, leaving male earnings (£258.6) at 87.5 per cent of the Great Britain figure. The relative deterioration recorded for each group is in marked contrast to the changes noted between April 1988 and April 1989, when average male earnings in Wales showed little change compared with Great Britain, while female earnings had actually displayed a relative improvement.

Table 11.4 also contains average earnings figures for 1980 and 1984, which clearly show the considerable relative deterioration in Welsh earnings over the decade compared with Great Britain. Between 1980 and 1990 average male earnings are shown to have increased by 117 per cent in money terms, compared with the 137 per cent increase calculated for Great Britain. The respective percentage increases in average female earnings are 139 and 156. The figures indicate that female earnings in Wales are catching up with average male earnings at a faster rate in Wales than in Great Britain. At April 1990 average full-time earnings of all female employees amounted to nearly 70 per cent of the figure for their male counterparts, compared with 63 per cent in 1980. This relative improvement was greater than that calculated for Great Britain, from 63 per cent to 68 per cent.

Table 11.D (Appendix) compares the Welsh earnings figures reported for April 1990 with those for other regions in Great Britain. Compared with the 1989 rankings, Wales remained with the lowest average male earnings, having dropped to the bottom of the manual male earnings league behind the South

TABLE 11.4
Average Gross Weekly Earnings: Wales and Great Britain
£'s. All Industries and Services. Full-time Employees on Adult Rates April

	Wales	GB	Wales as % GB
Manual males			
1980	111.3	111.7	99.6
1984	148.9	152.7	97.5
1989	209.8	217.8	96.3
1990	224.7	237.2	94.7
Non-manual males			
1980	132.5	141.3	93.8
1984	192.1	209.0	91.9
1989	280.9	323.6	86.8
1990	306.2	354.9	86.3
All males			
1980	119.1	124.5	95.7
1984	165.8	178.8	92.7
1989	238.6	269.5	88.5
1990	258.6	295.6	87.5
Manual females			
1980	67.7	68.0	99.6
1984	94.0	93.5	100.5
1989	131.8	134.9	97.7
1990	143.5	148.0	97.0
Non-manual females			
1980	78.5	82.7	94.9
1984	116.7	124.3	93.9
1989	180.5	195.0	92.6
1990	193.0	215.5	89.6
All females			
1980	75.4	78.8	95.7
1984	111.1	117.2	94.8
1989	168.0	182.3	92.2
1990	180.3	201.5	89.5

Source: New Earnings Survey, 1990; Welsh Economic Trends.

West. While retaining third place with respect to manual female earnings, the relative deterioration in the position of non-manual female employees saw earnings for all full-time females in Wales falling to second lowest amongst the regions, some 10 pence a week higher than female earnings in the North.

Table 11.E (Appendix) indicates the prevalence of low pay in Wales and Great Britain by showing the percentage of employees with average weekly earnings below £130. As in 1989, Wales is reported as having the highest percentage with respect to male employees, 7.5 compared with 5.2 for Great Britain, while 27.7 per cent of female employees had average weekly earnings below £130, compared with 21 per cent for Great Britain, placing Wales third highest in the regional rankings, compared with sixth in 1989. Comparisons of average earnings across broad occupational and industrial groupings are provided in Table 11.F (Appendix). The main feature compared with the pattern reported in the 1989 survey, is the relative deterioration in service industry earnings for all employee categories in Wales compared with Great Britain. While non-manual males and females experienced a relative deterioration in all industry groupings, manual employee earnings in manufacturing for both males and females displayed a relative improvement.

The relative absence of higher-paid occupations in Wales is indicated by the fact that the New Earnings Survey records only 16 per cent of all full-time adult employees with average gross weekly earnings above £320. This was the lowest percentage of all the regions and compared with 24 per cent for Great Britain as a whole. This evidence is supported by figures from a variety of other sources showing low professional and managerial earnings in Wales. A quarterly survey for November 1990 produced by Inter Exec, the career management consultants, showed that average executive salaries in Wales, combined with the South West of England for the purposes of the survey, lagged behind those in all other regions of the United Kingdom.

AGRICULTURE

1990 was viewed as a particularly bad year for the United Kingdom's agricultural sector, which was characterized by plummeting incomes, soaring debts and growing uncertainty about the future. The continuing struggle against high interest rates and rising costs in the face of falling crop and livestock prices was aggravated by a succession of market disturbances. These included the Anglo-French lamb war, a flood of imported meat from eastern Europe at artificially low prices, and various worries about animal health which hit consumer confidence. The year ended with the breakdown of the latest round of talks on the General Agreement on Trade and Tariffs (GATT) in Brussels, largely because of disagreements concerning the reduction of agricultural protection policies.

The aggregate accounts for United Kingdom agriculture for 1990 show that the total income from farming is estimated to have fallen by 6.7 per cent during the year after allowing for interest, rent and labour costs, with farming income of farmers and spouses forecast to have fallen by 14.3 per cent. As in 1989, different sectors experienced varying fortunes, partly as a result of some major swings in producer prices. The main features included a continuing recovery in cereal production and a substantial decline in the average realized returns for

TABLE 11.5
Net product and farming income by country, 1989 and 1990

		(£ million)		Indices in Real Terms*	
		1989	1990 (forecast)	1989	1990 (forecast)
Net product					
United Kingdom		4,866	4,954	97.9	91.1
of which:	England	3,807	3,885	94.2	87.9
	Wales	275	284	98.7	93.0
	Scotland	504	541	114.5	112.1
	Northern Ireland	281	244	132.6	105.4
Farming income					
United Kingdom		1,513	1,296	107.3	84.0
of which:	England	1,148	967	91.9	70.8
	Wales	53	41	144.7	101.6
	Scotland	152	172	456.9	470.9
	Northern Ireland	160	116	174.5	115.6
Total income from farming					
United Kingdom		2,265	2,113	102.9	87.7
of which:	England	1,696	1,560	93.7	78.7
	Wales	146	145	102.2	93.0
	Scotland	212	239	205.4	211.3
	Northern Ireland	212	169	145.5	105.9

* Deflated by the RPI: 1985 = 100.
The figures for farming incomes cover farmers and spouses, while total incomes from farming reflect the total incomes from agriculture of the group with an entrepreneurial interest in the industry covering non-principal partners and directors and their spouses and family workers together with farmers and spouses.
Source: Farm Incomes in the United Kingdom, 1990, MAFF.

cattle and calves. Although the value of milk and milk products sold off the farm increased slightly, reflecting increased output for human consumption, income patterns for dairy farms continued to decline.

Provisional figures for the three main indicators of agricultural incomes for Wales, England, Scotland and Northern Ireland and the United Kingdom as a whole are given in table 11.5. They reflect the differences in the product mix in different parts of the United Kingdom and the changing profitabilities of the production of particular commodities. While total income from farming is forecast to have remained virtually unchanged in Wales between 1989 and 1990, the farming income of farmers and spouses is forecast to have fallen by some £12m (23 per cent) compared with the 1989 figure. In real terms the figure of £41m showed farming income at its lowest level since 1945. Other figures, given in the aggregate accounts for Welsh agriculture published by the Welsh Office in January 1991, indicate an increase in gross output of less than 1 per

TABLE 11.6
Agricultural labour force, Wales, June 1988, 1989 and 1990 (thousands)

	June 1988	June 1989	June 1990	% Change 1990/1989
Total farmers, partners, directors (doing farm work)*	34.9	35.3	35.0	− 1
Total wives/husbands of farmers, partners and directors*	11.9	12.0	11.6	− 3
Salaried managers	0.3	0.3	0.3	+ 2
Total other family workers*	5.1	4.8	4.9	+ 3
Total hired workers*	5.1	5.0	5.0	− 1
Total seasonal or casual workers	8.6	8.3	8.2	− 1
Total Labour Force	65.8	65.6	65.0	− 1
Youth Training Scheme Trainees	0.8	0.8	0.7	− 8
Family and hired workers:				
Regular whole-time	6.4	6.1	5.9	− 4
Regular part-time	3.8	3.7	4.0	+ 8
Total regular	10.2	9.8	9.9	+ 1
Total workers* (including seasonal or casual workers)				
Male	15.3	14.7	14.7	0
Female	3.6	3.3	3.4	+ 3
Total	18.8	18.0	18.1	0

* Full-time and part-time.
All figures exclude schoolchildren. All figures are rounded, but percentage changes are based on unrounded figures.
Source: Welsh Office.

cent in value terms, with the value of gross input showing a 1 per cent fall. Gross product is provisionally estimated to have increased by 2.8 per cent and net product by 3.2 per cent.

As in previous years the aggregate results for agriculture based on an industry-wide calculation can be complemented by data for individual farm businesses as reported in the Farm Business Survey in Wales for 1989/90. In broad terms, farm incomes were shown to have fallen substantially from their 1988–9 levels for virtually every farm category. Disregarding changes in breeding livestock values, net farm incomes fell by around 7 per cent in money terms on specialist dairy farms and by around 12 per cent on mainly dairy farms. On livestock rearing farms, the income falls were considerably larger, with net farm income down by around 65 per cent on hill sheep farms, 60 per cent on hill cattle and sheep farms, 70 per cent on upland cattle and sheep farms, and 83 per cent on lowland cattle and sheep farms.

Agricultural labour force figures for Wales are provided in table 11.6, as abstracted from the June 1990 Agricultural Census Results for Wales. The total labour force showed a 1 per cent fall from the 1989 figure, with the main change involving a reduction of around 7,000 in the number of farmers, partners and directors (together with spouses) doing farm work. The Census results for farm livestock (not tabulated) show a 1 per cent fall in the total dairy herd between June 1989 and June 1990 which was more than offset by a 5 per cent increase in the total beef herd producing a 1 per cent rise overall in the total cattle breeding herd. The total flock of sheep and lambs increased by 2 per cent to a new record level of 10,935,300, while the number of egg-laying fowls fell by 3 per cent and the pig-breeding herd by 2 per cent.

On the policy-making front there were no major changes to the EC's Common Agricultural Policy (CAP) regimes in 1990. The price-fixing generally froze common prices, although green pound devaluations meant substantial support price increases in the United Kingdom, amounting to 8.5 per cent in the beef sector, 10.7 per cent for crops, 6.8 per cent for milk and 11 per cent for sheepmeat. In addition, as a result of 1990 production levels, stabilizer mechanisms led to abatements to a variety of common prices set by the Council, including 11 per cent for sheepmeat in Great Britain. Among the specific measures introduced by the EC were amendments to the use of set-aside land, enabling its use for cereal production for industrial purposes, and a set of proposals adopted to assist smaller farmers and those in disadvantaged areas which included an additional 4 ECUs (some £3.12p) on the additional ewe premium in Less Favoured Areas (LFAs). The extension of the LFA scheme announced in the autumn brought disappointing news for Wales, with special aid extended to only some 9,000 extra hectares of farmland, compared with the 25,000 hectares applied for. The EC also produced a set of proposals on agriculture and the environment which involved significant changes to the rules for extensification, set-aside and Environmentally Sensitive Area (ESA) schemes.

Environmental considerations were also evident in policy measures introduced by the United Kingdom government, including the pilot Nitrate Scheme, a new Code of Practice for the Safe Use of Pesticides on Farms and Holdings, and the launch of the pilot Beef and Sheep Extensification Schemes aimed at reducing production of these commodities by the provision of annual compensation payments. Other developments included amendments to the terms of the Set-Aside scheme, changes to the Potato Marketing Scheme to give non-producer interests a greater influence in market management decisions and a four pence drop in the guaranteed price of wool.

The final months of 1990 were dominated by the GATT talks. With negotiations on most areas of trade liberalization reported to have gone well, their collapse was blamed on the continuing dispute between the EC and other countries over farm subsidies. All parties had tabled offers of reductions in agricultural support, with the EC offer involving a 30 per cent reduction over the period 1986 to 1996, together with associated reductions in border protection and export subsidies. Other participants wanted deeper cuts in the EC's level of farming support, with the United States particularly concerned with raising its grain and food exports to Europe in order to assist its own hard-pressed agricultural industry. Whatever the compensatory arrangements and safeguards to be incorporated in any eventual deal when the GATT talks were resumed, it was generally accepted that 1991 would see the dawn of a new era with a restructured CAP and a liberalized, market-orientated agricultural trading system exposing European agriculture to increased competition.

Despite claims that the main brunt of the proposed support cuts would be borne by the EC's largest producers and fall on products which were predominantly 'non-Welsh', the new arrangements, particularly with respect to livestock, were anticipated to pose a considerable threat to Welsh agriculture. Particular concern was expressed that any compensatory proposals designed to benefit small farms would not necessarily be to Wales's advantage, as Welsh farms, while smaller than the United Kingdom average, were larger than the EC average and considerably larger than the smallest European farms, such as those to be found in Greece and Portugal.

TOURISM

The 1990 tourist season was generally viewed as a poor one in Wales as long-run trends were aggravated by high interest rates and fuel price rises, which particularly hit 'impulsive' holiday breaks. In September the Wales tourist Board (WTB) launched a massive publicity drive to encourage end-of-year, second holidays with the offer of special cut-price autumn breaks in a wide range of establishments throughout Wales, but over the year tourist numbers were reported as showing a 9 per cent drop, with tourist spending falling by 5 per cent compared with 1989. Long-standing fears that Wales was losing out in the lucrative overseas tourist market were supported by figures in the WTB's Hotel Occupancy Survey for 1990, which showed that the percentage of hotel users who came from overseas had fallen below 10 per cent. The WTB repeated its perennial call for additional legislative powers enabling it to promote itself abroad or else achieve a greater presence for Wales in the British Tourist Authority's overseas marketing campaign.

The year saw the beginning of a radical restructuring of the WTB's organization. As part of its 'commercialization' programme many of the central services were to be transferred into the hands of private companies. Control of the WTB's central reservation service was taken over by Holiday Wales Ltd, while Tourism Quality Services Ltd began to take over responsibility for the system of inspecting and grading hotels and boarding houses, with the ability to offer its services to a variety of other organizations both at home and abroad. It was planned to hand over the running of the WTB's regional offices in North, South and Mid Wales to companies combining public and private interests and offering a wide range of marketing services to members or anybody else who cared to pay for them. Charges were to be introduced for both hotels and visitors for the bed-booking services supplied by Tourist Information Centres, which were also required to start selling a variety of goods, or increase their current sales, in a bid to cover costs. The latter move was viewed with particular concern in many areas because of the implications for increased competition for local shops. The WTB described the restructuring of its activities as an attempt to improve the standard of tourism services to individual operators and, through them, to customers. The Board claimed that it would liaise closely with the new companies in the initial stages, helping to draw up long-term development plans and seconding staff with the aim of ensuring complementation and avoiding duplication.

During 1990 the WTB's involvement in the Valleys Initiative continued with the relaunch of the 'Valleys Revisited' campaign. Designed to emphasize the changed nature of the South Wales valleys and their attractions and sights, a particular aim was the promotion of the area as a short-break destination. The WTB's emphasis on sensitive tourist development and increased local participation in rural areas was reflected in its support of a new strategy launched by the Taf and Cleddau Rural Initiative in Pembrokeshire, while other developments in rural tourism saw the growing importance of the farm holiday sector. November brought the announcement that the DBRW was to establish a new tourism department to work closely with hoteliers, private tour operators and local authorities, and plans were announced to flood overseas markets with publicity about tourist attractions and holidays in Mid Wales.

As in many other sectors of the economy, training was a particular focus of attention during 1990. In February the Welsh Joint Education Committee published a report on 'Tourism Education at Further and Higher Levels in Wales'. Financed by the Training Agency, the study's findings called for a co-ordinated and integrated programme of tourism education planning in Wales, and recommended the creation of a Tourism and Leisure Education and Training Task Force for Wales and a Centre for Education in Leisure and Tourism Support (CELTS). The report emphasized that as tourism and leisure is a multisectoral activity with an all-Wales orientation, there was an urgent need to tackle any potential duplication of efforts arising from the TEC system. The concern expressed in the report regarding a general lack of professionalism in the tourism industry was reflected in evidence during the year that a large number of businesses in the hospitality and tourist sector were failing early on in their existence through a lack of understanding of the industry and of sound business training.

INDUSTRIAL DEVELOPMENTS

Although 1990 saw announcements of a variety of new developments and expansions in many parts of Wales, the lasting impression is one of cutbacks and closures, which rapidly accumulated as the recession deepened. The casualties involved large as well as small firms, international names as well as local concerns, and included among them were some of the most successful enterprises of recent years.

During the year the Abercynon-based AB Electronics group, one of Wales's leading high-technology companies employing some 4,500 workers in South Wales, ran into major problems after years of successful expansion. In April the company announced that it was shedding 220 jobs at its Northampton plant and relocating at Abercynon in a bid to cut costs. September brought further bad news when the group reported that 200 jobs were to be lost in production, administration and engineering spread over the company's three assembly division plants at Abercynon, Rogerstone and Abercarn, and in October it was announced that Microloom Ltd, bought by the AB Electronics Group in March 1990 and the biggest company on the Hendy Industrial Estate near Llanelli, was to close with the loss of 150 jobs. The announcement in November of 90 jobs to be lost at AB's electronics factory at Edmundstown in the Rhondda was followed by fears of further job-shedding at AB plants as the outturn for the first half of 1990 threatened a loss for the first time since 1987 after adverse experiences in many markets, particularly data processing, defence, telecommunications and the automotive industry.

In the Llanelli area two significant announcements were those involving Avon Inflatables and UK Optical. Avon Inflatables, Dafen, announced in December that production was to stop for a month from mid-January 1991, with 180 workers laid off. The decision followed the dramatic collapse of the

US marine market on which the company had relied heavily for sales of its highly acclaimed range of dinghies and rigid-hull craft. Earlier in the year, in June, the UK Optical factory at Kidwelly had closed suddenly, with the loss of more than 200 jobs. The major reason for the shock closure was claimed to be the reduced demand for plastic lenses for spectacles at a time of fierce competition from cheap imports, with the scrapping of free eye tests also identified as a key factor. September brought further disappointment with the failure of Dyfed County Council and Llanelli Borough Council to persuade a Californian-based optics manufacturer to purchase the plant.

At Merthyr Tydfil the year began with confirmation of Hoover's £12m investment project involving the development of a new generation of washing machines. The good news was tempered, however, by job cutbacks which saw a further 200 redundancies added to those experienced in the previous autumn. The year ended with the announcement of 160 job losses and a wage freeze for the 1,300 shop floor workers for 1991. The main attention in Merthyr during 1990, however, focused on the town's second largest private sector employer, the Thorn Lighting bulb factory. With large losses reported at the plant, matters were brought to a head during the summer by the decision by the US giant GTE not to buy the Thorn Lighting Division from Thorn-EMI after the cost of the deal increased as the pound sterling strengthened against the dollar. The need to slim down the division brought fears of closure at the 550-employee plant, but November seemed to bring a reprieve after a takeover deal agreed by GE Lighting, part of the huge US General Electrics Corporation. The Merthyr factory was to come under the wing of the newly formed GE Thorn Lamps, with a guaranteed supply contract for the market-leading Mazda brand promising a four-year breathing space. Elsewhere in the lighting sector, it was announced in July that the Wellco plant on the Swansea Enterprise Park was to be sold just a year after the company had relocated its lighting operation from Hertfordshire to the purpose-built factory. The Swansea plant's new owners, the Electro Lighting Group, announced plans to relocate sales, marketing, purchasing and distribution activities to North-ampton. With the future of manufacturing being evaluated, 160 jobs were reported to be in the balance.

The debate concerning the strength and quality of the motor vehicle sector in South Wales continued during 1990. The view that the sector was still dominated by low skill levels, with production concentrated in routine assembly factories could be contrasted with WDA-sponsored studies drawing a positive picture of motor component manufacture, and evidence that poor recruitment and training standards were being rectified with greater attention being paid to increased investment in research and design. However, the industry came under considerable strain as a result of the slowdown in the demand for new cars. Typical of the repercussions was the announcement of the phasing-out of production by GKN Firth Cleveland at its factory on the Treforest industrial estate, with the loss of some 140 engineering jobs over the next two years. Other developments in the car components sector included the takeover of BSK aluminium, Llanidloes, a main supplier of components to the Ford Motor company by Bromsgrove Industries, and Valeo's planned closure of its Ammanford plant as the French-owned company announced a move to a new £20m factory at Gorseinon.

Foreign developments in the sector included the £9m contract announced by Llanelli Radiators, owned by the Japanese Calsonic International group, to supply cooling systems for a new range of British-made Japanese saloon cars. The Nissan Primera was the first new car to be produced at Nissan's Sunderland plant, and the contract replaced that for the supply of parts for the Primera's predecessor, the Bluebird. Elsewhere Bosch announced that it had signed a 'no-strike' deal at its new plant at Miskin, with the electricians' union, the EETPU, gaining sole recognition to represent the projected 1,200 workforce when production began in January 1991. By the end of 1990 Toyota had still to make a decision about trade union recognition at its new engine plant on Deeside, construction of which had begun in July. The Bosch and Toyota projects had both been announced in 1989.

Possibly the most significant development in the South Wales motor vehicle sector during 1990 was the announcement of a 'non-event' by the Ford Motor Company. April 1990 brought news that Zeta Phase II of the investment plans announced for Bridgend in 1988 was to be switched to Cologne along with £200m of investment. Whilst Ford remained committed to spending the greater part of £500m on the first phase of the development of its new lean-burn engine, which would take engine production to around 800,000 by the mid 1990s, concern was voiced about what would happen when replacement and redevelopment was due after 1997. It was feared that in the absence of second-stage investment the long-term future of Ford's South Wales operations was in doubt. Assurances were given that Welsh plants would have opportunities to compete for further engine programmes and other component manufacture through the 1990s, including bidding for the third phase of engine development code-named the Sigma project, which involved the production of the new breed of clean air engines intended to meet tough European anti-pollution laws. By the end of the year, however, considerable doubts had emerged regarding realistic hopes of securing the Sigma project in the face of competition from elsewhere in Europe, particularly Spain.

Citing 'business reasons' and 'the need to ensure continuity of supply' the formal emphasis for the change of plans by the Ford Motor Company was placed on the recent series of costly pay-deal strikes, but suspicions remained that a critical factor in the review of Ford's manufacturing plans for the 1990s was the sudden and recent developments in eastern Europe which had brought new market and cheap labour opportunities. To many observers the Ford Motor Company's decision could be viewed as reneging, and an example of the down-side of 1992 and the implications of the open market. The investment loss seemed to confirm the cynicism regarding the precariousness of inward investment promises, and was particularly embarrassing considering the grants and enticements which had been made available to attract the project.

Over the years, considerable Welsh Office assistance had also been provided to another big-name company that ran into major difficulties in 1990 – Laura Ashley. Founded in the mid-1950s, the Laura Ashley company had developed over the years into an international clothing, fabrics and home furnishings empire servicing an almost entire lifestyle, with over 450 shops world-wide and employing some 8,000 people. Recent years, however, had seen claims that, while the basic products remained popular and good, the manufacturing base was too clumsy and expensive and badly placed to compete with Far East rivals armed with cheap labour and unencumbered by the high sterling exchange rate which made exports expensive. Amidst reports of increasing mismanagement, 1990 brought a radical restructuring. The announcement that the group head office was to be moved from Carno, Powys, to join the retail group head office already located at Maidenhead in Berkshire, preceded the report that the year ending January 1990 had seen a pre-tax loss of £4.7m compared with a £20.3m profit in the preceding twelve months. The resignation of the company's chief executive in August was followed by the announcement that the Japanese retailing and restaurant group, Jusco, was to take a 15 per cent stake in the company. The package deal also involved the loss of control over Laura Ashley's US bedlinen distribution subsidiary, Revman Industries, and a reduced shareholding in Laura Ashley's existing joint venture in Japan. The company denied the 'rescue package' image of the deal and emphasized that the deal took advantage of considerable retail experience in the Far East, while Laura Ashley would retain 100 per cent brand control, so dictating what products were sold. Nevertheless many commentators saw the deal as providing the opportunity to embark on an otherwise alien rationalization and cost-cutting programme. The basic strategy was viewed to be an increasing focus on foreign sales, particularly in the US and the lucrative and fast-growing Japanese markets, with the company sourcing its manufacturing with cheaper labour from outside the United Kingdom. Laura Ashley's reorganization also saw the disposal of its non-core activities.

The worst fears seemed to be confirmed in September with the news of closures and cutbacks to begin in the spring of 1991. Over 1,000 United Kingdom-based jobs were to go in factory closures at Leeswood, Shrewsbury, Oswestry and Newtown. The curtain-making factory at Newtown was retained along with the factories at Gresford, Machynlleth and Caernarfon, but the year ended with further uncertainty surrounding the future of Laura Ashley in Wales, and many observers remaining unconvinced that the company's problems had been resolved. More reductions in Laura Ashley shareholdings were anticipated, together with a further dismantling of the company's Welsh connections. The major blow to the Mid Wales economy stemming from the Laura Ashley closures was accompanied by a variety of other job loss announcements in the area, including those by the Benson Group in Knighton and by Shopfix at Newtown.

Another major name to have an uneasy time during 1990 was Amersham International, the biochemical and healthcare group. April brought the announcement of a major cost-cutting exercise following 'very disappointing interim results', and in November it was announced that the diagnostic tests manufacturing facility in Cardiff, employing some 250 people, was to become jointly owned by the American photographic giant Kodak, and wholly owned in two years. Renamed Amerlite Diagnostics, the Cardiff facility, it was claimed, would benefit from enhanced marketing opportunities in the USA. The same month brought the announcement of a healthcare joint venture planned with a Soviet Union consortium of partners led by the Cardiology Institute, Moscow. An ownership change was also experienced by British Telecom's telephone manufacturing business at Cwmcarn in Gwent. The announcement of the £14m sale to Canadian electronics giant STC was accompanied by that of job losses at the repairs division due to BT withdrawing from telephone refurbishment and negotiations to sell the profitable labels business. Fears were expressed concerning STC's general 'state of health' and the fact that BT's commitment to purchase from STC plants would end after three years.

Closures and job losses in engineering were typified by August announcements concerning the collapse of EF holdings at its factory specializing in aluminium extrusion and fabrication on the Penallta Industrial Estate at Hengoed, Mid Glamorgan, and of Celtpress (Engineering) in Newport specializing in fabrication and machine-shop facilities. Redundancies announced at JPM Automatic Machines of Cardiff were blamed on changes in the gambling laws which had limited demand for a new range of 'one-arm bandit' amusement machines, while autumn brought news of the collapse of the Mainport Group of companies, which was a major employer in the Pembroke area.

The major closure in North Wales was that of the Brymbo steelworks in Wrexham. Despite the £8m investment promised in 1989 and the plant's recent good profitability record, the September closure announcement, involving 1,100 job losses, blamed the slump in car-industry demand, which normally provided 60 per cent of the plant's order books in specialist steel. Following the plant's closure, Brymbo's owners, Rotherham-based United Engineering Steel (UES), refused to sell the steelworks as a going concern despite active negotiations with local authorities and the WDA exploring various options to maintain steelmaking at the plant. Buyer search, it was claimed, was hampered by UES's desire to transfer Brymbo's order book to their other plants in Yorkshire and by UES's unwillingness to sell the plant to anyone who represented any sort of competition to it or any of its shareholders, which included British Steel. Slight compensation was provided by UES's donation of £250,000 to the North East Wales TEC, which was matched pound for pound by the Welsh Office, while November brought the announcement that a £5.5m factory building project was to be brought forward to help ease the effects of the Brymbo closure. Other job loss announcements in North Wales during the latter part of 1990 included those at Pilkington's Deeside insulation factory and at Castle Cement's Padeswood plant near Buckley. The end of the year also brought news of the closure of Sealink's Railfreight terminal at Holyhead at the end of its contract with Railfreight Distribution.

The Brymbo closure was in stark contrast to steel developments in South Wales, with the firming of British Steel's commitment to concentrate its hot-strip mill production in the region following confirmation of the Ravenscraig plant's closure in Scotland. In May British Steel announced an £83m investment at Llanwern, involving a new continuous casting machine intended to become operational towards the end of 1993, and in November the company announced plans to undertake a £172m modernization programme at Port Talbot, which would give the works an annual capacity of more than 4 million tonnes. Ongoing investment schemes at the Trostre tinplate works,

Llanelli, were accompanied by an internal restructuring which brought some redundancies, but end-of-year announcements at the Bryngwyn works brought fears for that plant's future. Redundancies at the Gorseinon plant came after a drop in orders for its specialist colour-coated steel stemming from the slump in the construction and building industries and uncertainty over Middle East contracts owing to the Gulf Crisis. In December 1990 some 17,900 workers were employed in the steel industry in Wales with crude steel production during the year reported as 5580 kt compared with 5793 kt in 1989.

In coal mining, December 1990 saw the last shift worked at the Mardy pit, the sole survivor among over 50 once worked along the Rhondda Valleys. Three hundred jobs were lost as coal working was concentrated at the adjoining Tower Colliery at Hirwaun, where Mardy coal had been wound up in recent years. Earlier in the year the Blaenant pit near Neath in West Glamorgan had been closed, with the loss of 580 jobs, while the end of 1990 brought the announcement of 280 job losses in the following spring at Bettws Colliery, Ammanford, the only British Coal mine left producing anthracite. There were also growing fears regarding the future of Deep Navigation near Treharris, Mid Glamorgan. Other job loss announcements in the coal industry included redundancy plans at the Aberpergwm washeries, near Neath, and at the Onllwyn open cast washery in the Dulais Valley run by a division of Ryan International under a British Coal open cast division contract, while the planned shutdown of the two remaining Disticoke batteries at the Coal Products United Furnacite plant at Abercwmboi in the Cynon Valley involved the shedding of 350 jobs out of a total workforce of some 425. Plans to redevelop the Abercwmboi works using an 'environmentally acceptable' system for producing smokeless fuel were refused by the local council. At the end of 1990 the five remaining deep mines in South Wales employed 2,364 workers, while 1,302 were employed, directly or as contractors, at British Coal's eight open cast sites. Output figures for the twelve months to end of December 1990 were 3.2m tonnes from deep mines and 1.7m tonnes from opencast operations.

As deep mining came to the brink of extinction the debate regarding the rundown of the South Wales coal mining industry continued. British Coal claims of geological unviability and lack of competitiveness were countered by claims of impossible targets, an obsession with privatization and short-termism in financial calculation at the expense of a complete energy and environmental strategy, and the distraction of electricity privatization. Critics claimed that British Coal's obsession with gaining long-term contracts in the electricity generating market meant sacrificing coal to an uncertain future with the specialized coal market increasingly left to imports and a growing private sector boosted by increased prices per tonne paid to independent mining companies. With the exception of the anthracite pit at Bettws, British Coal's South Wales operations were heavily dependent on coal sales to the Aberthaw and Uskmouth power stations, but the privatization of the electricity industry placed a major question mark over the future of the coalfield, as both electricity generators, National Power and Powergen, could contemplate increased profits by switching to a variety of foreign supplies to cut costs after the existing contract to purchase domestic coal ended in 1993. A preview of the future seemed to come with successive trial shipments of American, Vietnamese and Russian coal through Newport destined for Aberthaw. The year 1990 also brought reports of a feasibility study begun by National Power with a west Wales developer with the aim of establishing an import terminal at Milford Haven which could handle some 5 million tonnes of fuel a year.

Electricity privatization had clear implications for the electricity companies serving Wales with increased competition and potential loss of business a major concern. Particular fears rested on the fact that SWEB and MANWEB had an above-average dependence on industrial customers. This made them particularly exposed to loss of customers, as large industrial energy users looked to alternative energy sources, including the development of their own power generation. Competition with other regional boards and with the generators produced many business switches. British Coal opted to buy electricity direct from National Power, while SWEB lost the contract to supply power to South Wales's four biggest docks when Associated British Ports, owners of Barry, Cardiff, Newport and Port Talbot docks, announced that it would buy electricity from Southern Electric.

In contrast, the diversity of business ventures which privatization opened up is illustrated by SWE's participation in plans to construct a £700m gas-fired power station at Wilton, Teesside, a scheme intended to supply the adjacent ICI petro-chemical complex. The privatization of SWE also brought further concerns regarding the operations of another privatized Welsh-based utility, with Welsh Water's purchase of shares in SWE. The share purchase fuelled criticism regarding the investment and diversification policies of the group and the use of government cash injected into Welsh Water during its privatization to meet the cost of cleaning up water. The decision to allow private generators to sell power to the national grid brought a number of proposals for mini-power stations in Wales such as those at Cardiff, Deeside and Angle near Pembroke.

The end of the year brought the announcement of the first South Korean investment in industry in Wales, when the specialist steel company SAMMI acquired almost a quarter of Camborne Industries which owned Aberneath Industries at Briton Ferry. SAMMI bought the rights initially to market and subsequently to manufacture in North America and the Far East a range of specialist steel products incorporating an environmentally-friendly process called Novimax which had been developed by Aberneath. The new products possessed similar characteristics to those of pure stainless steel, but at a considerably lower price, and production was planned to begin during late spring 1991. Japanese-related developments during 1990 included a joint venture between the Gooding Group and the Sanken Electric Company to create a new manufacturing base, promising more than 500 jobs at Aber-amman in the Cynon Valley; and expansion plans were announced at the Yuasa Battery factory in Ebbw Vale and at the Kenfig plant of Orion Electric, the colour television and video cassette recorder company. In Cardiff, Dynic Corporation and C. Itoh joined forces in a £0.5m investment project to produce printer ribbons with an expected employment total of 105 people.

American developments were dotted throughout Wales. January brought the announcement of the building of a new £25m factory by the American plastics firm Viskase in the Swansea Enterprise Zone, to complement the company's plant in Fforestfach and its sister firm in the city's Maritime Quarter. Again, in the Swansea Enterprise Park, Alberto Culver announced a factory development promising 280 new jobs, while in Welshpool the Ohio-based Robinson and Mayers set up a small electronics factory, and at Rhymney Britcair's new factory, owned by the American Merck and Co., was opened in March. Other North American schemes included the establishment of a new company NEO (Wales) and plans by its Canadian parent for a roll service centre at Baglan, Port Talbot. The increasing German presence included Triumph International's factory plans at Panteg, Pontypool, and the choice of Bedwas, near Caerphilly, by DAS, the Munich-based insurance group, as the location for a new claims handling office. A major development in west Wales involved the £350m purchase of the American-owned Amoco refinery in Milford Haven by French oil giants Elf Aquitaine, who acquired a 70 per cent stake in the refinery as well as some 200 petrol stations in the United Kingdom. Despite Elf's attempts to dispel fears regarding the installation's future, uncertainty lay over the deal after the sale's referral to the Monopolies and Mergers Commission on the basis of the French gov-ernment's majority stake in the parent company.

A particularly significant development in Cardiff was that announced in June by British Airways concerning its intention to build its maintenance engineering base at Cardiff-Wales airport. The base was intended as the site for BA's contract to maintain its fleet of Boeing 747s, with a projected employment of 500 jobs. The announcement coincided with the official opening of BA's new £30m engine-overhaul factory at Nantgarw, and was followed in the autumn by news of two American aero-industry companies intending to begin manufacturing operations in Merthyr Tydfil in 1992 on the back of the planned maintenance complex. Other developments in Merthyr included the opening of the Pentrebach Business Centre, plans for a new distribution centre for BRS after winning a contract to distribute all Hoover products and the intention by Benka Electronics to create 75 new jobs over the next three years. Bluebird Toys announced that its workforce would double to more than 600 by September 1991, with the switching of all production currently handled at Swindon to Merthyr, which was to become the company's main manufacturing base.

A brief listing of other planned expansions and new developments reported for South Wales during 1990 includes a purpose-built freight park at Chepstow, a paper recycling plant on the old Byass Works at Aberavon, a new turkey processing plant at Abergavenny, an extension to a cosmetic firm factory at Talbot Green, expansions by a knitwear firm at Ammanford, redevelopment and expansions at the John Williams foundry business at Cardiff following a management buy-out, a stationery firm in Ebbw Vale and the creation of 200 new jobs by a new company, Oakdale Batteries, supported by British Coal Enterprises, on the Penyfan Industrial Estate. In Mid Wales the Original Welsh Pantry Co. Ltd, bought out by management from Nestlé, announced the building of a factory extension at Dolgellau, while Uniwire moved into a new factory on the Glanyrafon Industrial Estate at Aberystwyth. Acoustic Canopies Ltd moved to the Mochdre Industrial Estate, Newtown, Steriseal Ltd expanded into two units on the Maesllan Industrial Estate, while Brook Thomson Ltd of Brecon announced expansion plans for its welder-generator activities. North Wales developments included an extra jobs boost at British Aerospace's Broughton factory after an orders boom for Airbus, a new frozen food factory at Flint and a start made on the Parc Menai Business Park. In Wrexham the merger of Britain's largest cable manufacturer BICC with its rival company, Sterling Greengate, was reported to involve the transfer of production from Aldermaston with the creation of 100 new jobs.

Civil service gains continued during 1990 with 100 extra jobs provided by the Central Statistical Office, mainly in Newport, and the relocation of an

Inland Revenue department bringing 275 jobs to Wrexham. Confirmation was also given of the switch of another 300 jobs from London to Swansea. In contrast, news of a planned cost-cutting exercise at Morriston's Driver and Vehicle Licensing Agency near Swansea aroused fears of job losses. Other white-collar moves included the announcement that Lloyds Bank was to transfer much of its clerical and support work from central London to Swansea, creating 175 jobs, although the general cutbacks announced at the end of 1990 placed further developments in the banking sector in doubt.

In addition to the transport developments discussed in an earlier section, some others are also worthy of note. In November 1990 National Welsh, Wales's largest bus company, announced that it was to sell its Gwent and English operations to Western Travel of Cheltenham. Bought by the management in a buy-out in May 1987 as part of the government's privatization of the bus industry, National Welsh had experienced a troubled career. Unable to earn 'reasonable' profits, the company plunged into a large operational deficit during 1990 as difficult trading conditons were aggravated by fuel price rises and pressure on wages. The 'rescue package' also involved a management buy-out of the company's Chepstow-based engineering offshoot, Bulwark Transport Engineering, together with the axing of services and laying off of staff, but doubts remained regarding the company's health and the future of other bus routes. Also in November Sealink, acquired earlier in 1990 by the Swedish ferry operator Stena Line AB, announced its plans for its Wales–Ireland routes, which involved an investment of £12.5m at Holyhead and Fishguard and the net creation of 78 jobs at the northern port but a loss of 60 jobs in Pembrokeshire. The end of the year brought news that the immediate future of another Irish Sea crossing was assured with the cash-aid backing for the Swansea–Cork Ferry, which included the pledge of a £500,000 interest-free loan from the Irish government.

Property developments continued at a high pace throughout 1990, including plans for a high-tech business and residential village near Pen-llergaer, a business park at Landore and another at St Mellons, which was claimed to be the biggest in the M4 corridor. Prominent in these developments was the Swansea-based BJ Group, whose ambitions included plans for a joint venture in Australia's expanding commercial property market. At Nantgarw a major project involved the joint development between the WDA and Spen Hill Properties, a Tesco subsidiary, designed to create a multi-million-pound industrial and business park complex. Caerleon Land Development Company Ltd announced development plans for the town, while Flint town centre was the location for a multi-million-pound development involving new shops, leisure facilities and housing. Cardiff developments focused on the Cardiff Bay scheme and included a £125m facelift planned for a business and leisure complex, and a £37m office complex by Hyperion Properties, while the £150m development by Associated British Ports was the first big private investment announced for the Bay. At the other end of the scale, smaller businesses were helped by the opening of the Gabalfa workshops. The speculative nature of many headline-making projects was highlighted during 1990 by confused reports concerning the Tawe Vale Project. Announced in 1989, it was suggested that plans for the high-tech super-village at Llansamlet by the government-backed British Urban Development Corporation had been abandoned.

The developments listed in this section make up a selection only of those reported during the year. While it is impossible to maintain a full record of closures and cutbacks, a regular summary of new developments and expansion plans is provided in quarterly issues of *Labour Market Wales*, published by the Training Agency Intelligence Unit for Wales. It should be noted, however, that it is difficult to obtain or confirm precise investment and job creation figures for individual cases and to distinguish fully between new and safeguarded jobs. A distinction should also be made between the announcements of plans and firm commitments, and also between intentions or projections and eventual outcomes, which may well be overtaken by events such as the general onset of recession or, as in the case of the Ford Motor Company, a change of mind.

REGIONAL COMPARISONS

The latest available Regional Accounts, published in *Economic Trends* in April 1991, contain data referring to 1989 and the usual selection is included in table 11.G (Appendix). While the table shows Northern Ireland lagging behind all other regions of the United Kingdom across the board, Wales is recorded as possessing the lowest figures in Great Britain for GDP per head, personal income per head and personal disposable income per head. The provisionally estimated figure for GDP per head of £6,372 amounts to 84.6 per cent of the United Kingdom figure of £7,534. Per capita figures for personal income (£6,493) and personal disposable income (£5,310) are 84.2 and 86.3 per cent of the respective Untied Kingdom averages. The Welsh figure for consumers' expenditure per head at £4,888 is the second lowest in Great Britain, some £50 higher than that recorded for the North of England. Figures for average household income (not tabulated) show that the Welsh figure is 85 per cent of that for the United Kingdom. A breakdown by source shows that

TABLE 11.7
Unemployment by county: Wales, unadjusted, narrow base, December 1990

County	Male No.	Male Rate	Female No.	Female Rate	Total No.	Total Rate
Clwyd	8,146	9.8	2,631	3.8	10,777	7.1
Dyfed	7,933	12.8	2,711	5.4	10,644	9.5
Gwent	11,925	12.4	3,102	4.1	15,027	8.7
Gwynedd	6,896	15.8	2,603	6.9	9,499	11.7
Mid Glam.	16,510	15.9	3,923	4.7	20,433	10.9
Powys	1,649	7.9	629	3.6	2,278	5.9
South Glam.	11,897	11.8	3,002	3.3	14,899	7.7
West Glam.	9,744	13.1	2,361	3.8	12,105	8.9
WALES	74,700	12.8	20,962	4.3	95,662	8.9

Narrow base rates are calculated by expressing the number unemployed as a percentage of the number of employees in employment plus the unemployed. This contrasts with workface-based rates which involve adding the self employed to the denominator.

Source: Employment Department, Office for Wales.

the proportion of total household income accounted for by employment is 56 per cent in Wales, compared with 59 per cent for the United Kingdom, while social security benefits account for 8 per cent, compared with 6 per cent nationally. The latest county household income figures for Great Britain show Mid Glamorgan continuing to languish at the bottom, with a per capita figure of £5,024. At 76.6 per cent this is the only county figure which is less than 80 per cent of the national average.

Figures showing variations in unemployment and earnings within Wales are given in tables 11.7 and 11.8. Table 11.7 shows unemployment by county in December 1990. Although Mid Glamorgan now recorded the highest male unemployment rate, Gwynedd remained the county possessing the highest unemployment rate overall, as in 1989. All counties followed the national trend in showing increases in total unemployment and male unemployment over the year. Female unemployment rates were lower in all counties in December 1990 compared with a year earlier, apart from Powys which, along with Gwynedd, displayed an absolute increase in the female unemployment figure. The greatest increase in the total unemployment figure over the year was recorded in Powys, some 29 per cent, compared with the 9.8 per cent increase in the figure for Wales. The south-eastern counties of Gwent, Mid Glamorgan and South Glamorgan also showed increases above the Welsh figure. Figures for long-term unemployment in October 1990 (not tabulated) show all counties experiencing decreases in the number unemployed for over one year compared with October 1989, with Clwyd, Dyfed, Gwent and Powys all showing percentage decreases in excess of the 21 per cent fall experienced in

TABLE 11.8

Average gross weekly earnings: Wales and counties (£'s). All industries and services, full-time employees on adult rates, April 1990

County	Manual males	Non-manual males	All males	Manual females	Non-manual females	All females
Clwyd	239.0	–	267.3	–	193.8	174.3
Clwyd East	252.3	307.2	271.9	–	192.8	171.2
Dyfed (exc. Llanelli)	–	–	246.4	–	192.6	179.7
Gwent	222.8	303.9	250.8	–	179.3	168.9
Gwynedd	219.1	–	248.4	–	–	175.7
Mid Glam.	224.9	321.3	259.7	–	205.5	189.2
Powys	–	–	220.8	–	–	–
South Glam.	221.6	315.0	275.5	–	196.3	188.2
West Glam. (inc. Llanelli)	232.6	292.6	255.7	–	180.9	174.5
WALES	224.7	306.2	258.6	143.5	193.0	180.3

– denotes not available because sample requirements were not met.
Source: *New Earnings Survey* 1990.

Wales as a whole. Almost a quarter of all the long-term unemployed in Wales in October 1990 were to be found in Mid Glamorgan.

A study of unemployment rates for Travel to Work Areas (TTWAs, as reported for December 1990, shows thirteen TTWAs recording narrow base rates above 10 per cent, compared with ten in December 1989. The highest rates were again to be found in Pwllheli (16), South Pembrokeshire (15), Holyhead (14.1) and Aberdare (13.7). Other high figures were recorded by Machynlleth (12.5), Bangor and Caernarfon (12.1), Merthyr and Rhymney (11.6), Porthmadog and Ffestiniog (11.4) and Cardigan (11.1). Haverfordwest, Dolgellau and Barmouth, Llanelli, and Blaenau/Gwent and Abergavenny also registered total unemployment rates above 10 per cent. As in December 1989, Welshpool (4.5) and Carmarthen (4.9) recorded unemployment rates below 5 per cent.

Table 11.8 shows differences in average gross weekly earnings between the counties of Wales. As in previous years, South Glamorgan continues to record the highest earnings figures for all full-time males (£275.5), some 107 per cent of the Welsh average, with the highest figure for manual males recorded in Clwyd, with West Glamorgan having fallen behind relatively in comparison with the figures reported in the *New Earnings Survey*, 1989. The limited information on non-manual male earnings shows Mid Glamorgan with the highest figure, and that county also recorded the highest figures for female employees. A detailed study of Section E of the *New Earnings Survey*, 1990 shows that Dyfed, Gwynedd and Powys were three of only eight counties in

TABLE 11.9
Average price of semi-detached houses, 4th quarter, 1990

County	Price(£)	Other regions of UK	Price (£)
Clwyd	45,436	South East	81,591
Dyfed	44,881	East Anglia	56,497
Gwent	53,115	South West	64,955
Gwynedd	45,225	West Midlands	56,968
Mid Glam.	45,506	East Midlands	48,235
Powys	50,341	Yorks. and Humbs.	52,442
South Glam.	57,747	North West	56,291
West Glam.	44,988	North	52,745
WALES	48,316	Scotland	55,592
UNITED KINGDOM	62,284	Northern Ireland	31,201

Source: Halifax Building Society.

the whole of Great Britain which recorded average gross male weekly earnings of less than £250.

According to figures reported by the Halifax Buildng Society the quarterly rate of house price inflation in Wales during 1990 showed a continuing slowdown, with prices falling by 2.2 per cent over the last quarter. This left the annual rate of house price inflation at around the zero level. Evidence regarding the variations in house prices within Wales is contained in table 11.9. The highest-priced semi-detached houses are on average to be found in South Glamorgan, Gwcnt and Powys (for which no figures were quoted in 1989). Clwyd, Gwynedd and West Glamorgan, together with Wales as a whole, recorded lower average prices for semi-detached houscs in thc final quarter of 1990 compared with the corresponding period in 1989. Table 11.9also provides comparable figures for other regions of the United Kingdom and shows that only Northern Ireland and the East Midlands registered lower average house prices than Wales at the end of 1990.

Table 11.H (Appendix) gives figures for identifiable government expenditure by function for 1989–90 for Wales, England, Scotland and Northern Ireland, as well as the United Kingdom as a whole, as reported by the HM Treasury. The index of Welsh identifiable public expenditure per head as a percentage of the United Kingdom figure (106.8) is some three percentage points below that for 1988–9. This reflects a rise of 6.7 per cent in total expenditure in money terms in Wales compared with an increase of 9.6 per cent in the United Kingdom as a whole. it should be noted, however, that the coverage of identifiable expenditure in the 1989–90 exercise had been changed since the previous exercise, making for the need for greater care than in the past when comparing with earlier figures.

With the exception of the *Cambridge Regional Economic Review* (September 1990), independent forecasters, as noted earlier in this survey, identified a relatively bright future for the Welsh economy in the 1990s. The latest *National Westminster Bank UK Regional Review* (NWB, March 1991) and the January 1991 edition of *Regional Economic Prospects* (Cambridge Econometrics/Northern Ireland Economic Research Centre) displayed continuing optimism regarding Wales's prospects. Both expected Wales to weather the current recession better than it had done that of the early 1980s and forecast growth rates at or near the United Kingdom average to the end of the decade. The NWB forecast that the region's economy would contract by 1.3 per cent during 1991, with output growth showing an upward trend by the third or fourth quarter, fuelled by a recovery in the service sector and renewed growth in manufacturing. This upturn would lead to growth of 2.5 per cent in 1992, with the economy expected to sustain annual growth at this pace over the period 1992–6, producing better than average employment growth. The REP forecast that Welsh GDP would grow at 2.4 per cent per annum from 1992 to the end of the decade, a higher rate than that experienced by five other United Kingdom regions. Obviously any forecast must be treated carefully and can rapidly be overtaken by events. The above are no exception, based as they are on a variety of assumptions, both general and specific, including continuing gains to Wales's south-eastern corner from relocation and inward investment.

Regardless of the length and depth of the recession the future prospects of the Welsh economy depend on national and international developments. European considerations clearly dominate, whether it is the effect of ERM entry on domestic policies, revisions to agricultural support, the ability of businesses to withstand competitive pressures in the single market, the ability to continue to attract inward investment, the implications for regional policy or, ultimately, the effects of EMU.[1]

NOTES

1. For a detailed discussed of the European dimension see L. Mainwaring, 'Wales in the 1990s: External Influences on Economic Development', in *Regions, Nations, and European Integration: Remaking the Celtic Periphery*, ed. G. Day and G. Rees (Cardiff, University of Wales Press, 1991).

   This survey is based on information published or made available prior to 1 June 1991. As such, some 1990 figures were unavailable at the time, while others are liable to later revision. The survey also contains some updated or revised statistics for previous years which differ from those reported in earlier surveys. Further details concerning the compilation and interpretation of some key statistics are contained in previous surveys and are not repeated here.

The preparation of this survey was aided by a grant from the Sir David Hughes Parry Awards at UCW Aberystwyth. Grateful thanks for assistance in the collection of data are extended to various individuals and organizations, but in particular to Ms Anne-Marie Sherwood and Mr Meirion Derrick, Official Publications Unit, Hugh Owen Library, UCW Aberystwyth. Any errors and all views expressed are the sole responsibility of the author.

In addition to those specifically referred to in the text the principal sources used are: *Agriculture in the United Kingdom* (1990), MAFF; *Business Briefing; Economic Trends; Employment Gazette; National Institute Economic Review; Parliamentary Debates, House of Commons Official Report; Rural Wales Action*, DBRW; and various Welsh Office publications and press releases. Various statistics for earlier years are to be found in *Welsh Economic Trends* and the *Digest of Welsh Statistics*, both published by the Welsh Office.

APPENDIX
ECONOMIC REFERENCE TABLES

TABLE 11.A
Index of Production and Construction for Wales (a)

Seasonally Adjusted (b): 1985 = 100

Div./Class	1980 SIC description	Annual indices 1989	1990	Quarterly indices 1990 qtr.1	qtr.2	qtr.3	qtr.4	% Change over prev. year (c)
1–5	Production and Construction	121.8	124.1	125.2	126.9	124.4	119.8	– 1.8
1–4	Production Industries (revised definition)	119.5	121.3	123.0	124.2	121.3	116.8	– 1.4
1	Energy and Water Supply	89.6	90.6	94.9	93.8	90.5	83.4	– 6.7
11–12	Coal and Coke(d)	79	86	87	89	88	82	8.2
13–14	Ext'n of Min. Oil and Nat. Gas; Min. Oil Processing	89	83	93	92	80	66	– 26.5
15–17	Gas, Electricity, Other Energy and Water Supply	100	102	105	100	103	101	– 1.3
2–4	Manufacturing (revised definition)	131.6	133.8	134.4	136.5	133.9	130.4	0.0
21–22	Metal Manufacture	131	117	122	122	114	108	– 14.5
23–24	Other Minerals and Products	138	124	128	125	121	120	– 8.8
25–26	Chemicals and Man-Made Fibres	114	114	118	115	111	111	– 2.3
3	Engineering and Allied Industries	131.2	137.0	133.2	138.6	141.3	134.7	4.3
31	Metal Goods not elsewhere specified	131	134	136	143	128	129	– 3.0
32	Mechanical Engineering	108	101	105	100	104	95	– 9.4
33–34 37 }	Electrical and Instrument Engineering	148	154	150	153	160	151	4.6

35-36 Transport (inc. Motor Vehicles)	122	139	126	143	147	140	16.1
41-42 Food, Drink and Tobacco	135	151	149	154	152	150	8.0
43-45 Textiles, Leather, Footwear and Clothing	109	116	120	119	111	115	5.4
46 Timber and Wooden Furniture	159	145	150	148	139	144	-0.8
47 Paper, Printing and Publishing	152	171	168	168	173	175	6.1
48-49 All Other Manufacturing (inc. Rubber and Plastics	141	153	160	163	147	143	3.5
5 Construction	135.0	140.0	137.8	142.9	142.1	137.1	-3.5
Market sector analysis (e):							
Consumer goods	140.3	150.8	152.1	151.3	150.7	149.2	6.9
Intermediate goods	111.7	108.6	113.4	111.4	108.2	101.2	-7.2
Investment goods	120.7	128.1	124.5	132.5	131.4	123.9	3.7

Notes:
(a) The Index is compiled from 212 series, individually weighted according to their output in the base year (1985). All value figures are deflated to allow for the effects of inflation and the change in quality of certain products, by means of producer price indices calculated by the Business Statistics Office. A report on methods, sources and results is published by the Economic and Statistical Service Division, Welsh Office.
(b) To produce a meaningful comparison from quarter to quarter the output data for each industry are adjusted to take account of seasonal variations. The adjustments are made on the basis of relative performance between the same quarters in the past.
(c) Calculated by comparison of quarter 4 of 1990 with the final quarter of 1989.
(d) Coal and Coke output in 1985, the base year for this series, was artificially low because of industrial action in that year.
(e) The Construction industry is excluded from this analysis.
Source: Welsh Office.

TABLE 11.B
Employment: Wales, United Kingdom and Regions,[a] 1983, 1989 and 1990: June of each year Employees in employment. Thousands. Not seasonally adjusted.

	1983			1989			1990		
	Male	Female	Total	Male	Female	Total	Male	Female	Total
South East	3995	3087	7082	4058	3594	7652	3993	3645	7638
East Anglia	401	287	688	416	368	785	434	378	813
South West	857	658	1515	900	847	1747	921	850	1771
West Midlands	1127	815	1942	1127	931	2058	1150	947	2097
East Midlands	819	607	1426	838	718	1556	834	734	1567
Yorkshire & Humberside	1019	753	1772	977	891	1868	1018	911	1929
North West	1276	1026	2302	1276	1148	2424	1275	1151	2426
North	605	451	1057	588	514	1103	591	524	1114
Scotland	1060	839	1899	1020	937	1957	1031	942	1973
Northern Ireland	269	226	495	274	253	527	274	256	530
WALES	510	377	888	517	465	982	526	467	993
GREAT BRITAIN	11670	8901	20572	11718	10416	22134	11776	10550	22326
UNITED KINGDOM	11940	9127	21067	11992	10668	22661	12050	10806	22885

Note:
(a) Northern Ireland and United Kingdom not reported in previous years.
Source: Department of Employment.

TABLE 11.C
Unemployment: Wales, United Kingdom and Regions
Thousands. Seasonally adjusted. Claimants aged 18 and over, December 1989 and December 1990

	1989			1990		
	Total	Male	Female	Total	Male	Female
South East	342.3	247.7	94.6	456.7	340.6	116.1
East Anglia	33.5	24.0	9.5	45.0	33.4	11.6
South West	88.7	62.4	26.3	118.4	87.5	30.9
West Midlands	152.9	109.9	43.0	166.5	123.8	42.7
East Midlands	96.3	69.0	27.3	111.4	82.4	29.0
Yorkshire & Humberside	162.2	119.4	42.8	174.5	133.0	41.5
North West	238.1	176.3	61.8	249.0	189.7	59.3
North	125.0	93.9	31.1	129.0	99.4	29.6
Scotland	211.2	153.5	57.7	200.8	149.6	51.2
Northern Ireland	100.4	74.7	25.7	96.9	73.5	23.4
WALES	85.8	64.1	21.7	94.0	72.9	21.1
UNITED KINGDOM	1636.1	1194.7	441.4	1842.3	1385.8	456.5

Source: Department of Employment.

TABLE 11.D

Average gross weekly earnings: Wales, Great Britain and Regions
£'s. All industries and services. Full-time employees on adult rates, April 1990

	Manual males	Non-manual males	All males	Manual females	Non-manual females	All females
South East	255.3	404.0	344.4	164.9	244.6	232.5
East Anglia	237.2	333.9	281.1	141.9	198.3	185.6
South West	227.0	326.6	277.3	141.8	199.5	188.2
West Midlands	229.4	322.3	269.3	143.1	195.0	181.1
East Midlands	231.6	322.8	269.7	140.1	198.9	181.6
Yorkshire & Humberside	230.7	316.8	266.9	140.8	193.5	181.2
North West	233.1	322.6	274.7	143.8	199.8	186.9
North	231.6	314.5	265.2	141.0	192.5	180.2
Scotland	231.7	327.4	276.4	141.2	200.6	187.2
WALES	224.7	306.2	258.6	143.5	193.0	180.3
GREAT BRITAIN	237.2	354.9	295.6	148.0	215.5	201.5

Source: New Earnings Survey, 1990.

TABLE 11.E
Distribution of gross weekly earnings: Wales, Great Britain and Regions
£'s. All industries and services. Full-time employees on adult rates, April 1990
Percentage with weekly earnings less than £130

	Manual males	Non-manual males	All males	Manual females	Non-manual females	All females
South East	5.3	1.8	3.2	31.4	7.7	11.3
East Anglia	5.3	2.9	4.2	48.2	19.0	25.6
South West	8.1	3.8	5.9	46.9	18.9	24.5
West Midlands	7.5	3.7	5.9	44.4	20.8	27.2
East Midlands	7.0	3.7	5.6	47.9	19.6	27.9
Yorkshire & Humberside	8.2	4.0	6.4	48.5	21.0	27.4
North West	7.5	4.5	6.1	47.3	18.1	24.3
North	8.8	3.6	6.7	49.4	21.9	28.5
Scotland	8.6	4.3	6.6	47.2	20.3	26.4
WALES	10.9	4.1	7.5	44.9	21.8	27.7
GREAT BRITAIN	7.2	3.1	5.2	42.9	15.2	21.0

Source: New Earnings Survey, 1990.

TABLE 11.F
Average gross weekly earnings by broad industry and occupational groupings: Wales and GB
£'s. Full-time employees on adult rates, April 1990

	Manual males			Non-manual males			Manual females			Non-manual females			All males			All females		
	Wales	GB	% GB	Wales	GB	% GB	Wales	GB	% GB	Wales	GB	% GB	Wales	GB	% GB	Wales	GB	% GB
All industries and services	224.7	237.2	94.7	306.2	354.9	86.3	143.5	148.0	97.0	193.0	215.5	89.6						
All index of production industries	249.7	254.6	98.1	339.8	370.0	91.8	156.9	153.0	102.5	186.3	206.0	90.4						
All manufacturing industries	244.5	250.0	97.8	330.8	364.1	90.9	156.9	152.8	102.7	185.6	202.8	91.5						
All service industries	194.2	216.8	89.6	292.6	349.9	83.6	127.4	143.3	88.9	194.3	217.8	89.2						
All occupations													258.6	295.6	87.5	180.3	201.5	89.5
All manual occupations													224.7	237.2	94.7	143.5	148.0	97.0
All non-manual occupations													306.2	354.9	86.3	193.0	215.5	89.6

Source: New Earnings Survey, 1990.

TABLE 11.G
Regional Accounts 1989[a]

	GDP per head (b)		Personal income per head (c)		Personal disposable income per head (c)		Consumers' expenditure per head (d)	
	£	% of UK	£	% of UK	£	% of UK	£	% of UK
South East	9086	120.6	9047	117.3	7134	116.0	6725	118.6
East Anglia	7460	99.0	7786	101.0	6196	100.7	5700	100.6
South West	7187	95.4	7825	101.5	6312	102.6	5711	100.7
West Midlands	6898	91.6	7093	92.0	5694	92.6	5167	91.1
East Midlands	7131	94.6	7402	96.0	5945	96.6	5058	89.2
Yorkshire & Humberside	6649	88.3	6940	90.0	5560	90.4	5078	89.6
North West	6898	91.6	7042	91.3	5647	91.8	5386	95.0
North	6522	86.6	6671	86.5	5418	88.1	4837	85.3
England	7717	102.4	7883	102.2	6284	102.1	5800	102.3
Scotland	7021	93.2	7214	93.6	5600(e)	92.0	5205(e)	91.8
Northern Ireland	5758	76.4	6342	82.2	5277	85.8	4607	81.3
WALES	6372	84.6	6493	84.2	5310	86.3	4888	86.2
UNITED KINGDOM	7534	100	7711	100	6152	100	5669	100

Notes:
(a) Provisional.
(b) Factor cost, current prices.
(c) Personal income is the income both actual and imputed of the personal sector.
(d) Consumers' expenditure measures the expenditure of UK residents whether in the UK or abroad, both by households and private non-profit-making bodies. The estimates are based on the results of the Family Expenditure Survey.
(e) Owing to the introduction of the community charge, the Scottish figures are not comparable with the other figures.
Source: Regional Accounts, 1989, Central Statistical Office.

TABLE 11.H
Identifiable public expenditure 1989–90 (a)

	£ per Head					As a percentage of United Kingdom identifiable expenditure per head			
	England	Scotland	Wales	Northern Ireland	United Kingdom	England	Scotland	Wales	Northern Ireland
Agriculture, fisheries, food and forestry	18.7	43.3	36.9	115.4	24.5	76.4	176.9	150.7	471.9
Trade, industry, energy and employment	77.1	127.5	126.0	474.4	95.0	81.1	134.2	132.6	499.3
Roads and transport	97.0	136.9	120.6	82.6	101.3	95.7	135.1	119.0	81.6
Housing	70.6	126.7	59.0	168.8	77.7	90.8	163.1	76.0	217.2
Other environmental services	114.4	140.5	156.5	176.6	118.0	94.4	119.0	132.6	149.7
Law, order and protective services	135.9	158.7	114.5	440.7	145.3	93.5	109.2	78.8	303.3
Education and Science	401.6	550.0	406.8	} 593.8	420.9	95.4	131.9	96.7	} 141.1
Arts and Libraries	19.1	19.9	16.9		18.5	103.1	107.2	91.1	
Health and personal social services	495.1	641.9	529.4	607.5	513.0	96.5	125.1	103.2	118.4
Social security	893.6	987.0	1,011.9	1,074.2	912.9	97.9	108.1	110.8	117.7
Miscellaneous(b)	0.0	24.8	17.3	37.3	4.1	−0.9	608.7	424.4	914.4
Total	2,320.0	2,962.1	2,595.8	3,771.3	2,431.1	95.4	121.8	106.8	155.1

Notes:

(a) The term 'identifiable expenditure' refers to expenditure that can be identified from official records as having been incurred in a particular country. The coverage of identifiable expenditure has been changed since the previous exercise (1988–9) to produce a greater consistency of treatment between different types of expenditure. All expenditure on common services – for example, revenue and tax collection, financial administration – has been treated as unidentifiable. In previous years this category of expenditure was not treated in a consistent manner. This change does not appreciably affect the index of per capita expenditure between territories.

(b) 'Miscellaneous' includes net receipts of Land Registry in England and Wales and costs from the central administration of the Secretaries of State.

Source: HM Treasury.